Victor Mollo

# DIAMONDS

## Are the Hog's Best Friend

### Collected and Edited by Mark Horton

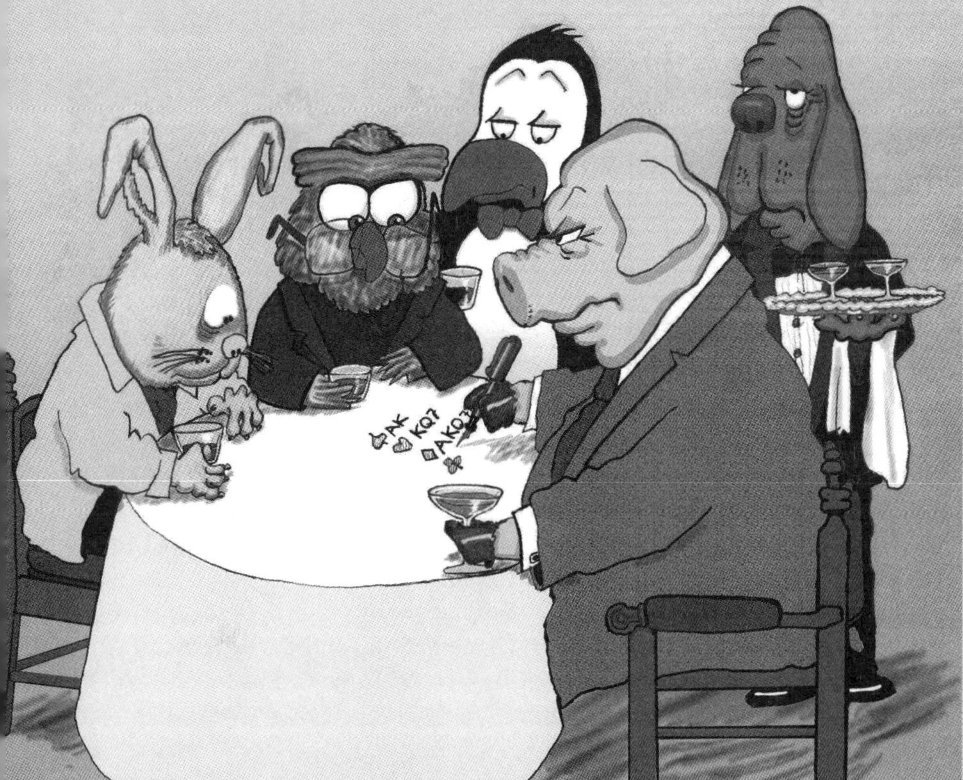

Master Point Press • Toronto, Canada

Text © 2013 The Estate of Victor Mollo
Cover image and illustrations © 2013 Bill Buttle

All rights reserved. It is illegal to reproduce any portion of this material, except by special arrangement with the publisher. Reproduction of this material without authorization, by any duplication process whatsoever, is a violation of copyright.

Master Point Press
331 Douglas Ave.
Toronto, Ontario, Canada
M5M 1H2   (416)781-0351
Email:       info@masterpointpress.com
Websites:   www.masterpointpress.com
             www.teachbridge.com
             www.bridgeblogging.com
             www.ebooksbridge.com

**Library and Archives Canada Cataloguing in Publication**

Mollo, Victor, author
    Diamonds are the hog's best friend / Victor Mollo ; illustrated by Bill Buttle.

Issued in print and electronic formats.
ISBN 978-1-897106-96-9 (pbk.).--ISBN 978-1-55494-243-5 (pdf).--ISBN 978-1-55494-475-0 (epub).--ISBN 978-1-55494-726-3 (mobi)

    I. Buttle, Bill, illustrator  II. Title.

| PR6063.O43D53 2013 | 823'.914 | C2013-902152-3 |
| | | C2013-902153-1 |

| Editor | Ray Lee |
| Copyeditor/Interior format | Sally Sparrow |
| Cover and interior design | Olena S. Sullivan/New Mediatrix |

1 2 3 4 5 6 7    17 16 15 14 13
PRINTED IN CANADA

# Publisher's Foreword

If by chance this is your first encounter with the Hog, the Rabbit, the Owl and all the rest of Mollo's wonderful characters, we envy you the joy of discovering them. Do not fail to find a copy of *Bridge in the Menagerie*, the book which began it all (now back in print at last!) and read this remarkable series from its very start. It is, correctly, the yardstick against which all other attempts at humorous bridge writing are measured.

This is one of four new collections of original Victor Mollo Menagerie stories, none of which have previously appeared in book form. *The Hog Takes to Precision* was published in 2011, *Swings and Arrows* will be available in 2014 and the final volume, *Last Call in the Menagerie*, will appear the following year.

*Ray Lee*
*Master Point Press*
*July 2013*

# Introduction

## SEARCHING FOR VICTOR MOLLO

Mark Horton, the editor of these latest Mollo books, has asked me to write about how these stories made it back into print. I was not part of the research that unearthed the scores of stories, but I did play a large part in taking those articles and getting them into a state whereby they could be included in this collection. Why, I hear you ask, was I selected for this onerous task? There were two reasons: firstly, I have a computer, a scanner and OCR software; secondly, I could not find a reason to say 'no' quickly enough.

The articles arrived in many formats: some in magazines, both small and large format, some as pdf files on disk and others as poor photocopies of the original Mollo typed stories. The actual physical process of scanning the documents represented no great problem, though the somewhat cheap OCR software I was using struggled considerably with hand diagrams and obviously the lower quality the photocopy the less accurate the character recognition. Thus the conversion to digital form was carried out as a fairly laborious manual process and took me about a hundred hours.

This, however, is by no means all there was to it. After reading about four or five articles, I got the feeling that I had seen one story somewhere else. The question was how to verify this. The reason I thought I recognized the story was that I am a bit of a 'Mollo-holic' — I have read and reread all the Menagerie stories many times (in fact I have actually hosted a dinner party where the dishes all came from the Mollo books) — so I tended to notice a repeat. So now the problem was how to develop a strategy to find any duplicates, and of course the answer was not to flick through all the books every time one had a nagging doubt. The solution I adopted was to create a database of all the deals in the existing Mollo books. Inspection revealed that noting the North spade holding would be a sufficient amount of data to rule out a large percentage of the deals as being a repetition.

So in the space of a morning I created an Access database of 372 hand records along with associated tables about the books so as to keep the database normalized according to Codd. Edgar F. Codd (August 23, 1923 — April 18, 2003) was the person who first codified rules for true relational databases; they are known as 'Codd's twelve rules' which of course means there are thirteen of them, numbered from zero to twelve. This ends the nerd interlude. A query form was set up so one could simply interrogate the database to see whether the North hand was unique; if it was not, then further research was undertaken. This approach removed a lot of the potential problems.

But not all. Just to confuse the issue further, there were cases where in two articles the deals were the same but the text was different and even a case where the texts were virtually the same but the deals different. And of course there were cases where the hands were rotated, e.g. North became South, etc., and also instances where the suits were manipulated, i.e. hearts and spades were interchanged. Only personal inspection and a thorough knowledge of all the articles brought these episodes to light. Am I sure we have a perfect solution? No, there is one deal that still nags me though I have reread everything and cannot find the duplicate; deep down I know I have seen it somewhere before but just do not know where.

So there you have it: that is how the Menagerie stories went from pieces of paper through various computers before reappearing on paper in this book. I hope you enjoy reading them, I know one of the reasons sometimes things took longer than they should is that I stopped to reread some interesting snippet. I can now say with some confidence that there are not many people out there who have read more Menagerie stories than I have, and I still look forward to rereading them all over again. Now excuse me while I go off and get some more chocolate and almond biscuits.

*Ron Tacchi*
*Vaupillon, February 2012*

# Contents

# The Chimp Joins the Griffins

'What's he like?' asked the Emeritus Professor of Bio-Sophistry, generally known at the Griffins as the Secretary Bird.

'Clueless, quite clueless,' replied Colin the Corgi.

We were discussing a new member, Charlie the Chimp, who had been playing at Colin's table during the afternoon session. His name wasn't really Charlie, but he looked like one and there was something distinctly simian about the way he jabbered and grimaced and waved his long hairy arms. Besides, he had to be addressed somehow and one couldn't keep on saying: 'No hearts, Mr. Bolvan-Bolvanovitch?' or 'Would you draw your card, Mr. Bolvan-Bolvanovitch?'

'And not only is he clueless,' went on C.C., 'but his eye is never on the ball. He is always prattling about hands that came up yesterday or the day before, or last year for that matter. There can be little doubt,' concluded Colin, 'that he will be a big and consistent loser.'

'Sounds a pleasant, unselfish sort of chap,' said the Hog approvingly. 'Clubbable and all that. Did you... er... form the impression, Colin,' went on H.H., 'that he is a man of substance?'

'Wouldn't like to say,' replied the Corgi cautiously. 'He was driving his Rolls himself when he arrived, but that's nothing to go by, of course. His chauffeur might have been having a day off or something.'

As we made our way to the card-room, the evening session was already in full swing.

'But I had nineteen, I tell you!' the Walrus was blaring across the room, 'and I would have got out of it for two down if the trumps had broken no worse than 3-2. What could I do against all six in one hand?'

Whatever disaster had befallen Walter the Walrus, Charlie the Chimp, his right-hand opponent, seemed to be taking it very well.

'It's like a hand my wife had on Tuesday,' he was saying. 'She went four down just as you did, but it would have been five down had I switched to a diamond, because...' The rubber was over the next hand.

The Hog and S.B., who now joined the table, drew each other, while the Chimp faced the Rabbit.

'What shall we play?' asked Charlie.

'Everything,' replied R.R. enthusiastically, 'Swiss, Baron, Fishbein, Texas, Flint...'

'Yes, yes,' broke in the Chimp, 'my brother met him at a congress in Harrogate last year, no sorry, it was Blackpool. They had a hand on which...'

'We play the usual,' announced the Hideous Hog in stentorian tones, to break up the Blackpool hand before it got under way.

'That means the Forcing H.H.' explained S.B. with a wry smile. 'We all play that here, you know. We have to.' There was a menacing gleam behind the pince-nez and the cold, bloodless lips curved down in a meaningful sneer.

It was not long before the Professor showed us what was in his mind.

```
        ♠  10 3 2
        ♡  10 9
        ◇  A 3 2
        ♣  A K Q 6 2
              N
          W       E
              S
        ♠  A Q
        ♡  A K 3 2
        ◇  7 5 4
        ♣  10 9 8 7
```

| West | North | East | South |
|------|-------|------|-------|
| Ch.Ch. | H.H. | R.R. | S.B. |
|  | 1♣ | pass | 1◇ |
| 1♠ | 2♣ | pass | 3NT |
| all pass | | | |

S.B. was practicing, or rather usurping, the H.H. system. He had every intention of playing the hand — and of not getting a diamond lead. Hence the typical Hog response of 1◇.

Charlie the Chimp opened the ◇K and the Secretary Bird hissed. When the Hog bid a suit he did not want led, people had the decency to lead another. Evidently this Charlie had no manners. Fortunately, the Emeritus Professor could see nine tricks, so he wasn't unduly worried — until Trick 4. Then the wild tufts of hair on either side of the bald dome rose in alarm for the ninth trick had suddenly vanished.

The Professor had ducked the ◇K, then, at Trick 2, he had gone up with the ace on the nine, the Rueful Rabbit following both times. The ♣A and ♣K came next and it was on the king, when the Chimp threw a spade, that the scales fell from his eyes, for the ♣J was still out and the suit was well and truly blocked. To unblock it, he had somehow to get rid of one of the clubs in the closed hand. Was that possible?

After a moment's reflection, the pince-nez flashed and the Emeritus Professor led a diamond. Let the Chimp take his winners. On the next diamond S.B. would discard a club from his hand and his troubles would be over.

Charlie the Chimp accepted the trick grudgingly, his mobile features registering acute suspicion. Then they took on an expression of cunning. Suddenly his eyes lit up and to the surprise of all concerned he led, not another diamond, but the ♡Q. The contract was now doomed. This was the deal in full.

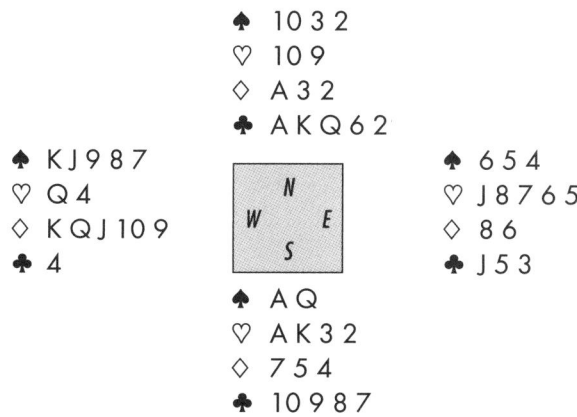

```
              ♠ 10 3 2
              ♡ 10 9
              ◇ A 3 2
              ♣ A K Q 6 2
♠ K J 9 8 7      N          ♠ 6 5 4
♡ Q 4        W       E      ♡ J 8 7 6 5
◇ K Q J 10 9     S          ◇ 8 6
♣ 4                         ♣ J 5 3
              ♠ A Q
              ♡ A K 3 2
              ◇ 7 5 4
              ♣ 10 9 8 7
```

'Fancy not cashing those diamonds!' exclaimed a kibitzer, deeply impressed by the defense.

'I recognized the situation at once' the jubilant Chimp told him proudly. 'That diamond was a Greek gift to trap me into a suicide squeeze. Only last Wednesday there was a hand just like it. Partner opened a heart and I bid two clubs, that is over an intervening spade, no, sorry, it was one notrump, I remember now and...'

'They never do that sort of thing to him!' hissed S.B., pointing an accusing finger at the Hideous Hog. 'He wouldn't get a crazy switch like that queen of hearts, not in a thousand years, so he'd make his contract and you would all genuflect, saying how clever he was.'

'Precisely,' agreed the Hog leering pleasantly. 'But tell me, how did you contrive to go down?'

'And how do you imagine that you would have made it?' countered S.B. belligerently.

'I should have played West for thirteen cards only,' replied H.H. 'He had bid a spade, remember, and he had shown up with five diamonds and a club. So how many hearts do you suppose he had? You didn't think of it, of course, but I should have cashed my top hearts before throwing him in with a diamond. Then he couldn't have exited with the queen of hearts, could he? As you so rightly observed just now, Professor, that sort of thing couldn't happen to me. I wouldn't allow it.'

'...and when I led my last club declarer threw the seven of diamonds, no, as you were, it was the nine of diamonds, because...' Charlie the Chimp liked talking about hands and he wasn't going to be done out of it just because no one was listening.

## An Unusual Trump fit

The Hog and S.B. were still exchanging asperities two hands later, hissing and jeering at each other, when the Rabbit dealt and opened 2NT on South's cards.

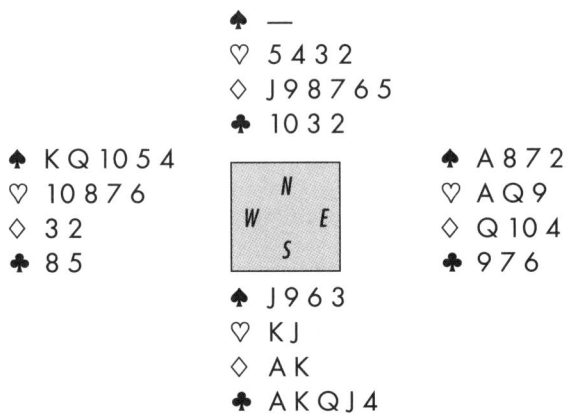

| West | North | East | South |
|------|-------|------|-------|
| S.B. | Ch.Ch. | H.H. | R.R. |
|  |  |  | 2NT |
| pass | 3◊ | pass | 3♡ |
| pass | 4♡ | all pass | |

If the bidding sequence appears in any way unusual it is largely because the Rabbit was playing Flint and the Chimp wasn't. He had forgotten all about it.

The Emeritus Professor opened the ♠K, which the Rabbit ruffed in dummy. After a diamond to his king and another spade ruff, R.R. looked round with satisfaction. Things seemed to be going well. Crossing to his hand with the ◊A he ruffed a third spade. Then he cashed a couple of clubs ending with the ten in dummy. With seven tricks in the bag, this was the position:

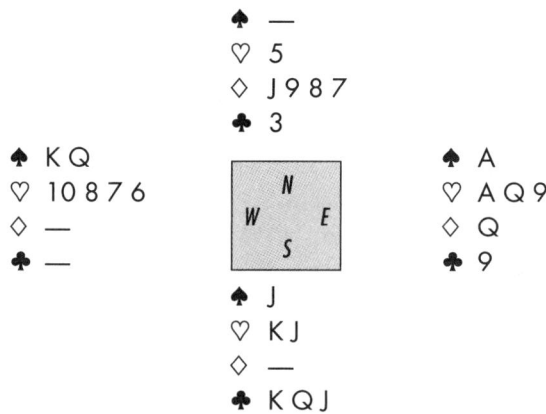

The Rabbit gaily played a diamond, ruffed with the jack in his hand and returned to dummy by ruffing his last spade. Now, as he led another diamond, the stage was set for the kill. Sitting with the ♡K over the Hog's ace-queen even R.R. could be certain of winning one more trick.

For several seconds H.H. could think of nothing offensive to say to his partner. The Emeritus Professor was in the same unhappy predicament.

'Curious hand,' observed Oscar the Owl, taking advantage of the momentary lull. 'No one seeing the two hands would wish to be in four hearts, yet it's the only likely game contract for North-South. In three notrump defenders lead spades and take the first five tricks. In five diamonds there are two hearts and a trump to lose, and against five clubs a not unlikely lead is a trump, leaving declarer with two spade losers in addition to a heart.'

'Yes,' said the Chimp, 'it's like that hand I was telling you about. If declarer leads...'

'Clueless,' said S.B. to himself in a sibilant whisper, 'quite clueless.'

## AN ADVENTUROUS CONTRACT

The rubber was soon over. When they cut again the Hog drew the Rabbit and it was the Professor's turn to play with our new Griffin. On the first hand the Hog reached an adventurous contract of 4♡. He must have thought it adventurous himself, for as R.R. tabled his hand, he didn't even scowl. 'Thank you partner,' he said with uncalled-for politeness, in the manner of one who liked his dummy.

```
            ♠  A J 9 2
            ♡  Q 10 7 6
            ◇  Q 6 2
            ♣  Q 4

                 N
            W         E
                 S

            ♠  Q 3
            ♡  A 9 5 4 3
            ◇  J 7 4
            ♣  K J 10
```

| West | North | East | South |
|------|-------|------|-------|
| S.B. | R.R. | Ch.Ch. | H.H. |
|  |  | 1NT[1] | 2♡ |
| pass | 4♡ | all pass | |

1.  12-14.

S.B. led the ◇10 to the Chimp's ace and king. Winning a third diamond with the queen, H.H. led dummy's ♡Q. Commenting on the hand later, the Hog explained that his only chance of not losing a trump trick was to scoop West's singleton jack. If he produced the bare king it wouldn't help, for then East would have a certain trick with the ♡J82, and as he had opened 1NT, he couldn't have a bare honor himself.

The ♡Q held the trick, but no jack appeared. Evidently the Chimp had been dealt a doubleton king and was afraid to go up with it in case it crashed his partner's singleton ace. After all, the Hog would have led dummy's queen had his own trumps been ♡J98543.

At Trick 5, after the ♡Q, H.H. led the ♣4 to his ten and West's ace. Another club came back.

'That club was a simple discovery play,' the Hog told us later. 'I had to find out who had the ace of clubs so as to take the right view in spades. Kindly don't interrupt,' he said severely to someone who was opening his mouth. 'East had shown up with ten points, the ace-king of diamonds and the king of hearts. Obviously, if he had the ace of clubs he couldn't have the king of spades as well, and vice-versa.'

After winning the club return in dummy, the Hog had led the ♠A then a small one. Charlie the Chimp played low and it was all over. These were the four hands:

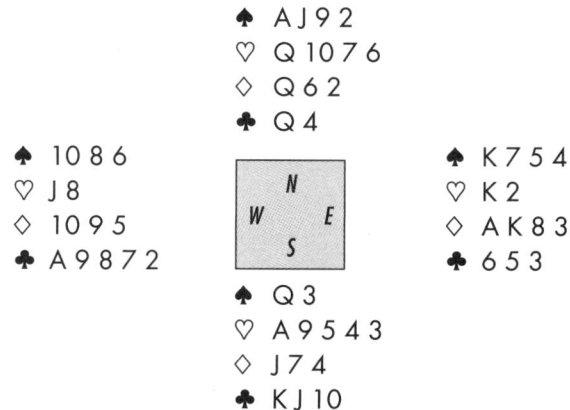

The Hog described his spade play as a pseudo ruffing finesse. 'The man in the street,' he said, with a sly look at Charlie, 'thinks declarer in that situation can't have the queen or he'd finesse the ordinary way. So why should he send his king to the chopping block for nothing? It isn't natural, not for the man in the street.'

It was a second or two before S.B. realized that two of the Chimp's kings had evaporated into thin air. Then he rose slowly from his chair, sparks flying from the bristly tufts over his ears, and bending forward he hissed at Charlie: 'Clueless.'

The Chimp responded at once. Rising in turn, he said with a courtly bow: 'Bolvan-Bolvanovitch, Boris Bolvan-Bolvanovitch at your service.'

# The Greeks Have No Word for It

'Anyone vulnerable?' asked Papa, who had strolled over after being cut out from another table.

'We shall be up after this hand,' replied the Emeritus Professor of Bio-Sophistry. His side was a game up and he was declarer in 4♠.

```
              ♠ J 9 3 2
              ♡ 7 4
              ◊ 9 7 6 5
              ♣ A Q 10

                  N
              W       E
                  S

              ♠ K Q 10 7 6 4
              ♡ A K 3
              ◊ 2
              ♣ 9 6 4
```

| West | North | East | South |
|------|-------|------|-------|
| W.W. | R.R. | H.H. | S.B. |
|  |  |  | 1♠ |
| pass | 2♠ | pass | 3♠ |
| pass | 4♠ | all pass |  |

The final contract was due to a routine misunderstanding. The professor, better known as the Secretary Bird, had raised the spades to the three-level preemptively, to shut out hearts. The Rabbit, busy with a muffin, had no time for such refinements and bid game automatically. After all, it needed only one more.

Walter the Walrus opened the ◊K and continued with the queen. S.B. ruffed, led a spade to Walter's ace, ruffed the diamond return and drew the last enemy trump. It was at this point that the Greek had inquired about the state of the rubber.

'I can, in fact, put my hand down,' S.B. assured him, 'for all that's left is a baby elimination. However, it usually saves time to play them out. Not all of us,' he added with a meaning wink in the direction of the Walrus, 'are as quick on the uptake as we might be.'

'What do you make the difference?' asked the Hideous Hog, turning to the Rabbit, one of whose New Year resolutions was to keep a running total of the score with every hand. 'Is that 230 I see?'

The Rabbit nodded gravely. The large, bold figures on his pad were unmistakable. There was 30 above the line, 60 and 150 below. The total, inscribed at the top of the 'We' column read: 230.

The Rabbit was proud of his new method of scoring, which showed at a glance when an extra trick would affect the rubber points.

Swinging his long, sinewy arms rhythmically, not unlike a metronome, the Secretary Bird cashed his two top hearts and ruffed the third in dummy. Then he trumped the table's last diamond in his hand and having eliminated the red suits, led a club.

'As you can see,' said the professor, 'even if the club finesse fails, I am home, for H.H. will have to lead another club into dummy's A10 or concede a ruff and discard.' The ♣Q, however, held the trick, the Hog following with the jack. S.B. looked up.

'Did you say that we were 230 up?' he asked with sudden interest. R.R. agreed. Returning to his hand with the last trump, S.B. led a club, finessing dummy's ten. The Hog promptly won with the king and scored the last trick with the ♡Q. One down. This was the complete deal.

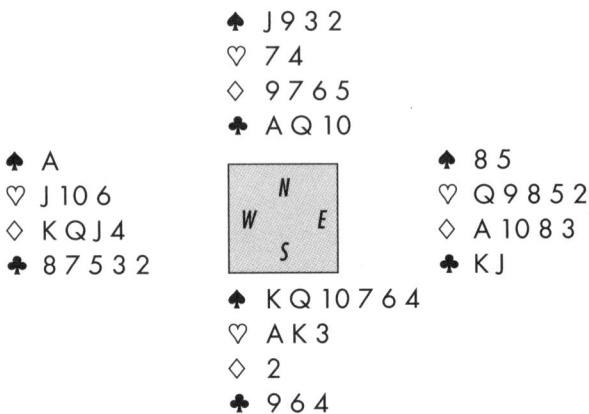

'Very cunning, H.H.,' observed Oscar the Owl. 'At the risk of a hundred points you defeated an unbeatable game.'

'You are too kind,' gloated the Hog happily, 'but I wasn't really risking anything, you know. I didn't like to contradict our friend, but I think he has made a slight error. The difference in the scores is 240, not 230 — or rather it was 240. Now, of course, it is 140. Ha ha! Anyway,' continued H.H., 'eleven tricks came to no more than ten, if you see what I mean, ha ha ha!'

Themistocles Papadopoulos looked pityingly at us all. 'Taking candy from children! You'd think that none of you had seen a falsecard before,' he said, adding contemptuously, 'I should like him to try that trick on me some day.'

H.H. leered back contentedly. 'Why,' he asked, 'should anyone try tricks on you? You trick yourself so much better than others do. For my part, I am strictly neutral. I don't care who fires the petards you hoist yourself upon. It's the bangs I like. Ha ha!'

The Hog slapped his thigh.

The rubber was soon over. Muttering dark imprecations and hissing in accompaniment, the Secretary Bird cut out and the Greek took his place. Before long, he was defending a contract of 5◊.

```
                    ♠ 762
                    ♡ 2
                    ◊ 1076
                    ♣ QJ10987
♠ J54
♡ KQ54            ┌─────────┐
◊ A54             │    N    │
♣ 632             │ W     E │
                  │    S    │
                  └─────────┘
```

| West | North | East | South |
|------|-------|------|-------|
| Papa | R.R. | W.W. | H.H. |
| | | | 2◊ |
| pass | 3◊ | pass | 3NT |
| pass | 4♡ | pass | 5◊ |
| all pass | | | |

The Greek opened the ♡K and noted with suspicion that as the Rueful Rabbit tabled his hand, the Hog said nothing. Not an oath, not an insult. Why not? Surely that dummy called for a few well-chosen words of vilification. Papa shook his head uneasily.

The ♡K brought the six from the Walrus and the three from the Hog. With one trick in the bag and the ace of trumps to come, the Greek looked anxiously for one more trick to beat the contract. Miracles apart, spades alone offered any real hope, so at Trick 2, Papa switched to the ♠4, bringing the queen from his partner and the ace from declarer. The ◊K came next. All followed and Papa held off. The Hog continued with the ♣A and ♣K — the Walrus contributing the five and the four — and then reverted to trumps. All followed again to the ◊Q, but Papa couldn't afford to play low a second time. If he did, H.H. would ruff a heart in dummy and throw two losers on the clubs.

The Greek took stock. Since the Hog had shown up with no more than five trumps and no ♡A, he badly needed the ♠K to make up the values for his opening two-bid. Papa's only hope of beating the contract was surely to kill dummy's entry to the clubs while he still had a small trump. That way the Hog would be kept to ten tricks. Having checked and crosschecked his calculations, the Greek led a low heart to knock out dummy's trump entry. Instead of ruffing, however, the Hog ran the heart up to his jack, and drawing the last trump, claimed the rest of the tricks. These were the four hands:

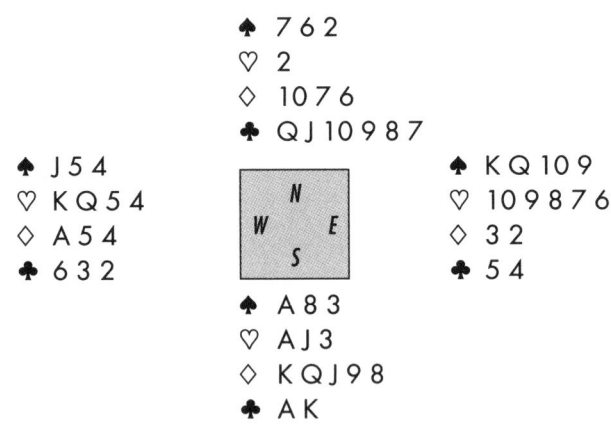

```
            ♠ 7 6 2
            ♡ 2
            ◊ 10 7 6
            ♣ Q J 10 9 8 7
♠ J 5 4              ♠ K Q 10 9
♡ K Q 5 4      N     ♡ 10 9 8 7 6
◊ A 5 4     W   E    ◊ 3 2
♣ 6 3 2         S    ♣ 5 4
            ♠ A 8 3
            ♡ A J 3
            ◊ K Q J 9 8
            ♣ A K
```

'That, my dear Papa, should teach you a lesson,' said the Hideous Hog severely. 'People who fall for Bath Coups shouldn't jeer at others.'

The Hog nudged Oscar in the ribs to make sure that he did not miss that quip about the Bath Coup. Papa's Adam's apple shot out three millimeters and there was a deep growl at the back of his throat, but nothing concrete materialized. Evidently, the Greeks had no word for it.

## CASTING SIGNALS BEFORE HOGS

The rubber was over and once more the cut brought Papa together with the Walrus. He chose the winning seats, dealt and passed. Then this hand came up:

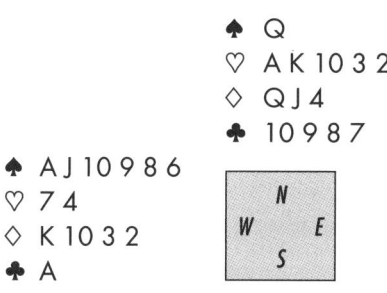

&spades; Q
&hearts; A K 10 3 2
&diams; Q J 4
&clubs; 10 9 8 7

&spades; A J 10 9 8 6
&hearts; 7 4
&diams; K 10 3 2
&clubs; A

| West | North | East | South |
|------|-------|------|-------|
| H.H. | W.W. | R.R. | Papa |
| 1♠ | pass | pass | 2♣ |
| 2♠ | 3♡ | pass | 3NT |
| pass | 4♣ | pass | 5♣ |
| all pass | | | |

The Hideous Hog opened the ♠A on which the Rueful Rabbit played the three and Papa the four. After gazing at the trick for nearly a second, H.H. continued with the ♠J, which Papa ruffed on the table. R.R. contributed the two and declarer the five.

Winning the next trick with the ace of trumps, H.H. led a third spade. Papa ruffed in dummy but the Rabbit overruffed with the jack and it was all over. This was the complete deal:

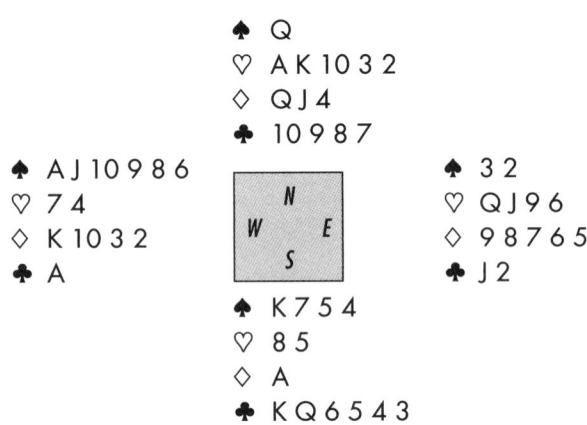

```
              ♠ Q
              ♡ A K 10 3 2
              ◇ Q J 4
              ♣ 10 9 8 7

♠ A J 10 9 8 6        N         ♠ 3 2
♡ 7 4           W         E     ♡ Q J 9 6
◇ K 10 3 2              S        ◇ 9 8 7 6 5
♣ A                             ♣ J 2

              ♠ K 7 5 4
              ♡ 8 5
              ◇ A
              ♣ K Q 6 5 4 3
```

'Well done, R.R.,' said Oscar, 'your three of spades broke the contract at the first trick. A most revealing card. If you had a doubleton, as you confirmed at Trick 2, Papa must have four spades. Allowing him six clubs, which seemed likely on the bidding, he could hardly have a loser in the red suits. So an overruff was the best, indeed the only chance. Truly a deadly signal.'

'Signal, indeed!' scoffed the Hog. 'He had heard that on partner's ace it is correct to drop the highest card. That three was an unblocking play, wasn't it, R.R.?'

'On the contrary,' retorted the Rabbit in a withering twitter, 'although you didn't recognize it, I gave you an unmistakable suit signal. Had I wanted a diamond switch, I should have dropped my two. Since I preferred hearts, I played my highest spade which happened to be the three. You were lucky to find me with the jack of clubs and... er...' R.R.'s voice trailed off as he became engrossed in another muffin.

'Why worry?' asked the Hog good-naturedly. 'So long as partner knows what your signals mean, does it matter if you don't know yourself?' H.H. was in a particularly good humor. He liked winning. He liked it better still that others should lose, especially Papa.

# Revenge Is Sweet

'I'll pay him out in his own coin,' fumed the Hideous Hog. 'All that crazy legal pedantry — sheer fanaticism... it would be immoral to allow such conduct to go unpunished... disgraceful...'

We were discussing over a bottle of madeira at the Griffins bar an incident which had occurred the previous night. The villain of the piece was the Emeritus Professor of Bio-Sophistry, known on account of his habits and appearance as the Secretary Bird.

Playing with the Rueful Rabbit, H.H. found himself in the unaccustomed role of dummy in a contract of 6♡.

The Professor, playing with Walter the Walrus, led out an ace. The Rabbit won the next trick and seeing no more losers, announced jauntily:

'All here. Drawing trumps.'

This was the trump position:

♡ K 9 8 6 5 4 3 ▭ ♡ A J 7

'One down,' said S.B. 'The queen of trumps doesn't come down.'

'Where is the queen?' inquired H.H. in a menacing voice.

'As it happens,' replied the Professor, 'I have the queen, not that it matters in the slightest.'

'On the contrary,' thundered the Hog, 'it matters a great deal. Since you have the queen, the Walrus shows out on the king of hearts and the finesse is automatic.'

'Declarer may not finesse. Law 72,' rejoined the Professor triumphantly. A jurist to his fingertips, he was now in his element.

'Anyway,' interjected Charlie the Chimp, who was kibitzing against the Hog, 'who said that R.R. would start drawing trumps with the king rather than with the ace?'

'Missing the ten as well as the queen,' retorted the Hog, 'it's elementary card play technique.'

'And since when,' countered the Chimp, 'has R.R. stooped to such trivia?'

Called in to adjudicate, Oscar the Owl, our Senior Kibitzer, pronounced in favor of the Professor. The last sentence in Law 72 left no room for doubt. The Owl read it out: 'Any question not specifically dealt with should be resolved in favor of the defenders.'

'Respect for the law is the mainstay of civilized society,' declared the Secretary Bird loftily, inscribing 100 above the line.

The Hog vowed vengeance, and it wasn't long before a suitable occasion presented itself. A couple of days later he found himself once more playing with the Rabbit against S.B., partnered this time by Charlie the Chimp.

East-West Vul. and 70
Dealer North

```
                    ♠ 5 4
                    ♡ A K 10
                    ◇ A 8 5 4 3
                    ♣ 7 5 4
   ♠ K                            ♠ A J 10 9 6 3 2
   ♡ 9 8 6 5 4 3 2                ♡ 7
   ◇ K 7                          ◇ Q 2
   ♣ K Q J                        ♣ A 3 2
                    ♠ Q 8 7
                    ♡ Q J
                    ◇ J 10 9 6
                    ♣ 10 9 8 6
```

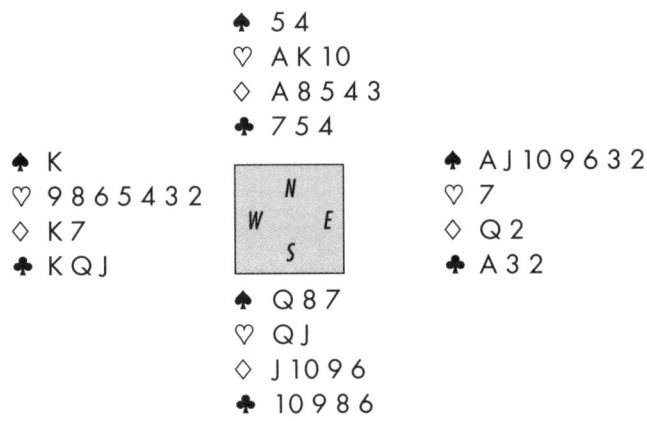

| West | North | East | South |
|------|-------|------|-------|
| R.R. | Ch.Ch. | H.H. | S.B. |
| | 1◇ | 1♠ | 1NT |
| dbl | pass | pass | 2◇ |
| 2♡ | pass | 2♠ | pass |
| pass | 2NT | dbl | all pass |

The Rabbit led out his three club honors, then the ♠K.

'Stop!' cried the Hog. 'It's my trick!' But he was too late.

'Premature lead by defender,' announced the Secretary Bird, and dwelling lovingly on each syllable he recited the provisions of Law 57.

The Rabbit gurgled. The Chimp smirked. The Hog growled but said nothing while the Professor considered his options, for the Hog, too, was thinking.

When he saw dummy, S.B. would have cheerfully settled for two down. Now, against this helpful defense, quite a rosy picture presented itself and it only required a little luck for the contract to be brought home.

'I accept the lead out of turn,' said the Professor after due deliberation, 'and I call on H.H. to play his highest spade.'

Without so much as a grunt the Hog produced the ♠A and placed it carefully in front of him, close to the edge of the table. The Rabbit had to stretch towards him to gather the trick.

'H.H. is taking it all very well,' observed a junior kibitzer.

'Surprisingly so,' agreed the Owl.

With downcast eyes the Hog turned to the Secretary Bird.

'It's a little embarrassing, Professor,' he began diffidently, 'but as my partner lent forward just now I couldn't help seeing the king of diamonds sticking out of the corner of his hand. I wouldn't allow it to influence my play, of course, but there it is. Isn't there a law...'

'Certainly there is,' broke in the Professor. 'Law 49 states explicitly: "Whenever a defender holds a card so that it is possible for his partner to see its face, such a card becomes a penalty card."'

'Do you mean,' asked H.H. in his silkiest voice, 'that this card must be played at the first opportunity?'

The Secretary Bird looked at him suspiciously. All this meekness was quite out of character.

'I... er, I mean...' the Rabbit was trying to say something.

'Kindly stop dithering,' the Hog told him, 'and leave the king of diamonds on the table.'

'What are you up to?' hissed the Secretary Bird. The wild tufts of hair over his ears bristled angrily.

'Is that king of diamonds a penalty card to be played at the first opportunity?' demanded the Hog. There was nothing meek about him now.

'It is,' agreed S.B., 'but I could waive the penalty.'

'Respect for the law is the mainstay of civilized society, if I may quote your words,' jeered the Hog, and as he spoke he led the ♠J, deftly scooping the ◇K.

A moment earlier the contract was unbeatable. Now it was unmakeable. The Secretary Bird came in with the ♠Q, cashed a club and two hearts and continued with the ace and another diamond, hoping against hope to find the Rabbit with the queen.

It was not to be. Having jettisoned his partner's king, the Hog had a certain entry with the $\diamond$Q. Three down.

The Rabbit was thoroughly mystified. 'You know,' he told me later at the bar, 'I don't believe H.H. could possibly have seen that king of diamonds. It wasn't, as he said, sticking out of the corner of my hand. It was at the other end, next to the two of hearts and I had my hand over it. I wonder what made him do it? Still,' went on the Rabbit, striking a more cheerful note, 'it didn't cost us a trick, for we could take only one diamond anyway, so despite my carelessness we got them down, and that's all that matters, isn't it?'

# Tainted Revenge

Waiting to cut in, I sat behind the Count, and, needless to say, my sympathies were entirely with him. I like the Count. Everybody does. He sports a monocle and a cavalry moustache and he showed me once, swishing his umbrella, how the hussars of old cut their enemies down with their sabers. On this occasion the prime enemy was Papa the Greek. Papa, I may say, is only an extract from an unpronounceable polysyllabic name, though under any other name he would have been equally unprepossessing. Supercilious and conceited, he has somehow persuaded half the club that he is a good player and the entire club that it is his special prerogative to have the last specious word in any and every argument.

So, as you can see, I had a personal interest in the rubber and in the 3NT contract which would, I hoped, bring it to an end.

The Doctor, sitting North, opened 1♣; East, whom we all suspect of being a tax inspector, but who pretends to a neutral coloring as a philatelist or a taxidermist or something equally unreal, passed, and the Count responded 1◊.

I had a quick look round — I was, when all is said and done, waiting to cut in — so I will show you what I saw before telling you what I heard.

The cards had been dealt like this:

```
                    ♠ A K J
                    ♡ 10 8 5
                    ◇ 10 9 8 7
                    ♣ A K 6
   ♠ Q 8 4                        ♠ 10 9 7 6 2
   ♡ A K Q 6          N           ♡ 4 3 2
   ◇ J 6 3        W       E       ◇ —
   ♣ Q J 3            S           ♣ 9 8 7 5 4
                    ♠ 5 3
                    ♡ J 9 7
                    ◇ A K Q 5 4 2
                    ♣ 10 2
```

This was the auction:

| West | North | East | South |
|------|-------|------|-------|
| *Papa* | *Doctor* | *Philatelist* | *Count* |
|  | 1♣ | pass | 1◇ |
| 1♡ | 1♠ | pass | 2◇ |
| pass | 2♡ | pass | 2NT |
| pass | 3NT | all pass | |

The Doctor's 2♡ was, of course, a directional asking bid. I should have mentioned earlier, perhaps, that the Doctor is a man of profound erudition who reads everything that is published on bridge as on medicine and is determined to get his full money's worth out of every line on both subjects. He practices what he preaches, notably Kock-Werner, Gingervan, Texas, Arcofac, Jacoby, Corn Oil and directional asking bids. Sometimes the patient fails to live up to the diagnosis. Then he has to pay for it. The Count knew from bitter experience what was wanted of him and he bid 2NT manfully. The Doctor raised him to 3NT and Papa shot the ♡A, ♡K and ♡Q across the table. The Count brightened visibly when the *soi-disant* philatelist (or taxidermist, as the case may be) followed to the third round, but I could not help wincing. The diamonds were blocked and unless the Greek played his last heart, allowing the Count to rid dummy of one of those lethal diamonds, the contract was doomed. Holding both black queens, Papa could hardly go wrong and I began to search for another table that might be up first. Before I had time to swirl an eyeball the Greek led the thirteenth heart.

Hope quickly yielded to despair when the Count tossed a small club from dummy, remarking in his best idiomatic English, as he spread his hand on the table: 'All here and tricks for the fire.'

The granite diamond sequence in dummy remained untouched to mock him and I held my breath. But all was well. 'Quite foolproof. Ten top tricks' announced Papa and nobody thought of questioning that direct descendant of the Delphic Oracle.

It was a sore temptation. I admit that it would have given me much pleasure to point out to the Greek that he had conceded, through sheer ignorance, a contract which was, at that stage, utterly unmakeable. He had thrown it through bad defense, though declarer had failed to take advantage of his blunder. Alas, I could say nothing without upsetting the Count, who had claimed the contract in all innocence.

I was still wondering how I could puncture Papa's insufferable conceit without embarrassing the Count, when East dealt:

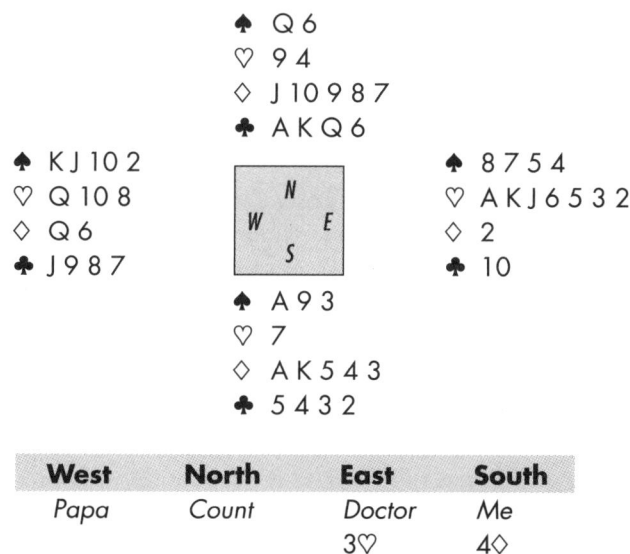

|  | ♠ Q 6 |  |
|---|---|---|
|  | ♡ 9 4 |  |
|  | ◇ J 10 9 8 7 |  |
|  | ♣ A K Q 6 |  |
| ♠ K J 10 2 |  | ♠ 8 7 5 4 |
| ♡ Q 10 8 |  | ♡ A K J 6 5 3 2 |
| ◇ Q 6 |  | ◇ 2 |
| ♣ J 9 8 7 |  | ♣ 10 |
|  | ♠ A 9 3 |  |
|  | ♡ 7 |  |
|  | ◇ A K 5 4 3 |  |
|  | ♣ 5 4 3 2 |  |

| West | North | East | South |
|------|-------|------|-------|
| Papa | Count | Doctor | Me |
|  |  | 3♡ | 4◇ |
| pass | 5◇ | all pass |  |

Papa led the ♡Q. The Doctor took it over with the king and continued with the ace.

At this stage, I might have almost spread my hand. Unless the Greek had all three missing trumps, I was home. Either the clubs would break 3-2 or I would discard one from dummy on my ♠A, after setting up the queen. For beyond any shadow of a doubt the Greek had the

♠K. East had shown up already with a suit headed by the ace and king, and I knew that he would as soon cure a patient by some shady, unorthodox means as open a three-bid with an ace-king *and* a king.

I ruffed the second heart, played the ace of trumps, to be on the safe side, and led a small spade to dummy's queen. The Greek duly went up with the king and began fidgeting. Some five minutes later, when his trance was nearing the halfway mark, I realized with horror what I had done. That ace of trumps at the previous trick was no safety play. It was a piece of criminal folly, for if Papa had the ◇Q I was doomed — if he played it, of course. The king of trumps, I now realized, was the only remaining entry to my hand and though I had set up dummy's ♠Q, I could no longer get back to cash the ace, and to the bitter end I should be locked in dummy. I was soothing myself with the thought that the clubs might break decently after all. Alternatively, Papa might not have the ◇Q and even if he had, he might not lead it.

My pulse was still unsteady when Papa came to the rescue with a spade. A few seconds later I noted, not without satisfaction, that the Greek had four clubs and the ◇Q. This time there was no reason to spare his feelings. I apologized to the Count, adding: 'My carelessness gave Papa the chance to defeat the contract; not a serious risk, perhaps, but one that I should have avoided.'

Raising a supercilious eyebrow, the Greek interrupted me with, 'Yes, yes, my friend. I agree that you did what you could to lose the contract, but it was not in your power. If I returned the queen of trumps, as you suggest, even you — forgive me for putting it so plainly — could have found no possible way to go down.

'As you can see,' he went on, 'my spades were KJ102 and I should have been hopelessly squeezed in the black suits — without malice aforethought on your part, of course. You would have been forced to play all your winners all down the line and in the five-card ending I could not keep four clubs and two spades. You would overtake dummy's queen and find, to your surprise, no doubt, that your nine was good.'

Of course, the argument was blatantly dishonest. Until he saw my hand Papa did not know that I had the ♠9. He had failed to spot the obvious defense and was trying to cover up with a hastily improvised squeeze fantasy. Unfortunately, I did not spot the fraud until it was too late to expose him, but I was resolved to make him pay for his effrontery. I did not have long to wait. Revenge is sweet and I had it in full measure on the last hand of the rubber. These were the hands:

```
                    ♠ 10 4 2
                    ♡ A J 9 5
                    ◇ A Q 2
                    ♣ A J 9
   ♠ A Q J 9 7 5 3        ┌─────────┐        ♠ K 8 6
   ♡ 7                    │    N    │        ♡ 4 3 2
   ◇ 10 9 8 6             │ W     E │        ◇ 7 5
   ♣ 10                   │    S    │        ♣ Q 8 6 5 3
                          └─────────┘
                    ♠ —
                    ♡ K Q 10 8 6
                    ◇ K J 4 3
                    ♣ K 7 4 2
```

| West | North | East | South |
|------|-------|------|-------|
| Papa | Count | Doctor | Me |
|      |       |        | 1♡ |
| 1♠ | 3♣ | pass | 3◇ |
| 3♠ | 6♡ | pass | 7♣ |
| pass | 7♡ | all pass | |

Having the king of partner's suit and a void in spades into the bargain I felt that I had something to spare. Papa led the ♣10 and it was, of course, all over. As the learned doctor was not slow to point out, the Greek had selected the only one of his thirteen cards which would give me the contract.

Papa tried to defend himself. A spade lead, he argued, could do no good, since I clearly had none, but I would never expect him to lead a singleton against a grand slam and it might upset my calculations. Besides, seeing the ten fall I could always take a backward finesse. That was a typical piece of sophistry which I was happy to demolish.

'My dear Papa,' I told him, 'even though you claim to have guessed that I had the nine of spades on that five diamonds hand, I am compelled to confess that I would not have discovered your ten of clubs until after I had played the king from my hand. In fact, without your invaluable help I would have planned to finesse in the normal way — we cannot all have second sight, you know — and would have gone down. Only one down, it is true,' I added, sprinkling a little salt on the open wound, 'but still a difference of some 2,500, I fancy.'

Then, quickly collecting my winnings, I was out of the room before he could recover his equipoise and his habitual effrontery.

I reached home in time to watch my wife finish the packing. Her niece, Maria, who was coming with us to Palma, had been helping her and I knew she would appreciate the story of the Greek's discomfiture. She has been taking lessons, and though the finer points of the hand would elude her, being a woman she would enjoy the personal side.

As I put myself down on a particularly recalcitrant suitcase I told her about the hand. She frowned. 'Your Mr. Papa,' she said, 'cannot be a very good player. There was no need for him to pretend that you would have taken a backward club finesse. The contract was unbeatable on any lead.'

I explained patiently that since the trumps were 3-1, I could not discard one of dummy's clubs on my fourth diamond and then ruff two clubs in dummy. Maria waited till I had finished and went on: 'You ruff dummy's three spades in your hand, using two top trumps and one of dummy's aces as entries. Then you enter dummy with the other ace and draw the last trump. Isn't it called a dummy reverse?'

Of course. Absurdly simple. How could I have missed it? And what a good thing that I should be away for a month. I could just imagine Papa's insufferable sarcasm. He would have collared me at the Club next day, pinning me down to a seat in full view of the public. With a smile of studied contempt, in a pitying tone of voice, he would have lectured me at length on the simple technique of dummy reversals. Of course, he would have claimed that the whole picture had been clear to him from the start and a lot of gullible people would have believed him!

It was a hot day and perhaps I looked a little flushed. 'Of course,' went on Maria, 'you would have made your slam without difficulty. It is simply that you were teasing your Greek. Isn't that so?'

Just then the telephone rang. Maria lifted the receiver and I heard her say, 'Who's that? Oh! What name did you say? No, they left for Gatwick five minutes ago. They will be in Capri for the next month.'

'It was Mr. Themistocles Papadopoulos. I thought you did not wish to be disturbed,' she said.

'Quite right,' I assured her, 'but I don't think that they use Gatwick any more. And what made you think of Capri, anyway?'

'I thought he might follow you,' replied my niece. 'A sort of safety move, isn't it called?'

One day, I think, when Maria has had more experience, she will make a first-class partner.

# Partner is Purely Incidental

'Partnership understanding will be the ruin of bridge. There's far too much of it,' declared the Hideous Hog, dispatching the last of the oysters.

We were dining at the Unicorn, and, while we waited for the *bécasse au fumet*, H.H. propounded his philosophy of bridge.

'It was all very well,' he went on, 'to be dazzled by the beautiful language of bidding when it was the prerogative of a chosen few. Today, with all our points and tables and conventions, we require no partner to be beautiful. We can do it out of a book, any book, and Heaven knows they are cheap enough to borrow.

'Why, even the Rabbit,' pursued the Hog bitterly, 'can often tell the difference nowadays between a force and a signoff. Yes, things have come to a pretty pass when he can turn up his Blackwood chart and work out, there and then, how many aces he holds — well, up to a point anyway.'

'Would you like to abolish partners altogether or only to do away with your own?' inquired Colin the Corgi, the facetious young man recently down from Oxbridge.

'Like the poor and the sick, partner will always be with us' replied the Hog solemnly, his eyes glued to a nearby trolley on which M. Merle was preparing the woodcock's sauce.

'Mind you, there's a place for partner, too,' he added, 'so long as it is clearly understood that opponents come first, last and all the time.

'Duplicate is the wolf in sheep's clothing,' continued the Hideous Hog. 'It's to duplicate that we owe the pernicious notion that bridge is primarily a get-together between points-conscious, system-sharing, convention-mongering partners, whose mission is not to engage in a duel with the enemy, but to exchange coded messages with each other.'

Before we could say a word, the Hog interrupted us. 'Think,' he cried, 'how stimulating it would be if every player, instead of being shackled to a partner he secretly despises, were forever pitted against his favorite opponent! How much better we should all play! Yes, even I could rise to still greater heights...'

M. Merle lit the cognac and the flames shot up, providing a Wagnerian background to the Hog's lofty but turbulent thoughts.

'Would you pick the Rueful Rabbit as your constant foe?' asked Colin, moving away his glass before the Hog could get at it.

'No, no one can be brilliant against that Rabbit. He's far too bad,' replied H.H. with feeling. 'How can you hit a man if you can't find him, and how can you find him if he does not know where he is himself? Of course you miss the target.'

'Would you prefer Papa?' ventured Oscar the Owl.

'A most desirable adversary,' agreed the Hog, 'too cunning, too clever, a born exhibitionist and above all, insufferably conceited. Why, there are times when he thinks he's me!'

## H.H. ON ETHICS

Half a woodcock later the Hog returned to the theme. 'Consider the ethical aspect,' he began. 'Your foe is entitled to take every advantage of you and to hit occasionally below the belt, because you can do the same to him. You wield the same weapons. But what weapon have you against someone else's partnership understanding? Of course if North plays with South, hand after hand, match after match, year after year, they will develop an insight into each other's methods. What sort of art is that? But let it once be recognized that partner is purely incidental and most of the problems in ethics begin to evaporate.

'With a fair field and no favor, the game regains the reality of which duplicate has all but robbed it. East meets North, and South meets West with no quarter asked or given. Partners come and go, canceling each other out, but the master reaps a just reward for bending opponents to his will, reading their thoughts and making them dance to his tune.'

'Take that grand slam of Papa's yesterday...'

# HOIST ON HIS OWN CRACKER

I remembered the hand well. I was sitting with my back to the card table, writing a rude letter to the London Electricity Board, when I heard this sequence behind me:

| North | South |
|-------|-------|
| C.C. | Papa |
| | 1◇ |
| 2♠ | 3♡ |
| 5◇ | 5NT |
| 7◇ | pass |

The Hog, who was on Papa's right, doubled. At this point, the steward came in to call to the telephone the Hog's partner, an inconspicuous clean-shaven young man of uncertain age, who parted his hair on one side.

'Show me your hand, Papa,' said Colin the Corgi, 'it will pass the time. And for once I'll know what you have.'

'No, no,' replied the Greek, 'it's a bad habit.'

'Why not ask me,' suggested H.H., seeing a chance to needle Papa. 'I will tell you every card. He has five diamonds and four hearts. His first two bids show that. Three aces are certain for he did not check on aces. The fourth you have yourself, my dear Colin. It's the ace of trumps. And since you've shown another top honor...'

The Hog's partner returned at this point, and, after reviewing the bidding, opened proceedings with the ♠4.

Turning away from the Electricity Board, I looked at the Greek's hand and his dummy. H.H. was, as stated, East.

```
        ♠ K Q 10 3
        ♡ J
        ◇ A K 8 7
        ♣ K J 4 2

              N
          W       E
              S

        ♠ A 2
        ♡ A K 7 3
        ◇ Q 10 5 4 2
        ♣ A 6
```

Winning the trick in his hand, Themistocles Papadopoulos pondered deeply. As he gazed at dummy he frowned and his hairy spatulate fingers beat a rhythmic tattoo on the table. Papa was sorely puzzled by the Hog's double. Then, with a sudden exclamation, he sat up excitedly in his chair. Evidently the scales had fallen from his eyes.

'Ha!' he cried 'you think you are clever, my friend, because you know my hand, and so you should for you can trust my bidding. But I am more clever than you for I know why you doubled.'

With a flourish he spread his hand on the table and in the manner of a Sherlock Holmes lecturing a gathering of Watsons, he proceeded to lay bare the dark recesses of the criminal mind.

'This, of course, is no Lightner Double, for our friend has not ruffed a spade and his partner would have led a heart had he been dealt eight of them. As you can see, we have all the high cards. Therefore, the double can only be based on the trump position. Now if they were divided, the double would make no sense. So the ◇J963 are in one hand. But only a lunatic would reveal such a holding by doubling a grand slam. It follows that H.H. has a void and that he doubled to protect his partner's trumps and to fool me! But as you say in English, he will be hoisted on his own cracker. Yes, for Papa can catch both the jack and nine now that he knows where they are. First the queen from hand, then the ten to trap the jack, then a finesse against the nine. Like this...'

The Hog's partner, who had been growing rather restless during Papa's discourse, greeted the ◇Q with a small spade. The Greek gasped. For several seconds he was speechless. Then he repeated his own words '...only a lunatic would reveal...'

This was the deal:

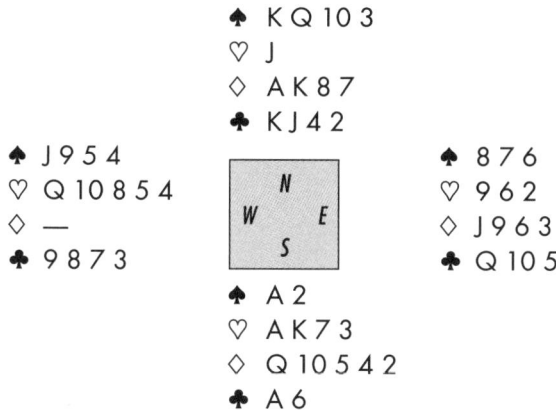

                    ♠ K Q 10 3
                    ♡ J
                    ◇ A K 8 7
                    ♣ K J 4 2

    ♠ J 9 5 4                           ♠ 8 7 6
    ♡ Q 10 8 5 4        N               ♡ 9 6 2
    ◇ —           W          E          ◇ J 9 6 3
    ♣ 9 8 7 3           S               ♣ Q 10 5

                    ♠ A 2
                    ♡ A K 7 3
                    ◇ Q 10 5 4 2
                    ♣ A 6

'Thirty-four points,' murmured the Walrus to the Rabbit. 'He should have made it, you know.'

'I am surprised Papa did not guess it,' observed R.R. 'What else could H.H. have doubled on but the trumps?'

The Hog laughed uproariously at Oscar's description of Papa's discomfiture. Other people's misfortunes appealed to his keen sense of humor, but none gave him so much pleasure as Papa's.

'Of course,' he added by way of a postscript, 'in this situation, a player less scrupulously ethical than I am can try another stratagem. On partner's opening spade he throws a heart. Needless to say, partner asks, 'No spades?' and he promptly finds one. But a doubt has been conjured up in declarer's mind. If East thought he had no spades, why did he not ruff, he will ask himself. Surely it could only be because he had a void. Naturally, for my part I would not dream...'

'That reminds me,' I broke in, 'of another hand you played against your favorite foe, the hand Oscar called "The Treble Chance". You remember...'

'No, no,' exclaimed the Hog, 'It's a dull hand. Nothing in it. Let me order another bottle of Krug...'

'You are too modest H.H., always hiding your light under a bushel. Please tell us,' pleaded Colin.

The deal had occurred a fortnight or so earlier.

# THE TREBLE CHANCE

'Last hand,' announced the Walrus. 'I promised my wife to be home at seven.'

'Well, it's only twenty past,' pointed out H.H.

'I know,' said W.W., 'but it's getting foggy and it will take me longer than usual to get back. I've parked my car miles away and I may have to wait for a taxi.'

South dealt this hand to Papa:

<pre>
        ♠ 4 3 2
        ♡ Q 10 2
        ◇ Q 3
        ♣ A Q 6 4 2
</pre>

| West | North | East | South |
|------|-------|------|-------|
| Papa | W.W. | S.B. | H.H. |
|      |       |      | 1♣ |
| pass | 1♡ | pass | 2NT |
| pass | 3NT | all pass | |

Papa had already detached a small club from his hand when his partner, the Emeritus Professor of Bio-Sophistry, led the ♠K.

'Lead out of turn,' called the Hog in a flash. 'I'll have a club from you, Papa.'

The Secretary Bird turned on him with a characteristic hiss: 'You are not entitled to call for a lead,' he said with some asperity. 'Surely you know the law H.H. Allow me to draw your attention specifically to Section 56, sub-section one on page 30 of the laws. You will find that you may bar a spade lead or treat the king as an exposed card or require...'

'Oh, a truce to all this legal pedantry!' cried the Hog. 'If I broke the laws as often as you do I, too, would know them backwards.' Then, turning to Papa, he added grandly: 'Lead what you like. I waive my rights.'

The Greek replaced the ♣6 and hesitated. Finally, since there was no penalty, he decided on the ♠4, partner's suit, and dummy came into view.

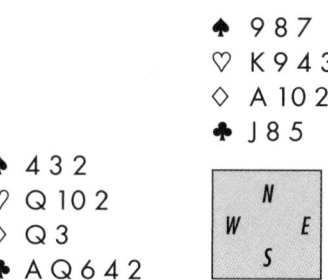

```
              ♠ 9 8 7
              ♡ K 9 4 3
              ◇ A 10 2
              ♣ J 8 5
♠ 4 3 2
♡ Q 10 2          N
◇ Q 3         W       E
♣ A Q 6 4 2       S
```

The Secretary Bird's ♠Q held the first trick, H.H. contributing the six. The ♠5 followed. Winning the trick with the jack, the Hog crossed to dummy with a heart to the king and led the ♣5, to which S.B. played the seven. The Hog put on the ten and Papa was in with the queen. The Greek studied the situation closely. There was clearly no future in spades or for that matter in hearts. Diamonds seemed to offer the best chance and Papa boldly led the queen.

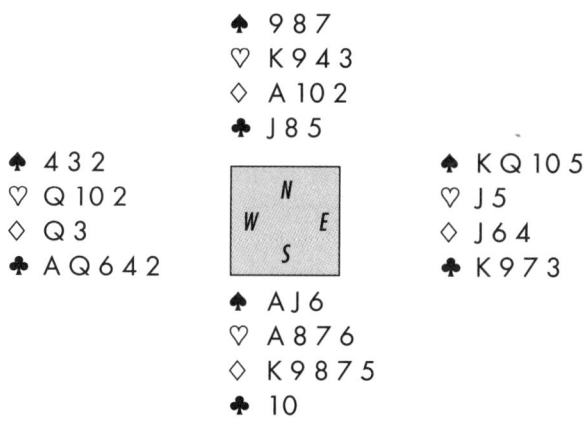

```
              ♠ 9 8 7
              ♡ K 9 4 3
              ◇ A 10 2
              ♣ J 8 5
♠ 4 3 2                        ♠ K Q 10 5
♡ Q 10 2          N            ♡ J 5
◇ Q 3         W       E        ◇ J 6 4
♣ A Q 6 4 2       S            ♣ K 9 7 3
              ♠ A J 6
              ♡ A 8 7 6
              ◇ K 9 8 7 5
              ♣ 10
```

The Hog won with the ace in dummy and followed with the ten, finessing successfully against East's jack. His contract was fulfilled with five diamonds, two spades and two hearts.

'How many points did you have?' asked Walter the Walrus suspiciously.

'Only sixteen,' lied the Hog, 'but as it was the last hand I thought you would forgive me for stretching a point — so long as I made the contract.'

Oscar the Owl emitted a soft, tuneful hoot. 'Bid clubs. Call for a club lead. Lead clubs yourself. Then no one else dare touch the suit.

That, I suppose, is what is known as the Treble Chance. Yet even so, you had to locate the jack of diamonds. Your guessing, H.H., is always accurate.'

'Guessing!' repeated the Hog scornfully. 'Do you suppose, then, that Papa would have led the queen if he had been dealt the jack as well? Don't you know that he never leads a true card when he has more than a singleton?'

## Papa Looks Into the Future

With all trace of embarrassment gone, the Hideous Hog chuckled good-humoredly as I recalled his devious practices against Papa.

'This reminds me of another unusual hand I played against him,' he said, emptying a small bottle of kirsch absent-mindedly over his pineapple. 'You know the hand I mean, the one he promised to keep from the Press so that you should have it exclusively for your next book, ha ha ha!'

The hand in question belonged undoubtedly to South-East, but it may be noted for the record, that though their respective partners were purely incidental, as the Hog would say, he was himself playing with the Rabbit, while Papa had cut Colin the Corgi.

I was sitting behind the Greek, who dealt and bid 1♠.

```
            ♠ J 8 3
            ♡ 9 8 7 6 5
            ◇ A 4 2
            ♣ 7 6
            ┌──────────┐
            └──────────┘
            ♠ A K 6 5 4
            ♡ 4
            ◇ K Q 10 5
            ♣ K Q 8
```

| West | North | East | South |
|------|-------|------|-------|
| R.R. | C.C. | H.H. | Papa |
|      |       |      | 1♠ |
| 2♡ | 2♠ | pass | 4♠ |
| all pass | | | |

The Rabbit led the ♡K, then the ace, which Papa ruffed. His ♣K at the third trick was won by the Rabbit's ace and this was followed by another heart for the Greek to ruff. H.H. threw a club. Next came the ace of trumps, which brought the two from the Rabbit and the seven from the Hog. Now the Greek played his ♣Q, ruffed a club in dummy, and followed with the ♠J, on which H.H. played the ten.

After a short pause, Papa went up with the king, picking up the Rabbit's nine. Then he spread his hand face upwards on the table. We knew from experience that some brilliant coup was about to be demonstrated and the more experienced kibitzers picked up their newspapers.

'All here,' announced Papa, 'but the hand is of some interest as an illustration of the art of card reading. Simple, yet striking.

'You will observe that I have lost two tricks, a heart and a club, and must lose a third, a trump to the queen. The contract depends, therefore, on not losing a diamond. Well, you are no doubt asking yourselves, how I can be so certain of that?'

R.R. fidgeted. The Hog grunted but said nothing. I felt sure that Colin was looking for some cutting remark and that he had nearly found one, when Papa resumed.

'It's really quite simple, you know. R.R. has shown up with five hearts. His partner followed twice, you may recall, and then failed. He has followed three times to the clubs and twice to spades, and we know that he has the queen left, for with ♠Q10 H.H. would have covered the jack. That comes to eleven cards — five hearts, three clubs and three spades. Therefore R.R. must have two diamonds, just two and no more. So, I play the king, then a small one to the ace, and if the jack has not dropped I finesse knowing that I cannot fail. Pretty, don't you think?'

It was at this point that Papa offered to donate the hand to me, for my next book.

'Meanwhile,' suggested Colin, 'if you have concluded your peroration, perhaps we can play out the hand without having to wait for the book to see the happy ending.'

With a look of scorn at his partner, the Greek went through the motions — first the ◇K, then a low one to the ace, then the 'marked' finesse.

Tremulously the Rabbit produced the jack.

'Impossible,' cried the Greek. 'You can't have it. You've revoked. Look again...'

A loud guffaw from the Hog drowned the rest of the sentence. These were the four hands:

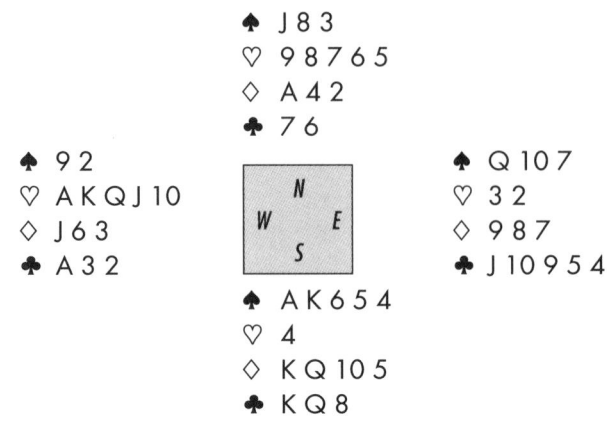

```
                    ♠ J 8 3
                    ♡ 9 8 7 6 5
                    ◇ A 4 2
                    ♣ 7 6
  ♠ 9 2                              ♠ Q 10 7
  ♡ A K Q J 10          N            ♡ 3 2
  ◇ J 6 3           W       E        ◇ 9 8 7
  ♣ A 3 2               S            ♣ J 10 9 5 4
                    ♠ A K 6 5 4
                    ♡ 4
                    ◇ K Q 10 5
                    ♣ K Q 8
```

'My dear Papa,' gloated the Hog, 'since you are without doubt the most energetic falsecard specialist in the Western Hemisphere, allow me to commend to you my little ten of trumps, from ♠Q10, on your jack. It's something new for your repertoire.'

'Why...?' began the Greek.

'Because,' answered the Hog, 'every card was indeed marked. You had shown up with a singleton heart and I had the remaining clubs myself. Unless you had a losing diamond there was no hope for us.'

'But...' tried the Greek once more.

'No, no,' went on the Hog, 'you looked like having the king-queen on the bidding. Besides my falsecard could not cost a thing. It was too incredible to be believed. But I must admit that even a very good player would have fallen for it. Even I might have been taken in.'

# The Rabbit's Secret Weapon

For no apparent reason the Rabbit has played well twice within the space of less than a week. There are rumors and speculations, but so far no one has discovered the cause.

The first time it happened was in a 4♠ contract against the Professor of Bio-Sophistry, better known as the Secretary Bird, and Charlie the Chimp. The Rabbit's partner was Timothy the Toucan, and this was the deal:

## Secretary Bird
## & Rueful Rabbit

Neither Vul.
Dealer West

```
                    ♠ A Q 10 5 2
                    ♡ 6 4
                    ◇ A 6 4
                    ♣ A 3 2
   ♠ 7 3                              ♠ 4
   ♡ A 10 9 8 3        N              ♡ Q J 7 5
   ◇ K J 7        W         E         ◇ 10 9 8
   ♣ Q J 5            S              ♣ 10 9 8 7 6
                    ♠ K J 9 8 6
                    ♡ K 2
                    ◇ Q 5 3 2
                    ♣ K 4
```

| West | North | East | South |
|------|-------|------|-------|
| S.B. | T.T. | Ch.Ch. | R.R. |
| 1♡ | dbl | 2♡ | 3♠ |
| pass | 4♠ | all pass | |

The Professor led the ♣Q. The Rabbit won in his hand, drew trumps in two rounds, crossed to the ♣A and ruffed a club. Then he paused to regroup.

'The hearts and diamonds are all wrong. One off,' whispered Oscar the Owl, who was sitting next to me and had, as usual, seen all four hands.

Having studied the unpromising situation, R.R. led the ♡4 from dummy. As the Chimp played the ♡J, the Toucan suddenly sprang to life, pointing out belatedly that the previous trick had been won in the closed hand.

'How surprising that you of all people, Professor, didn't notice it,' said the Hideous Hog, who was kibitzing against the Chimp.

The Secretary Bird hissed.

'Sorry. My fault entirely. I should have warned you,' apologized T.T.

'Better late than never,' said the Hog with a meaningful look.

The Rabbit, who had detached the ♡K, put it back, hesitated, and after muttering to himself for a while, played the two.

Left on play, the Chimp switched to the ◇10. The Rabbit played low, winning with the ace in dummy. He continued with a heart to his king, and after that there was no defense. All S.B. could do was to choose between leading a diamond to R.R.'s queen or presenting him with a ruff and discard.

'I was mistaken,' admitted O.O. 'I assumed he would go up with the king. The Professor would win, put Charlie in with the ♡Q, and a diamond return would kill the contract stone dead. Ducking that first heart was brilliant. A very unusual endplay, R.R. Remarkable.'

I didn't see the Rabbit for several days. Before I could discuss the hand with him, he had distinguished himself again.

It was towards the end of the afternoon session. The Hog and I cut out. Papa the Greek and the Rabbit took our places. Before either side had scored, this hand came up.

Neither Vul.
Dealer East

```
              ♠ 7 6 5 4
              ♡ Q 6 4
              ◇ A 5 3
              ♣ Q 7 2
                  ┌─────────┐
                  │    N    │
                  │ W     E │
                  │    S    │
                  └─────────┘
              ♠ A Q 8 2
              ♡ A K 9 7 5 2
              ◇ 4
              ♣ 10 4
```

| West | North | East | South |
|------|-------|------|-------|
| S.B. | W.W. | Papa | R.R. |
|  |  | 1♠ | 2♡ |
| 3♣ | pass | 3◇ | pass |
| pass | 3♡ | pass | pass |
| 4◇ | pass | pass | 4♡ |
| all pass | | | |

The Secretary Bird led the ◇J. As always, R.R. played quickly to the first few tricks. Leaving planning to the planners, he didn't believe in taking his fences before he came to them. Going up with the ◇A, he led a heart to his king, then another to the queen. When both defenders followed twice, the Rabbit deduced that there were no more trumps out, so he began to look around.

Assuming the spade finesse to be right, there were two losers in clubs and two in spades (don't forget that East bid spades, so they won't split 3-2). Hoping perhaps to find the Professor with the ♣AK so dummy's queen could be set up for a spade discard, the Rabbit was about to play the ♣10. The card was already in mid-air, visible to all, when Papa stopped him. 'You're on the table,' he warned.

'You're usurping dummy's prerogative,' hissed the Secretary Bird.

'Sorry,' stammered Walter the Walrus. 'I, er...'

'Never mind, Walter,' consoled Papa. 'There's no penalty. Declarer can expose all his hand if he likes. He can play any suit, any card.'

A sibilant, unfriendly sound from S.B. interrupted him.

'Oh dear, this is so confusing, so very confusing,' muttered the Rabbit. After an animated conversation with himself, he finally led dummy's ♣2. These were the four hands:

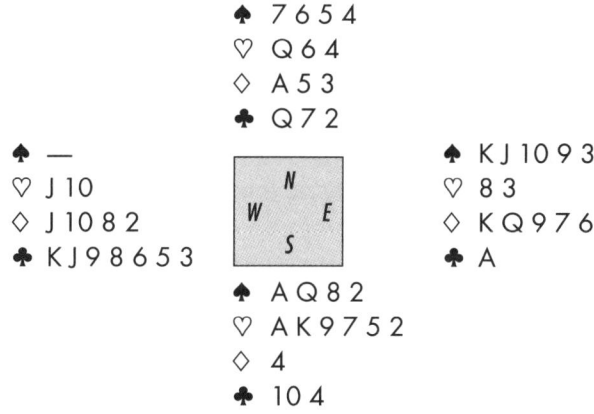

```
              ♠ 7 6 5 4
              ♡ Q 6 4
              ◇ A 5 3
              ♣ Q 7 2
♠ —                              ♠ K J 10 9 3
♡ J 10            N              ♡ 8 3
◇ J 10 8 2    W       E          ◇ K Q 9 7 6
♣ K J 9 8 6 5 3   S              ♣ A
              ♠ A Q 8 2
              ♡ A K 9 7 5 2
              ◇ 4
              ♣ 10 4
```

A spade return from Papa was won by the queen and now a club to dummy ensured the contract.

'Extraordinary!' spluttered the Greek. 'What an unnatural way to play the clubs!'

'Not a bit of it,' retorted the Hog. 'If the Professor had both the ace and king of his suit, he would have surely led one of them. And if you had either, it had to be a singleton, for you could hardly have fewer than ten cards in spades and diamonds on your bidding — and you had followed twice in hearts. Elementary, my dear Themistocles.'

'Are you suggesting that the Rabbit worked that out?' asked Papa with a contemptuous curve of his lips.

Mimicking S.B., the Hog produced a very creditable hiss.

Over a madeira before dinner, I asked R.R. to explain his reasoning, and I reminded him of that brilliantly timed throw-in on the 4♠ hand a few days earlier.

Looking rather coy, the Rabbit let me in on his secret. 'I've been reading a textbook on bridge psychology,' he told me. 'It isn't as difficult as it sounds, but there's a technique in applying it. First you find out what your opponents want, then you do the opposite.

'Now take that 4♠ contract you mentioned. It was odd, as H.H. pointed out, that the Professor, who's always so quick on the trigger, for once claimed no penalty. Why not? I was going to play up to my ♡K, of course, and he could have made me play from my hand, in which case I would play a small one. Evidently he didn't want that. So I did it, and it worked out surprisingly well, just as the book says.'

'And what made you lead a low club from dummy this afternoon?' I asked.

'That wasn't quite so straightforward,' admitted R.R. 'Papa warned me just in time not to play from the wrong hand. Had I done so, I would have had to play from dummy. Clearly, he didn't want that, though I couldn't think why. The Professor, however, intended this time to penalize me. He wanted one thing, Papa wanted another, a 50-50 chance, as you might say. But as always, one fifty is better than the other. Papa is the stronger player, so I trusted him and did the opposite of what he, not S.B., wanted me to do.

'Psychology is a great thing,' concluded the Rabbit. 'Other people think things out, do your work and direct you and all you have to do is go the other way.

# Getting a Count on Dummy

It was the first rubber after dinner. The Rueful Rabbit cut Timothy the Toucan. Walter the Walrus faced Charlie the Chimp. Compelled to kibitz, the Hideous Hog was strictly neutral. So long as the Chimp lost he didn't care who won.

Bouncing unsteadily in his chair, the Toucan suspected that after the magnum of Latour '61 with the pheasant it was a grave error to go on to the white Chateauneuf with the *zabaglione*. His distribution felt distinctly unbalanced and he looked apprehensively at the Rabbit, who was sipping a cherry brandy.

A little flushed no doubt, but eager and alert, the Rabbit looked full of confidence as he dealt the first hand.

Neither Vul.
Dealer South

```
              ♠ —
              ♡ K 4 3 2
              ◊ K J 9 6 4 2
              ♣ 4 3 2
```

```
                  N
              W       E
                  S
```

```
              ♠ A K Q 7 6 3 2
              ♡ A Q J 9 6
              ◊ —
              ♣ A
```

| West | North | East | South |
|------|-------|------|-------|
| W.W. | T.T. | Ch.Ch. | R.R. |
|  |  |  | 2♣ |
| dbl | pass | pass | 2♠ |
| pass | 3◊ | pass | 3♡ |
| pass | 4♡ | pass | 5♣ |
| pass | 6♡ | dbl | all pass |

It was a relief to the Toucan to be dummy. He tabled his hand and the Rabbit shook his head. 'We've missed it,' he murmured under his breath. 'I knew I should have gone on, but over the double 7♡ could be so misleading.'

The Walrus led the ♣K.

Seeing at least fourteen winners and no losers anywhere, the Rabbit intended to play the hand slowly, lingering pleasurably over every trick. First he laid down the ♡A on which the Walrus threw a club. Next he decided to ruff a spade so at Trick 2 he led the ♠2, covered by the Walrus with the five. The Rabbit called for dummy's ♡2.

'I think not,' said the Chimp with a gleeful smirk. Standing behind him, H.H. smiled malevolently.

'I'm ruffing...' began the Rabbit. Then he stopped in his tracks as with quick, nimble fingers the Chimp detached and held to the light the ♠4, which had been nestling in dummy with the ♣32.

The Toucan dipped his long red nose in shame. The heat in the room was stifling.

The Rabbit scrutinized the card closely. Alas, there was no doubt about it. That little club was a spade. The poor Toucan had mixed up his three black cards and the Rabbit hadn't noticed it.

'Cheer up, Timothy,' said the Rabbit. 'It's as much my fault as yours. In fact,' he added as a thought suddenly struck him, 'we should have all spotted it. How odd that no one did.'

'Are you accusing me?' cried W.W. indignantly. 'Am I supposed to sort out your twos, threes and fours for you?' The Walrus knew all about points and signals and the higher side of bridge. Splitting hairs over deuces was all well for professionals, but a man in his position had more important things to think about.

On the ♠5 the Chimp parted with the ◇7. The Rabbit blinked, 'Having no spades?' he asked incredulously,

'I've looked diligently among my clubs and I can't find a single one,' replied the Chimp with a chuckle.

This was the deal:

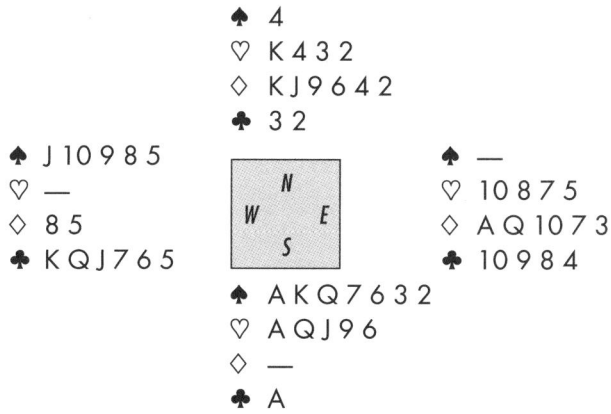

```
                    ♠ 4
                    ♡ K 4 3 2
                    ◇ K J 9 6 4 2
                    ♣ 3 2
  ♠ J 10 9 8 5                        ♠ —
  ♡ —                 N               ♡ 10 8 7 5
  ◇ 8 5           W       E           ◇ A Q 10 7 3
  ♣ K Q J 7 6 5       S               ♣ 10 9 8 4
                    ♠ A K Q 7 6 3 2
                    ♡ A Q J 9 6
                    ◇ —
                    ♣ A
```

A euphoric grunt from the Hog should have warned the Chimp that a big dark cloud hovered over the silver lining.

The Walrus gathered the trick won so unexpectedly by his ♠5 and continued with the ♣Q. He reasoned that if declarer had a losing diamond it couldn't run away. A club might.

The Rabbit ruffed and paused to count the spades. A recount confirmed that there were still four out against him and that he would, therefore, have to ruff one. Before doing so he took another round of hearts with his queen, just to make sure that the Walrus really had none and that a finesse against the ten would succeed. Reassured by this combination of safety and discovery plays, R.R. ruffed a spade with the ♡K and, finessing on the way back, drew trumps and claimed the rest.

Gloating as was his wont the Hog turned to the Chimp. 'You realize, of course, my dear Charlie, that the contract can't be made without declarer's spectacular gambit at Trick 2, giving up a trick to a low spade. Whether he lays down a top spade or crosses to the ♡K to lead the spade from dummy — which you don't ruff, of course — he has two inescapable losers.

'What a pity,' added H.H. mockingly, 'that you didn't spot that little spade lurking among the clubs until it was too late. Somehow I don't think that R.R. would have played the same way had he had a complete count of dummy from the start.'

# Coups by Dummy

*(A story with this title appears in Masters & Monsters, but this version involves two different deals and some new text.)*

Monsieur Merle, the head waiter, bowed and departed. The Rabbit had settled the particulars of his salad and was relaxing over a glass of madeira when I joined him at the bar of the Unicorn.

'Ye-es,' he said slowly, giving me a faraway look, 'a little avocado pear, finely sliced to blend with the tarragon leaves...'

Blushing deeply, as he realized that he was no longer speaking to Monsieur Merle, the Rabbit quivered and subsided guiltily on his stool. 'What's the news?' I asked. I had not been to the club for several days and I wanted to put the Rueful Rabbit at his ease by changing the subject.

'Well,' he began, 'the Hog has been rude to several members, very rude...'

'I meant *new* news,' I explained.

'Oh, I see' the Rabbit reconsidered the situation, nodded to himself, frowned and resumed with an air of perplexity.

'As a matter of fact, a very curious thing happened last night. For the first time since I have known him, H.H. deliberately picked the losing seats.'

It was certainly out of character, for the Hog made a point of choosing the winning line.

I must have looked impressed for the Rabbit went on eagerly: 'I thought you'd be surprised. Let's ask him why he did it. There must be some good reason and I am sure that between us we can get it out of him. You ask the questions and I'll order the drinks. He'll be here soon.'

'We've been discussing luck and superstition,' was my opening gambit when the Hog joined us a few minutes later. 'Many people seem to believe that cards tend to follow the seats. You yourself have been known...'

'Nonsense,' interrupted the Hog with his usual vehemence. 'How could anyone but an advanced imbecile find a connection between the position of a chair and the distribution of a pack of cards? Only morons, cretins, quarter-wits...'

'Why, then,' broke in the Rabbit 'do you make such a fuss about it? You have sworn at me before now, when I have cut you and had the choice, for failing to take the winning line. Why, if you don't believe in it yourself?'

'Because, my dear sir,' replied the Hog warmly, 'I do not go through life, like some people, thinking only of myself. Few of the best men or the biggest winners are to be found among egocentrics. Of course I don't believe in seats, but my partners do, even if they sometimes prefer not to have their superstitions shown up in public. Some of them,' he continued pointing an accusing finger at the Rabbit, 'are less jittery and don't shiver quite so much if they expect luck to be with them.

'But, of course,' said the Hideous Hog, pushing his empty glass firmly towards the barman, 'that is a side issue. In fact, quite a case can be made for a nervous partner. At least he does not get ideas above his station. Don't let us make too much of him. Apart from partner, there are two other opponents to consider and one or both may be depressed and even demoralized by being confined to the losing seats, especially if they have lost two or three rubbers in them already.

'It is not enough to love your neighbor,' went on the Hog sententiously, seizing a glass which had been left *en prise*. 'You should defer to his weaknesses and cherish his superstitions. Trust him. He will not let you down.

'Besides,' he added as an afterthought, 'even if there is no real advantage in taking the winning seats, what possible virtue can there be in picking the losing ones?'

'Why, then,' cried the Rabbit, 'were you so insistent last night on giving up the winning seats and forcing Walter into Colin's chair, just after you and he had won a large rubber?'

A crafty smile spread over the Hog's rosy face. The corners of his fleshy mouth curved outwards and as he cast down his eyes a gleam of malicious contentment escaped from under his left eyelid.

'There's such a thing as tactics,' he explained. 'As you must have observed, that Walrus of yours is one of Europe's foremost hypochondriacs. In every breath of fresh air he sees a wave of pneumonia. As it happens, my partner, Colin, had a particularly draughty seat and every time the door opened a cold air stream hit him in the ribs, as it were. So I thought, ha ha! What a good spot it would be for your precious Walter. He'd be so scared about his health that he wouldn't know one card from another. Ha ha ha! Every time the door opened... ha ha!'

'But that's unfair,' exclaimed the shocked Rabbit.

'Unfair?' repeated the Hideous Hog incredulously. 'You of all people say that! And how often have you bid risky games and slams only because your horoscope for the day, vouchsafed to you by your favorite newspaper, told you to speculate boldly? You invoke the occult for sordid personal gain, you shamelessly exploit esoteric knowledge, and you have the nerve to speak of unfairness to me, to me of all people!

'And what do you know,' went on the Hog, working himself up into a noble fury 'of the ethics of strategy? Have you studied the works of the great military thinkers, Clausewitz, Ludendorf, Wagner...?

I thought I heard a hissing noise somewhere.

'...you have a duty to your partner. You owe it to him to win.'

This time the hiss was unmistakable and a scathing voice said, 'That, no doubt, was one of Mozart's military maxims.'

Looking up, I could see behind the glint of pince-nez, a small round head and projecting from it two tufts of hair growing wildly at right angles. It was, of course, the Emeritus Professor of Bio-Sophistry, on leave from one of Ghana's most ancient universities. Parked behind a pillar, which obscured him from view, the Professor must have heard every word we were saying. As he now stalked out of the room, the Hog snorted contemptuously. 'That Secretary Bird. I don't know why I play with him, though one must be clubbable, I suppose. After all, he is a consistent loser.'


## Perfect Timing

Looking into the card room later that afternoon, I saw that H.H. had again cut R.R. as his partner, 'for the fifth time in four rubbers,' to quote the Hog.

As I walked up to them, the Emeritus Professor was dealing, cigarette in hand, flicking ash all over the table as was his custom. His partner, Walter the Walrus, protested loudly. 'A filthy habit,' he bellowed, scooping up the cigarette ash with a card. 'If you must poison your lungs, not to mention ours, why should the cards be contaminated as well?'

I sat behind South, the Rabbit, who dealt at love all.

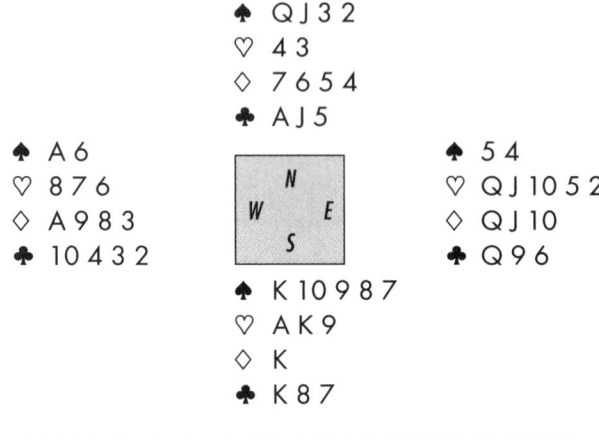

                ♠ Q J 3 2
                ♡ 4 3
                ◇ 7 6 5 4
                ♣ A J 5

♠ A 6                              ♠ 5 4
♡ 8 7 6          N                 ♡ Q J 10 5 2
◇ A 9 8 3    W       E             ◇ Q J 10
♣ 10 4 3 2       S                 ♣ Q 9 6

                ♠ K 10 9 8 7
                ♡ A K 9
                ◇ K
                ♣ K 8 7

| West | North | East | South |
| --- | --- | --- | --- |
| S.B. | H.H. | W.W. | R.R. |
| | | | 1♠ |
| pass | 2♠ | pass | 3♠ |
| pass | 4♠ | all pass | |

The Secretary Bird, as we all called the Professor, opened with the ace and another trump. Winning the second trick, the Rabbit played his two top hearts and ruffed the third.

Then came a diamond from dummy to the queen, king and ace. The S.B. returned another diamond. R.R. ruffed and pondered. Weighing up his chances, he could see four trump tricks, two hearts and a heart ruff and two top clubs. The tenth trick could only come from the club finesse which, of course, was wrong. The Rabbit played his ♣K and was about to lead another, when he stopped short and suddenly exclaimed: 'Oh dear! You all have a card too many. I mean I haven't as many as you have. You people must have gone wrong somewhere or... er...'

'If I may intrude,' ventured a junior kibitzer diffidently, 'there's a blue card on top of the red deck. I did not like to say anything before... Peregrine is so cross if we juniors utter a word — but I saw that gentleman (pointing to W.W.) place it there inadvertently when he removed this gentleman's cigarette ash.' A nervous nod in the direction of S.B. punctuated the end of the sentence.

The blue card, now brought into the open, revealed itself as the deuce of diamonds.

'Declarer has revoked, I think,' ventured S.B., but there was little conviction in his voice.

'Sorry, partner,' said the Rabbit miserably 'I... er... we... they...'

'What!' roared the Hideous Hog at the Emeritus Professor. 'You turn the table into a dustbin, to clear up your mess your partner forcibly seizes my partner's card and...'

'Oh very well, I am prepared to wash out the hand,' announced the Secretary Bird with the air of a nobleman of old renouncing his *droit de seigneur*.

'Really?' cried the Hog. 'You are good enough to agree most graciously that a cold game should not be scored against you. Words fail me.'

'Well, what do you want?' asked S.B. and W.W. in unison.

'Nothing to which we are not entitled,' replied the Hog with hauteur. 'The pack is not faulty. The deal was correct. Only one card is not in its appointed place. It must, therefore, be restored and played at the first opportunity.'

'Whenever you wish. I mean, er...' offered the Rueful Rabbit, anxious not to upset anyone.

'At the first opportunity,' commanded the Hog. 'Now!'

'Here it is then,' said the Rabbit apprehensively, ready to withdraw at the slightest sign of opposition.

The Walrus took the trick on the 'better late than never' principle, but that was the end of the defense. Whether he gave declarer a ruff and discard or led a club into dummy's tenace, the result would be the same. The endplay had been timed too well.

'As you know,' the Rabbit told me afterwards, 'I don't like that sort of thing, but fortunately it made no difference to the result. I might have lost a club, of course, since the queen was offside, but then I would not have lost that little diamond, if it had not turned up, I mean. So it came to the same thing, really, didn't it?'

# HONORS COUNT

North-South Vul.
Dealer West

♠ J 9
♡ 6 5
♢ A J 10 9 8
♣ K J 9 7

```
      N
   W     E
      S
```

♠ A K 10 8 6
♡ Q 4 3
♢ K Q 5
♣ 6 5

Against silent opposition, North-South bid as follows:

| North | South |
|-------|-------|
| H.H. | R.R. |
| pass | 1♠ |
| 2♢ | 2♠ |
| 3♠ | pass |

The Secretary Bird opened with the ♡K and ♡A on which his partner, the Walrus, played the jack, then the two. After a pause the ♣4 followed. Which card should the Rabbit play from the table? While he looked at the ceiling for inspiration, I tried to work out the hand.

Why had S.B. switched to clubs after receiving so much encouragement from his partner in hearts? I could think of one reason only — the fear that the Walrus could not overruff dummy and would thereby give vital information to declarer. That information could only refer to the ♠Q and it followed that the S.B. had been dealt that queen singleton or more likely doubleton. And in that case he was hardly likely to hold an honor in clubs, as well, for with an eleven count and a six-card major he would have surely opened the bidding.

It appeared, therefore, that the Rabbit was destined to lose two clubs and that the contract would hinge on his play of the trump suit. Presumably, he would finesse and go one down.

Someone jogged R.R. out of his daydream — I learned later that he was wondering where he had parked his car — and he settled on dummy's ♣J.

The Walrus won with the queen and returned a trump. Going up with the ace, and picking up S.B's seven, the Rabbit continued with the ◊K.

I saw H.H. look up sharply. Why was not the Rabbit drawing trumps? Next to dealing, it was the best part of his game and there appeared to be no reason at all for the ◊K. Ominously, the queen followed the king and by this time there could be little doubt that R.R. was playing the hand in notrump.

The Hog was about to say something, but caught his breath and waited patiently until a low diamond had been played from dummy.

'Sorry, partner,' he said then, transferring the ♠J, which had been nestling between the red suits, to dummy's right. 'I always forget.'

The hint, however, was wasted. The Rabbit's thoughts were far away and he was about to continue, automatically, with the ◊5 when the Hideous Hog spoke again.

'Any honors partner?' he asked.

'Who? What? Honors? N-no, no honors.' The spell was broken.

'Your hand,' snarled the Hog as R.R. was about to play dummy's ♠J. After that there was no longer any play for losing the contract.

'You know,' the Rabbit told me afterwards in strict confidence, 'I had quite forgotten that spades were trumps. But you can see now that the Hog is not as unscrupulous as they make out. He did not breathe a word until it was too late for me to get into dummy to take the trump finesse. Luckily the queen dropped, but he could not know that, could he?' These were the four hands:

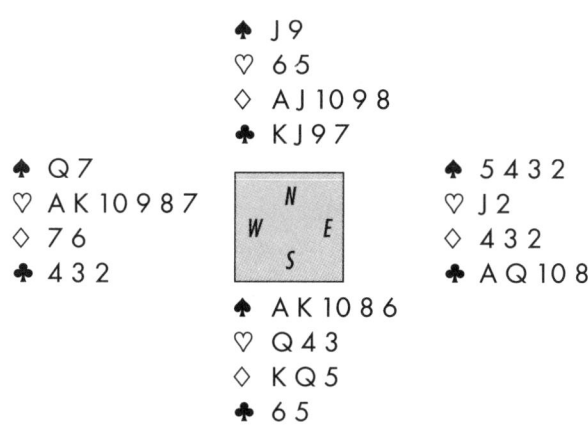

# NOBLESSE OBLIGE

On the next hand the Emeritus Professor failed to lose a 3NT contract, making it game all. Then the Walrus dealt this:

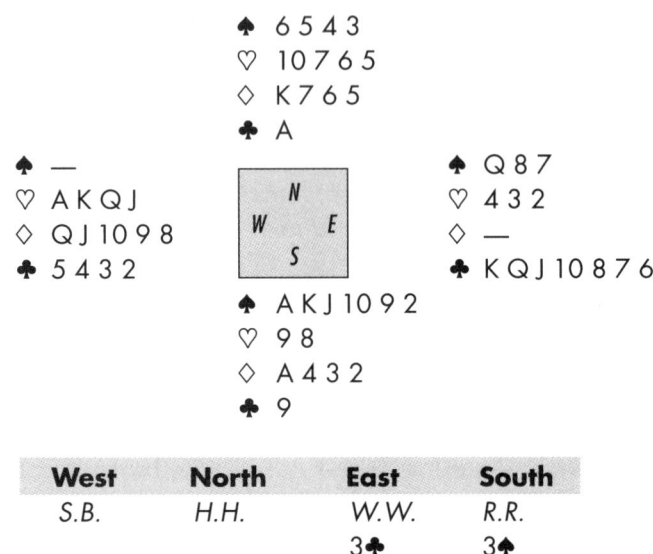

♠ 6 5 4 3
♡ 10 7 6 5
◇ K 7 6 5
♣ A

♠ —
♡ A K Q J
◇ Q J 10 9 8
♣ 5 4 3 2

♠ Q 8 7
♡ 4 3 2
◇ —
♣ K Q J 10 8 7 6

♠ A K J 10 9 2
♡ 9 8
◇ A 4 3 2
♣ 9

| West | North | East | South |
|------|-------|------|-------|
| S.B. | H.H. | W.W. | R.R. |
|  |  | 3♣ | 3♠ |
| 4♣ | 4♠ | all pass |  |

The Professor would have done well to bid 5♣, but knowing nothing of partner's void in diamonds, he feared that a sacrifice might prove too costly, and he was not entirely without hope of breaking the contract. After all, the Rabbit was playing the hand.

The ♡K, ♡A and ♡Q, in that order, were led to the first three tricks. The Rabbit ruffed on the third round and played his ace of trumps. Seeing West show out, he crossed to dummy with the ♣A to take the marked finesse in trumps.

Back in his hand with the ♠J, he was about to play the king when the Walrus, setting down a cup of coffee, turned abruptly and jolted R.R.'s elbow. The nine of trumps, the end card in his hand, dropped accidentally on the table.

'Sorry,' apologized the Walrus, 'clumsy of me, but they do put these tables in the most awkward...'

'My fault, really, I er...' chittered the Rabbit, and he was about to pick up the card when H.H. stopped him.

'I am afraid,' he said gently but very firmly, 'that the card has been played. Much as it is against our interests, we must observe the rules.'

'No, no,' protested the Walrus, 'it was my fault entirely. I could not possibly take advantage of it. I would not dream...'

The S.B. hissed softly. Something was wrong, but what was it?

'Please pick it up,' implored W.W.

'Your sentiments do you credit,' said the Hog, inclining his head. '*Noblesse oblige.* Nevertheless that card has been played.'

'Quoting Stradivarius, I suppose,' jeered the Emeritus Professor in an audible aside.

The Hog pushed the ♠9 towards the Walrus, saying in his silkiest voice: 'Play anything, my dear Walter, anything you like. There's no need at all to be embarrassed. It's the luck of the game. Another time it might be in our favor.'

Slowly, reluctantly, the Walrus gathered the trick, which had fallen so unexpectedly to his queen of trumps, and having nothing left but clubs, led a club.

The Rabbit discarded a diamond from his hand, trumping the club in dummy, returned to the closed hand with the ◇A, and for want of anything better to do, led out his trumps. On the last one, West was hopelessly squeezed in the red suits, the three-card end position being:

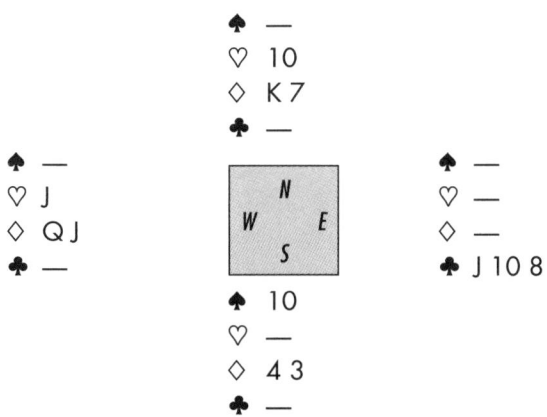

The unnatural loss of the trump trick had been compensated at once by the ruff and discard, and at the same time, it rectified the count for a squeeze against S.B. Had the Rabbit ducked a diamond, not that it would have occurred to him, the Secretary Bird could have broken up the squeeze by leading the ♡J.

For the squeeze to operate a trick had to be lost, but it had to be lost to East and not to West.

'Well played,' said the Hog. The Rabbit looked startled. He was not in the habit of receiving compliments. But the Hog was perfectly sincere. He thought that dummy had played very well.

# Equality of Confusion

Lord Mortsbury, President of International Morticians Inc., and his export manager, Jeremy Joybell, came to the Griffins for practice. They had qualified to represent Andorra in the forthcoming World Pairs for the Babel Bowl, organized by the Papuan Bridge Federation, and had devised a system to counter other systems. The key to it was that every bid had at least two entirely different meanings.

'But how will you know which is which?' asked Oscar the Owl.

'We won't,' replied Mortsbury, 'but no one else will either.'

'And they won't know that we don't know,' pointed out J.J., 'so we'll gain on balance.'

'Surely it's all rather confusing. Won't the authorities object?' persisted O.O.

'All progressive systems are not only allowed but encouraged,' Mortsbury hastened to assure him. 'The Papuans believe that it's the only way to ensure fair play. Since many pairs are bound to be at a disadvantage, not knowing the codes and ciphers of the others, everyone should be in the same boat.'

'Equality of confusion,' chipped in Colin the Corgi, the facetious young man from Oxbridge.

'Of course,' explained J.J., 'every pair must notify every other pair of its system, giving full details thirty days in advance, but as no one will have the time or the inclination to read, let alone absorb, this mass of information, it's only a formality.'

## CONFUSION WORSE CONFOUNDED

Who would give the morticians the practice they so badly needed? The Hideous Hog had an early dinner engagement, Papa the Greek was to lecture the Magicians' Circle on Vanishing Tricks. The Walrus, the Mule and the Secretary Bird could find no partners. So it fell to the

Rueful Rabbit and Timothy the Toucan to provide the opposition. Soon this hand came up.

Both Vul.
Dealer East

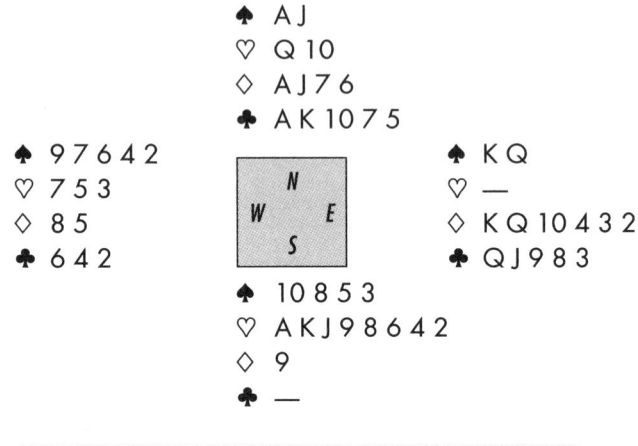

```
                    ♠ A J
                    ♡ Q 10
                    ◇ A J 7 6
                    ♣ A K 10 7 5
   ♠ 9 7 6 4 2                      ♠ K Q
   ♡ 7 5 3           N              ♡ —
   ◇ 8 5         W       E          ◇ K Q 10 4 3 2
   ♣ 6 4 2           S              ♣ Q J 9 8 3
                    ♠ 10 8 5 3
                    ♡ A K J 9 8 6 4 2
                    ◇ 9
                    ♣ —
```

| West | North | East | South |
|------|-------|------|-------|
| J.J. | T.T. | Mortsbury | R.R. |
|      |       | 2NT | 4♡ |
| pass | 5NT | pass | 7♡ |
| all pass |  |  |  |

J.J. explained that Mortsbury's opening 2NT showed a two-suiter in either the majors or the minors and a range of 8-22 non-vulnerable and 0-14 vulnerable.

'The reverse vulnerability syndrome is a feature of our system. It will fox opponents no end,' he added gleefully.

The Rabbit took in the situation at a glance. Clearly Mortsbury couldn't have a two-suiter in the majors, so he would be quite safe in making his natural bid of 4♡. The Toucan likewise had no problem. So long as R.R. had the ♡AK there should be tricks to burn. So the grand slam was reached in two rounds of bidding.

Joybell led the ◇8 and the Rabbit counted. Twelve cold tricks were on view, so surely he could develop a thirteenth. There was much to be said for Harpagon's approach in Molière's *Miser*. 'There'll be eight of us to dinner,' he told his cook. 'To be precise, there'll be ten, but if there's enough for eight there'll be enough for ten.' So at bridge. Where there are twelve certain tricks there's usually a thirteenth to be had.

The Rabbit went up with the ◇A and reeled off trump after trump, always a pleasant pastime, discarding from dummy two clubs and two diamonds. On the penultimate trump he reluctantly threw the ♠J, the only card he could spare, leaving this position with Mortsbury still to play:

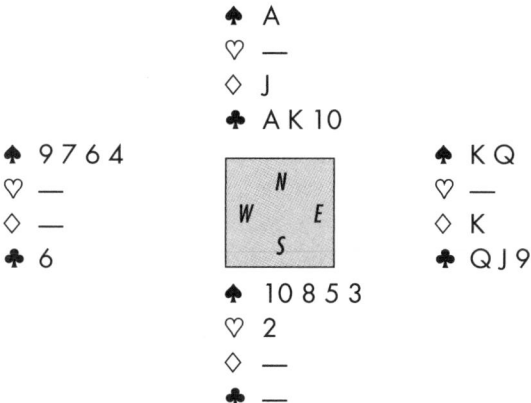

```
              ♠  A
              ♡  —
              ◇  J
              ♣  A K 10
♠ 9 7 6 4                        ♠  K Q
♡ —              N               ♡  —
◇ —          W       E           ◇  K
♣ 6              S               ♣  Q J 9
              ♠  10 8 5 3
              ♡  2
              ◇  —
              ♣  —
```

Hoping that J.J. had the ♠10, he let go the ♠Q. He had no alternative, but it made R.R. wonder. Could such an experienced a player as Mortsbury have bared the ♠K? Had the Rabbit's discard of the ♠J from dummy pulled the wool over his eyes? R.R. dearly would have liked to cash his last trump, in case it squeezed Mortsbury, but he realized that dummy would be squeezed first. So, with tremulous fingers, he led a spade, and his heart gave a jump when the ace brought down the king.

'That's the trouble with these sophisticated systems,' the Rabbit told me later. 'It's such a strain having to remember everything that you get bemused. Marmaduke never would have bared the ♠K had he been playing something simple.'

## A Textbook Situation

Soon we were joined by the Secretary Bird and the Hog, who apparently had forgotten about his early dinner engagement. They were just in time to kibitz, or rather to umpire, the deal below. I was sitting behind the Rabbit, who had been dealt:

♠— ♡ K J 9 6 5 ◇ A K Q 10 ♣ A K Q J

After two passes, Mortsbury, East opened 1♡. J.J. explained that this showed either 0-2 hearts and 0-6 points or else 5=0=4=4 with a void in hearts and 19+ points. Non-vulnerable, as they were, it also could be a hand with the values for a conventional 2NT opening.

What would the Rabbit do? He couldn't double — that would guarantee spade support. His minors weren't long enough to warrant 2NT. He was much too good to pass.

After due reflection R.R. bid 2♡. As expected, the Toucan called 2♠ and the Rabbit, again as planned, bid 2NT. T.T. persisted with 3♠, posing a serious problem for the Rabbit. Doubtless, 3NT would be the best contract, but having taken the bit between his teeth, would the Toucan pass? Expecting to find a doubleton opposite, certainly not a void, would he not careen into 4♠? How could he be saved from self-destruction?

Suddenly the Rabbit had an inspiration. He would call 4♡. If the Toucan read it as a slamward move, agreeing spades, he would doubtless invoke his favorite Blackwood, and R.R. would pass 4NT with alacrity. If, pursued by the Furies, the Toucan insisted on spades, the Rabbit would bid 4NT himself. Whether T.T. showed one ace or none, either minor would provide a better spot than spades, and 100 honors would soften the blow.

Hearing 4♡, the Toucan, his long red nose aglow, bounced excitedly in his chair. He saw it all. Mortsbury had two hearts at most. He had but one himself. Clearly the Rabbit had six or seven and didn't want any other suit as trumps. So, all his troubles over, he passed and 4♡ became the final contract.

Jeremy Joybell led the ♠J.

```
            ♠ Q 9 7 6 4 2
            ♡ 2
            ◇ J 7 5
            ♣ 8 6 2

                 N
              W     E
                 S

            ♠ —
            ♡ K J 9 6 5
            ◇ A K Q 10
            ♣ A K Q J
```

The Rabbit recognized the situation at once — he had seen it many a time in textbooks and he knew exactly what to do.

He would shorten his trumps, cash the winners in the side suits and wait for West, with nothing but trumps left, to ruff and lead into his trump tenace. If he could do that twice he would make his contract.

Ruffing the first trick, R.R. overtook the ◇10 with dummy's jack and ruffed another spade. Next he cashed the ◇KQ, then the ♣AKQ. When all followed, he gave a sigh of relief and exited with the ♣J. As expected, J.J. ruffed, but Mortsbury overtook the ♡3 with the ♡7 and returned the ♡8. A hot defense. The Rabbit couldn't remember seeing it in any textbook and he now was reconciled to going one down. He inserted the ♡9 and, much to his surprise, held the trick. He still had an exit card in the ◇A, but instead of ruffing, J.J. discarded a spade. This didn't add up, for all his remaining cards should have been hearts.

Mortsbury ruffed with the third of his two trumps, and worse still, returned another trump. The Rabbit, completely bemused, inserted the ♡J and so scored his tenth trick. Blushing a deep crimson, Mortsbury was profuse in his apologies.

These were the four hands:

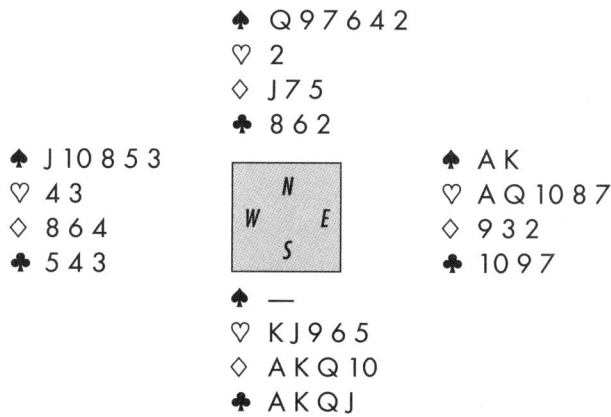

'I am terribly sorry,' began Mortsbury. 'We've had so little experience. I completely forgot. I just didn't think.'

There was a gleam in S.B.'s pince-nez. 'A serious irregularity,' he said severely. 'The umpires would certainly impose a substantial penalty. A bid not in keeping with the advertised system is a breach, a grave breach...'

'I think not,' broke in the Hog. 'What my learned friend is forgetting,' he went on, addressing the morticians, 'is that when all progressive methods are allowed there is nothing against first-in-hand psyches. Marmaduke made a natural bid, and since the system rules it out, it becomes *ipso facto* a psych. There's nothing wrong with it so long as there's no undisclosed understanding between partners.'

'You know,' the Rabbit told me over coffee and cognac after dinner, 'if I were to put my mind to it, I am sure I could devise a system that no one would understand. Perhaps,' he went on with a far away look in his eyes, 'I've been playing one all along without knowing it.'

# A Spirited Defense

*(This story appears in* Bridge in the Fourth Dimension, *but there are alterations to the text and the third deal is different.)*

'Double dummy problems!' exclaimed the Hog, breathing contempt into every syllable. 'Anyone can do them, that is if they have nothing better to do. It's just a question of time. Try everything, starting with the weirdest plays. Sooner or later you're bound to hit the solution. And you needn't waste time on anything that anyone would ever do in real life. Just chuck away an ace or two. Trump a couple of winners. You'll get there in the end.'

The bar at the Griffin was almost empty. Five of us were sitting round a magnum — the Hog, the Rabbit, the Toucan, the Owl and I. Champagne before dinner was a new departure, but when the Hog announced that sugar was the greatest killer of our age and that he would give up madeira till Lent, the Toucan, who was in the chair, saw the point at once. He had supreme faith in the Hog's judgment and he accepted unquestioningly his pronouncement that all champagne was entirely free of sugar but that the '59 vintage was even freer than the others.

'Those problems,' went on the Hog, 'mean nothing at all for they ignore human reflexes and they make no allowance for speed. Neither do textbooks for that matter, yet it's sometimes better to play the wrong card quickly than the right one slowly.'

Encouraged by our silence the Hideous Hog raised a podgy forefinger and proceeded to explain. 'This, of course, is the classical situation,' he said, flourishing a bit of paper on which he had scribbled:

A Q J 9 8 4

K 3

'Declarer is in three notrump. There are no side entries to dummy and he runs the ten, on which partner plays the two, showing three cards. You are East and you duck, hoping that declarer will repeat the finesse, fail, and cut himself for evermore from the table. Naturally. But you would do better to win the trick than to pause before ducking, for the pause would give the whole show away and you wouldn't make your king at all.

'Sometimes,' pursued the Hog, 'speed is its own reward. You don't have to know what you are doing so long as you do it quickly. Try this hand on which I happened to be sitting East a couple of days ago.'

♠ A 10
♡ A Q J
♢ Q J 3 2
♣ A 6 5 3

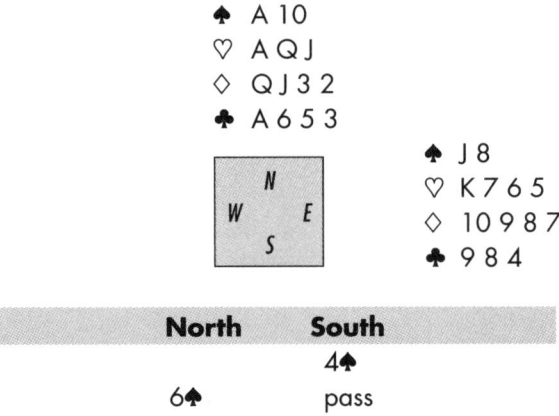

♠ J 8
♡ K 7 6 5
♢ 10 9 8 7
♣ 9 8 4

| North | South |
|-------|-------|
|       | 4♠    |
| 6♠    | pass  |

'West opens the queen of clubs which declarer wins with the king in the closed hand. He leads the ten of hearts and plays dummy's queen. What should you do?'

'Return a diamond,' volunteered the Toucan. 'Declarer may be hoping to get rid of a losing diamond on a heart.'

'I duck,' hazarded Oscar the Owl. 'It's usually the correct technique.'

'I, too, duck,' declared the Rabbit with unaccustomed confidence.

'Why?' asked H.H.

'Because,' explained R.R., 'no one in a slam would really think of ducking, so unless I was intended to do something different, if you see what I mean, you wouldn't be asking me, would you?'

'True,' conceded the Hog, snorting gracefully. 'Yet neither you nor Oscar have a clue as to what it's all about. You haven't asked yourselves, any of you, why declarer should embark on the heart finesse, before drawing trumps. Yet that is surely the key to it all, 'the dog that didn't bark in the night,' as Edgar Allan Poe put it — or was it Simenon? Anyway, if declarer wanted to get rid of a diamond, he could do it *after* drawing trumps. That's why Timothy gave the wrong answer. You and Oscar gave the right one, though for the wrong reason or rather for no reason at all. And yet you would have beaten the contract, just as I did. The mere fact that you didn't know what you were doing would have made no difference, so long as you did it quickly. This was the deal:

```
              ♠ A 10
              ♡ A Q J
              ◇ Q J 3 2
              ♣ A 6 5 3
♠ Q 7                            ♠ J 8
♡ 4 3 2          N              ♡ K 7 6 5
◇ K 6 5 4    W       E          ◇ 10 9 8 7
♣ Q J 10 2       S              ♣ 9 8 4
              ♠ K 9 6 5 4 3 2
              ♡ 10 9 8
              ◇ A
              ♣ K 7
```

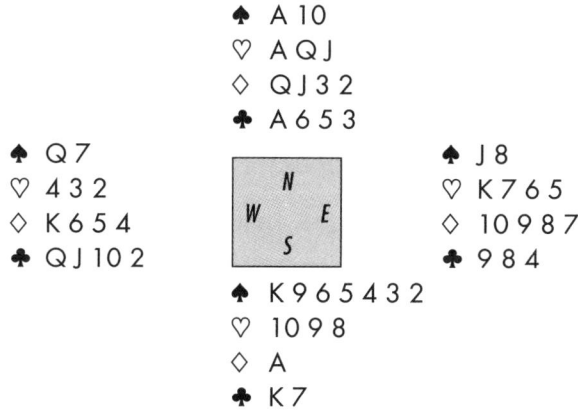

'Now you can see why declarer took the heart finesse before touching trumps,' said the Hog, certain that no one could see anything. 'If the finesse succeeded, he could afford a safety play in trumps. If it failed, he couldn't. It was as simple as that.'

'What happened?' asked the Toucan eagerly.

'Naturally,' replied the Hog, who had been hoping that someone would have the decency to ask him, 'declarer crossed back to his hand with the ace of diamonds and led a trump, inserting dummy's ten to insure himself against a four-nil trump break. He did, too, of course, in a manner of speaking. But he couldn't insure himself against my having the king of hearts, which came into its own in due course — after I had made my jack of trumps.

'I need not point out,' pointed out the Hog, 'how fatal it would have been for me to pause, even for a few seconds, before playing low to the first round of hearts. It would have given the whole show away and declarer would never have considered that safety play which meant so much to my jack.'

## FIND THE LADY

Emptying someone's glass absent-mindedly, the Hog wrote down another hand and passed it round.

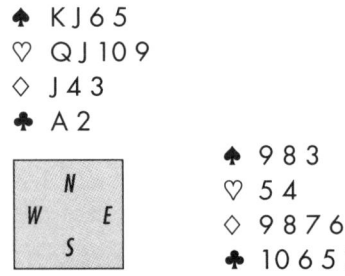

♠ K J 6 5
♡ Q J 10 9
◇ J 4 3
♣ A 2

♠ 9 8 3
♡ 5 4
◇ 9 8 7 6
♣ 10 6 5 3

| West | North | East | South |
|------|-------|------|-------|
| 1♡ | dbl | pass | 2♡ |
| pass | 2NT | pass | 3♠ |
| all pass | | | |

'North-South had a partscore, which is why the bidding stopped at three spades, I suppose. I was sitting East, as you have probably guessed since those are the sort of hands I hold most of the time. Anyway, partner started with the king and ace of hearts, the king and ace of diamonds, on which declarer threw the queen, and a third diamond to dummy's jack. Everyone followed to everything and our side had taken four tricks. At this point declarer led dummy's queen of hearts. Over to you.' With a sweeping gesture, H.H., took us all in.

'I ruff and return the ten of clubs,' suggested Timothy the Toucan.

The Hog greeted the suggestion strictly on its merits. With a half-hearted sneer, he turned away.

'Trump with the nine to promote something,' ventured the Rabbit.

'I discard a club,' announced O.O., some ten seconds later.

'Perhaps...' I began.

'You are all hopelessly wrong,' declared H.H.

'Impossible,' protested the Owl. 'Between us we have covered every solution and none at all. One of us must be right.'

'Not at all,' retorted the Hog, 'for you all took ages, over twenty seconds, in fact, and that's inexcusable. But first let me ask you, Oscar, why didn't you trump that queen of hearts?'

'Because,' explained the Owl, 'I suspect that this hand is a little like the last one. If declarer wants to discard a loser he can do so after drawing trumps. More likely, he is concerned about the trumps. Maybe he is missing the queen and hopes that I will give myself away by ruffing if my trump holding is worthless and refusing to ruff if I have the queen. To protect partner who has, presumably, that missing queen, I refuse to ruff. Q.E.D. Quite simple.'

'Too simple,' broke in the Hog. 'So simple, in fact, that had you really started with ♠Qxx you wouldn't have taken so long to decide what to do. That pause of yours showed clearly that you didn't have the queen.'

'How clever!' cried T.T., admiringly. 'You could see it all at a glance and you played quickly, as you always do, and you didn't ruff as R.R., and I would have done and...'

'Oh, but I did ruff,' interrupted the Hog baring his teeth in what may have been intended as a smile.

'But surely...'

'I mean to say...'

T.T., and R.R., protested simultaneously.

'Only, you see,' went on H.H., softly, 'my holding wasn't ♠983, but ♠Q93, and I ruffed precisely because it seemed so foolish a thing to do. But I did it in a jiffy and declarer didn't think that anyone could be so clever so quickly. It was all a question of speed, as I've been telling you. The same play in the same situation may convey several different messages. It's just a matter of timing.'

Emilio, our barman, came round to remove the empty magnum.

'No,' said H.H., shaking his head hesitantly 'I don't think that I should have any more.'

'...er ...' murmured the Toucan — or perhaps he was only clearing his throat.

'Well, if you absolutely insist,' said the Hog, 'I'll make an exception as it's so near Christmas. But this time make it only a bottle. It isn't just the sugar, you know, liquids tend to put on weight.'

# ONE OVER THE EIGHT

We all felt that we had had enough and sat back. 'While you kill the bottle,' resumed H.H., 'I'll show you one more hand to bring out the importance of the speed motif. It isn't a perfect example in some ways, but it's seasonal for it came up at Oscar's Christmas party last year.'

'I still remember that Latour '45,' murmured Colin the Corgi, who had come up to join us.

The Rueful Rabbit looked a little apprehensive, I thought, and his nose twitched nervously as the Hog wrote down a hand.

```
        ♠ 5 4 3
        ♡ 7 6 3
        ◇ J 10 2
        ♣ A 4 3 2
            N
        W       E
            S
        ♠ A J 7
        ♡ A K 5
        ◇ A 9 3
        ♣ K Q 10 9
```

| North | South |
|-------|-------|
|       | 2NT   |
| 3NT   | pass  |

'I was South,' said the Hog. 'West led the king of spades, which I ducked. The jack of hearts came next and I ducked again. I won a second heart and looked round. Somehow I had to make two diamond tricks and my best chance was obviously to lead low towards dummy. That way I could play East for the ◇KQ, losing the first trick to one honor before finessing against the other. Or else, West with ◇Qxx might go up with the queen. Anyway,' went on the Hog, 'I played a small diamond and our... er... West followed with the six.' As the Hog paused a bead of perspiration rolled down the Rabbit's forehead.

The Hideous Hog gave a derisive snort. 'You do not ask me,' he said accusingly, 'at what speed West played his little diamond. Yet surely that is all-important.  If he produced it smoothly, as if he had not a care in the world, you might conclude that East had both honors.  If, as in this case, West frowned and pondered — and let me tell you that he was a perfectly ethical player — you would know that he had an honor, probably $\Diamond$Qxx or maybe $\Diamond$Qxxx.  Be that as it may, dummy's jack lost to East's king and I won the spade return with the ace and...'

'And then,' broke in Colin, who was no respecter of persons, 'you cashed your clubs and your ace of hearts and threw West in with a spade to lead away from his queen of diamonds.  Three notrump bid and made.  Elementary, my dear Watson.  We expect better than that of you.'

'The result has nothing to do with it,' retorted H.H., with some asperity.  'I was illustrating a point, the importance of playing quickly, so...'

'Stop, stop,' cried the Rabbit, who was in obvious distress.  'I know you are jeering at me.  All right, there's no need for these meaning looks.  I was West and... er... I mean, it was a Christmas party and well...'

'I remember it clearly now,' interposed Oscar the Owl.  'After expressing generous appreciation for my Latour and sampling the Clos de Vougeot '55, you did honor to...'

'Eight cherry brandies,' said H.H., in icy tones.

'No, no, I swear it was only seven,' protested R.R., indignantly.

'But what happened?' asked the over-inquisitive Toucan.

'I did what any sane declarer would do,' replied H.H., 'that is against a sane defender.  I had lost three tricks and won two, so I cashed five winners, the four clubs and the ace of hearts and I watched the discards.  Our friend, R.R., followed to the heart and to two rounds of clubs.  Then he threw the eight of spades and the ten.  So I put him in with a spade.  Who wouldn't?'

'Well?' cried T.T.

'Coming in with the queen of spades,' went on the Hog, scorn giving way to anger in his voice, 'that Rabbit produced, not a diamond, but the thirteenth heart!'

'To which he had no right,' observed Colin, 'having shown already five spades, three hearts, three diamonds and two clubs.'

We looked at the full deal:

```
              ♠ 5 4 3
              ♡ 7 6 3
              ◇ J 10 2
              ♣ A 4 3 2
 ♠ K Q 10 8 2                      ♠ 9 6
 ♡ J 10 8 2        N               ♡ Q 9 4
 ◇ Q 6        W         E          ◇ K 8 7 5 4
 ♣ J 8            S                ♣ 7 6 5
              ♠ A J 7
              ♡ A K 5
              ◇ A 9 3
              ♣ K Q 10 9
```

'You can all see what happened, can't you?' went on the irrepressible C.C. 'Moved by the Christmas spirit, by the Latour, the Clos de Vougeot and by eight cherry brandies, our friend had a heart mixed up with the diamonds and he did not discover his mistake until it was too late not to profit by it. That was it, wasn't it R.R.?'

The Rabbit shook his head ruefully. 'No, no,' he said in a weak voice, 'it wasn't a heart. It was a spade which became... er... entangled with the diamonds. But really,' he added miserably, 'I didn't have eight cherry brandies. It was only seven.'

# A Visit from the Americans

The Griffins rubbed their eyes when they saw the names go up on the notice board. For the gala pairs event, held in honor of New York's visiting Salamanders, the Hideous Hog had picked as his partner none other than Walter the Walrus, one of the three worst players in Europe. The two others, the Rueful Rabbit and Timothy the Toucan, had entered together.

'That points merchant!' scoffed a Griffin.

'A walking abacus,' said another contemptuously, for the Walrus was one of those players who believe that it is better to go down honorably with the correct point count than to slip into some makeable contract by shady means.

Over dinner, Oscar the Owl, our official kibitzer, told us the inside story of the Hog-Walrus partnership.

'The Hog,' he explained, 'is trying to sell the Americans a patent for a pocket computer which will tell a player, in every situation, exactly how many points he should have for his bid, in less than two-fifths of a second after he's made it. Walter is financing the venture.'

'Are the Americans interested?' asked someone doubtfully.

'All the Hog expects of them,' answered O.O. reassuringly, 'is a grant-in-aid to supply computers to underdeveloped areas. That sort of thing always appeals to them, you know — and still more so to the Hog, of course.'

An hour later the players were trooping into the card room to take their places. 'Concentrate on your dummy play,' I heard the Hog say to the Walrus. 'You turn the cards so elegantly and arrange them so neatly. It's much the best part of your game. Stick to it, Walter, and leave the — er — mechanics to me.'

# A Bird in the Bush

I was sitting North-East, between the Walrus, who was dummy, and one of the Salamanders, when this hand came up:

```
            ♠ A K 9
            ♡ 5 4 3 2
            ◊ 4 3 2
            ♣ J 10 9
                          ♠ J 6 5 3
         ┌──────────┐     ♡ 7 6
         │    N     │     ◊ J 10 8
         │  W    E  │     ♣ 7 6 5 3
         │    S     │
         └──────────┘
```

| North | South |
|-------|-------|
| W.W.  | H.H.  |
|       | 2♣    |
| 2NT   | 3♡    |
| 4♡    | 4NT   |
| 5◊    | 6♡    |
| pass  |       |

The bidding was straightforward. H.H.'s 2♣ showed at least 23 points and his rebid indicated a playable heart suit. W.W.'s 2NT was the standard response on a balanced 7-9 point hand. Before calling the slam the Hog checked for aces.

West opened the ace of trumps, H.H. following with the nine, and continued with the eight to declarer's ten. The Hog barely paused to grunt before leading a spade to dummy's king and returning to the closed hand with a club to the ace. Then, in quick succession, he reeled off the ♣K and ♣Q and three trumps. West followed to the clubs, but having no more trumps he had to find three discards. He had played the deuce to the first spade trick and now he parted with the ♠7 then the ♠4 and finally with the ◊7.

Which four cards should East keep to the end? Declarer had shown up with five hearts, three clubs and a spade. Was he left with one spade and three diamonds or with two of each? It was reasonable to place him with the ◊AK on his 2♣ bid, but he could not have the queen as well — or the ♠Q for that matter — since he would then have twelve tricks on top.

My Salamander pondered deeply before playing to the last heart. West had produced three spades and was marked with the queen. That left no more than one remaining spade for declarer, and thus, three diamonds. Yes, it all dovetailed nicely. Every card fitted into its appointed place. With a clear picture of the deal before him, East shed a diamond, retaining ♠J6 and ◊J10. Thereupon the Hog tabled his hand claiming the last four tricks for his ◊AK65. These were the four hands:

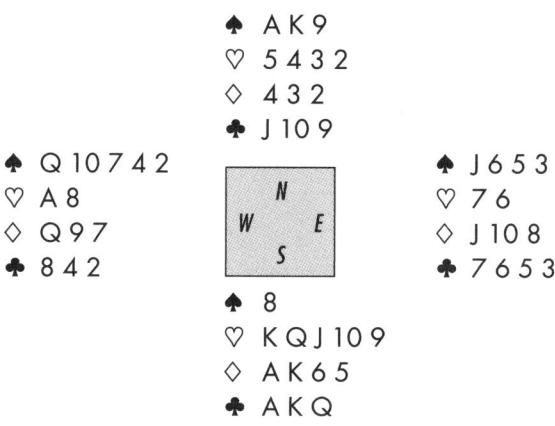

```
                    ♠ A K 9
                    ♡ 5 4 3 2
                    ◊ 4 3 2
                    ♣ J 10 9
  ♠ Q 10 7 4 2                        ♠ J 6 5 3
  ♡ A 8           ┌─────────┐         ♡ 7 6
  ◊ Q 9 7         │    N    │         ◊ J 10 8
  ♣ 8 4 2         │ W     E │         ♣ 7 6 5 3
                  │    S    │
                  └─────────┘
                    ♠ 8
                    ♡ K Q J 10 9
                    ◊ A K 6 5
                    ♣ A K Q
```

'Your ace of spades was invaluable, Walter,' chortled the Hideous Hog; 'worth at least 8 points, even though it didn't take a trick.' In deference to our distinguished visitors, he stopped gloating after a mere minute or so.

'Since you were relying on a pseudo-squeeze,' inquired the Owl, who was kibitzing with me, 'why play a spade at all?'

'To create the idea that I had two of them, of course. After all, I wouldn't have played as I did, cutting myself off from dummy, with a singleton, would I now? Which only goes to show,' jeered the Hog, 'that a bird in the bush is often worth two in the hand. Ha ha!'

# THE HOG SHOWS OFF

Throughout that evening, the Hideous Hog was on his best behavior. Once or twice he snarled at opponents. Occasionally he hurled an epithet or two at partner. But jeers and sneers apart, his conduct was a model of dignity and decorum. He nearly had a lapse, though, on this board:

```
        ♠ 10 8
        ♡ 7 6 3
        ◇ A 8 7 6
        ♣ A 10 5 3
            N
        W       E
            S
        ♠ J 6 5
        ♡ A K
        ◇ K Q 4 2
        ♣ K Q 8 2
```

| West | North | East | South |
|------|-------|------|-------|
| Salamander | W.W. | Salamander | H.H. |
| | | | 1◇ |
| 1♠ | 2◇ | pass | 3NT |
| all pass | | | |

Once more the Hideous Hog and Walter the Walrus were opposed to a pair from the visiting Salamanders. West led the ♠4 and even before dummy was down the Hog pursed angrily his thick, fleshy lips. One had to make allowances for foreigners, of course, but since he, the Hog, had bid 3NT confidently after hearing the spade overcall, shouldn't that rude Salamander have led some other suit? H.H. was not amused.

East won the first trick with the ♠Q and the next one with the king. Then he switched to the ♡J. Grunting with relief, the Hog seized the trick with the ace and set about the diamonds. All followed to the king, but on the queen East threw a heart. The kibitzers shook their heads. Things looked bad for the Hog. H.H. paused, then tabled his hand with a flourish. 'I will just take my nine tricks' he announced, banging down the ♡K demonstratively, to impress the gallery, 'two hearts, three diamonds and four clubs.*'

'We have just 26 points between us,' broke in the Walrus who liked to put first things first, 'so I don't know how you can be so certain.'

'And who said that the clubs would break?' asked a kibitzer rashly.

The Hog turned on him. 'Kibitzers should be seen and not heard,' he bellowed 'and some of them should not be seen either. Can't you see that I've played the king of hearts? And hasn't it occurred to you that West has only thirteen cards? We know he has six spades since East couldn't find a third one. We know he has four diamonds since East showed out on the second round. If, then, he has one heart only, he must have two clubs and the suit breaks. Conversely, if West follows to the king of hearts, he must have one club or none. So I cross to dummy with a club to the ace and lead the ten and run it, unless East covers. If he does, I win in my hand, enter dummy with the ace of diamonds and play a low club finessing against the nine. Why, the meanest master must see that...'

'I wonder if they have Hogs in America?' I heard one Griffin ask another as H.H. went on declaiming.

'If they have, I don't suppose they'd admit it,' replied his companion. 'I mean, would you?'

## Inspired Dummy Play

The gala duplicate in honor of New York's Salamander Club had reached the halfway stage. The Hideous Hog admitted modestly that with Walter the Walrus as his partner he did not expect to score more than eighty per cent. The Rueful Rabbit was jubilant. Things were going his way and he felt sure that he and Timothy the Toucan were four solid bottoms over average. Perhaps there were worse players in the States than these two, but I was inclined to doubt it and I decided to watch their encounter with the leading pair from the Salamander Club.

---

* Aside to Alvin Landy: We hasten to admit that the opponents could summon the director and probably stop the Hog from taking any finesses as punishment for so loose a claim. But sometimes editorial license must be allowed to outweigh legal writ. Besides, the Hog can always claim that he was interrupted in the midst of making his statement and by, of all things, a kibitzer!

It was a Howell movement and there occurred at this point a slight hitch. The Rabbit went to table six. His partner, the Toucan, made for table nine. Proceedings were held up for several minutes before they were reunited at table seven where they were due to meet the Americans. Little time was lost while the Rabbit tried to grab the cards from the wrong slot of the wrong board, but it all added to the delay and the Rabbit's fingers twitched nervously as he picked up his cards:

```
        ♠ K 9 3 2
        ♡ Q 4 2
        ◇ —
        ♣ A K 7 6 5 4
```

```
            N
        W       E
            S
```

```
        ♠ J 6 5
        ♡ A K J 10
        ◇ A 6 3
        ♣ J 10 9
```

| North | South |
|-------|-------|
| R.R. | T.T. |
|  | 1NT |
| 2♣ | 2♡ |
| 3♣ | 3NT |
| 4♡ | pass |

West led the ◇5 and the Toucan ruffed with the deuce in dummy and played the three from his hand on East's seven. West shook his head. The red four in dummy was a diamond, not a heart.

The Toucan apologized, replaced the deuce of trumps with the four of diamonds and gave up the trick. The Rabbit blushed. 'It's all this hurry,' he said apologetically. 'Doesn't give one a chance to sort one's cards properly.'

Both the Salamanders urged the Toucan to take back his low diamond and to play another. East, in fact, was quite insistent, but the Toucan would not hear of it and neither would the Rabbit.

Having won the first trick with the seven, East returned another diamond and T.T., apparently thinking that the deuce of trumps was an exposed card, ruffed in dummy. Overtaking the ♡Q with the king, he drew trumps and ran the ♣J. East won and cashed the ♠A, conceding the rest.

The complete deal was:

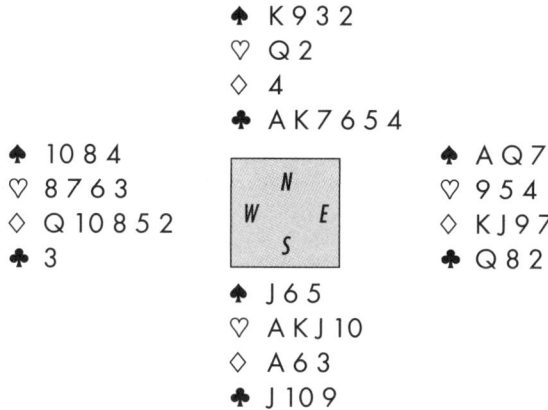

```
                    ♠ K 9 3 2
                    ♡ Q 2
                    ◇ 4
                    ♣ A K 7 6 5 4
  ♠ 10 8 4                              ♠ A Q 7
  ♡ 8 7 6 3          N                  ♡ 9 5 4
  ◇ Q 10 8 5 2    W     E               ◇ K J 9 7
  ♣ 3                S                  ♣ Q 8 2
                    ♠ J 6 5
                    ♡ A K J 10
                    ◇ A 6 3
                    ♣ J 10 9
```

'A bottom, I fear,' sighed the Toucan, 'for, of course, I didn't have to lose that first diamond.'

'Amazing,' exclaimed the Rabbit, who was looking at the traveling scoresheet. 'No one else has made it. Someone even managed to go three down.'

Oscar the Owl blinked sagely. 'Don't you see, Timothy,' he said, 'if you win the first diamond with the ace, ruff another and draw trumps, East will come in with the queen of clubs and give his partner the lead with a diamond. West can cash three diamonds and lead a spade through dummy's king for three down. You can't stop him.'

'No, no,' protested the Toucan, 'I would take the club finesse before drawing trumps. Then East couldn't hurt me with a diamond.'

'True,' agreed the Owl. 'He would return a club. West would ruff and put East in again with a spade for another club ruff. That, no doubt, is what happened when someone went two down. In fact,' added O.O., 'you can only make the contract by holding up the ace of diamonds deliberately — a fine, fine play — or by mixing up the red cards a bit. The latter isn't so scientific, but it's more likely to happen in real life, a better percentage chance, shall we say.'

# A VERY SMALL LOSER

Timothy the Toucan was declarer once more on the next deal.

```
        ♠ A 10 6
        ♡ J 7
        ◇ A K Q
        ♣ A K 3 2

            N
        W       E
            S

        ♠ Q J 9 8 7
        ♡ 10 9 8
        ◇ J 10
        ♣ 6 5 4
```

The Rabbit, North, opened 2NT and raised the Toucan's 3♠ to 4♠.
West led the ♡K, continued with the queen and switched to a diamond.

At this juncture, a kibitzer, who had been trying desperately to keep
silent, could contain himself no longer. 'There's a card on the floor,' he
stammered. 'Perhaps I shouldn't say anything but, er, well...'

The Rabbit dived hastily under the table and came up with the
deuce of hearts. 'Fortunately it's a very small card,' he said guiltily, 'so
it shouldn't matter, but if you'd like an average do say so, please.'

The Tournament Director ruled that the deal must stand and the
Toucan explained reassuringly that the third heart made no difference
whatever. He had three inescapable losers in the side suits and the
contract hinged purely and solely on catching the king of trumps.

T.T. proceeded to cash dummy's diamonds, discarding his third
heart, and ruffed the deuce of hearts, which had been restored to its
rightful place in dummy. The object of the play was to get back to his
hand for the trump finesse and as he explained later, he could have just
as easily discarded a club on the diamond and ruffed a club. The heart
was purely incidental.

The queen held the first trick in trumps and dummy's ten won
the second. When East showed out the Toucan shrugged his sloping
shoulders, but sooner than surrender at once he went through the

motions. He cashed the ♣A and ♣K and continued with another to East's queen. This was the deal:

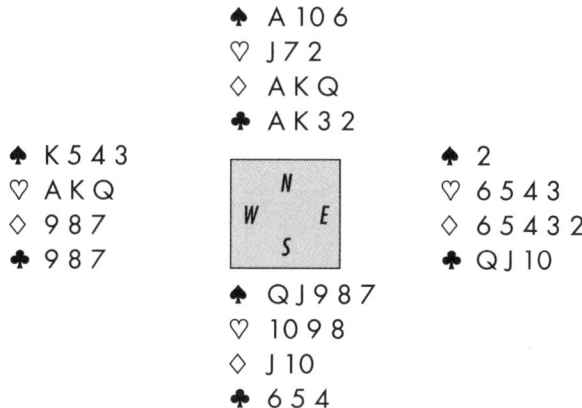

```
                  ♠ A 10 6
                  ♡ J 7 2
                  ◇ A K Q
                  ♣ A K 3 2
  ♠ K 5 4 3                      ♠ 2
  ♡ A K Q          N            ♡ 6 5 4 3
  ◇ 9 8 7      W       E        ◇ 6 5 4 3 2
  ♣ 9 8 7          S            ♣ Q J 10
                  ♠ Q J 9 8 7
                  ♡ 10 9 8
                  ◇ J 10
                  ♣ 6 5 4
```

and the three-card end position was:

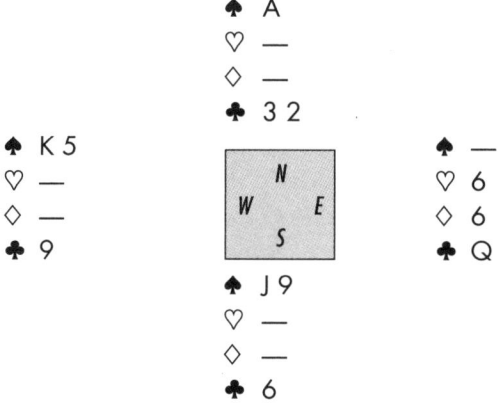

```
                  ♠ A
                  ♡ —
                  ◇ —
                  ♣ 3 2
  ♠ K 5                         ♠ —
  ♡ —              N            ♡ 6
  ◇ —          W       E        ◇ 6
  ♣ 9              S            ♣ Q
                  ♠ J 9
                  ♡ —
                  ◇ —
                  ♣ 6
```

Winning the third club with the queen, East had perforce to lead a red card. The Toucan ruffed and West's king was smothered.

'Bad luck,' he said politely, but afterwards he told me in confidence, 'I could never have made it, you know, if he hadn't gone up with the king of trumps. Why didn't he discard something?'

# The Hog &
# Colin the Corgi

# Diamonds Are the Hog's Best Friend

We were dining with Oscar the Owl at Arbour Lodge, his house in Birdcage Walk, overlooking St. James's Park. Oscar, Senior Kibitzer at the Griffins, was taking a party to the Unicorn that night and the conversation naturally turned to the phobias and idiosyncrasies which tended to keep apart the members of our two clubs.

Oscar quickly put his finger on one of the basic ideological differences. When a Griffin picks the highest card, he selects automatically the winning seats. It stands to reason. One takes the lucky line to have the better cards. But to imagine, as do most of the Unicorns, that the choice of cards, the red or the blue, can make the slightest difference to one's card-holding is sheer superstition, and we Griffins regard it as childish.

Peregrine the Penguin, Oscar's opposite number at the Unicorn, shook his head. Looking at it with an open mind, he felt that seats and cards affected the situation in equal measure.

'A more serious bone of contention,' he argued 'is your insistence on the weak notrump. We all play the strong. Why must you be different?'

'And why do you play goulashes after a throw-in?' countered Oscar. 'We don't, and it's so unnecessary.'

'What do you think?' I asked the Rueful Rabbit.

'For my part,' replied R.R, 'I am quite happy at the Unicorn in the summer. Their cucumber sandwiches are just as good as ours but I must say that in the winter I like muffins with my tea. Why do they give you those anemic crumpets at the Unicorn?'

'You are all wrong,' broke in the Hog, who had just disposed of his final portion of lobster mousse. 'It's fear of the unknown that keeps people from visiting each other's clubs. Call it, if you like, the partner complex. Some players rightly suspect that they are pretty awful, yet for some inscrutable reason they are averse to being insulted by strangers. Others, less concerned with their own shortcomings, are haunted by the dread of meeting partners even worse than they are. A Griffin steels himself to be butchered by the Ra... by the er... the devil he knows. But at the Unicorn he may cut the Walrus or that odious Secretary Bird. He will be slaughtered as before, but not in the same familiar fashion, and most people are conservative about that sort of thing. They like to feel massacred in their own way or not at all.'

The Hog had more to say on the subject, but just at this point he was interrupted by Falcon, Oscar's butler, who held before him a large dish of asparagus. First to be served, H.H. was not slow to make the most of his chances. With a swift, dexterous movement of his powerful wrists he neatly severed all the green tips from the stems. Then he transferred them *en masse* to his plate. For a moment we were all too taken aback to speak. The Penguin was the first to recover and he admonished the Hog severely.

'Other people besides yourself, H.H.,' he said indignantly, 'like asparagus tips.'

'But not as much as I do,' replied the Hog with simple dignity, helping himself to melted butter.

It only remains to add that Monsieur Corbeau, Oscar's chef, excelled himself with the *Bombe Nesselrod*. A magnum later we were on the way to the Unicorn.

For the first rubber of the evening the Hideous Hog cut the Rueful Rabbit against Walter the Walrus and Colin, the facetious, Corgi-shaped young man just down from Oxbridge. I found a seat between Walter and the Rabbit. This was the first hand, with North the dealer. W.W. had just decided to open 1NT when H.H. called 1◊.

```
                    ♠ A 3 2
                    ♡ J 10 2
                    ◇ 9 8 7 6
                    ♣ J 4 2
    ♠ Q J 9        ┌─────────┐
    ♡ A K 9 3      │    N    │
    ◇ A Q 3 2      │ W     E │
    ♣ 10 9         │    S    │
                   └─────────┘
```

| West | North | East | South |
|------|-------|------|-------|
| W.W. | R.R. | C.C. | H.H. |
|      | pass | pass | 1◇ |
| pass | 2◇ | pass | 2♡ |
| pass | 2♠ | pass | 3NT |
| dbl | all pass | | |

It should be pointed out in all fairness to the Rabbit that he fidgeted nervously throughout the auction. He did not like his raise to 2◇, still less his bid of 2♠. But he was not encouraged to bid notrump, in case he ended up as declarer, so what could he do?

The Walrus breathed stentoriously, rolling his top-heavy thorax from side to side of the table. A look of distrust lit up his normally expressionless eyes. He had heard of the Hog's devious bidding methods and he felt certain that something underhand was afoot.

After fingering several red cards and replacing each one, in turn, he finally settled on the ♠Q.

The Hog went up with dummy's ace and Colin contributed the eight. Next came the ♡2, the six from the Corgi and the queen from the closed hand. Winning the trick with his king, Walter continued with the ♠J. Colin echoed with the six and H.H., capturing the trick with the king in his hand, led the ♡4 towards dummy.

The Walrus came in again with the ace and led forth his ♠9, which Colin overtook with the ten. The seven, the thirteenth spade, followed. The Hog threw a small diamond and it was W.W.'s turn to discard.

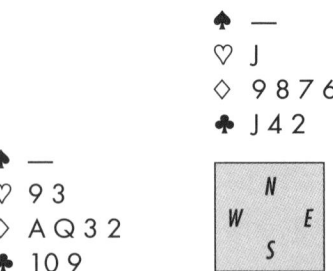

```
            ♠ —
            ♡ J
            ◇ 9 8 7 6
            ♣ J 4 2
♠ —
♡ 9 3          ┌─────────┐
◇ A Q 3 2      │    N    │
♣ 10 9         │ W     E │
               │    S    │
               └─────────┘
```

For quite a time the Walrus seemed reluctant to let go any of his cards.
There was so much to be said against parting with any one of them. If
he unguarded the ♡9 it might easily cost a trick, for had not H.H. bid
hearts at some stage? The ♣9 would look distinctly encouraging. The
◇Q was a certain trick. Should he throw it away? Dejectedly, he began
a high-low signal with the ◇3. Colin promptly led a club and it was all
over. The complete deal was:

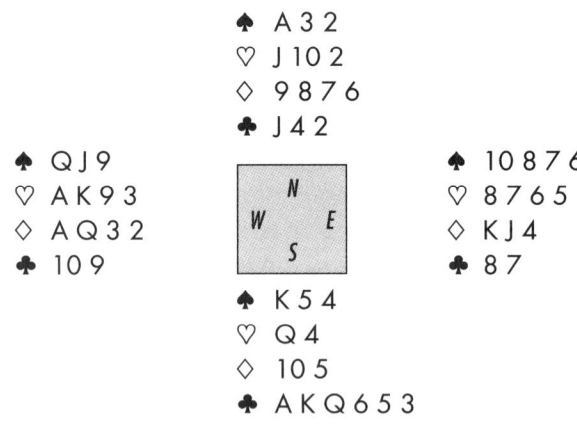

```
               ♠ A 3 2
               ♡ J 10 2
               ◇ 9 8 7 6
               ♣ J 4 2
♠ Q J 9                          ♠ 10 8 7 6
♡ A K 9 3      ┌─────────┐       ♡ 8 7 6 5
◇ A Q 3 2      │    N    │       ◇ K J 4
♣ 10 9         │ W     E │       ♣ 8 7
               │    S    │
               └─────────┘
               ♠ K 5 4
               ♡ Q 4
               ◇ 10 5
               ♣ A K Q 6 5 3
```

'Couldn't you lead a diamond?' demanded the irate Walrus.

'Easily,' replied Colin, 'I am afraid that seeing your signal I did not
even try. Or do you look upon the three as encouraging?'

'Did you expect me to throw the queen?' thundered Walter.

'No, no. That would have broken the contract. No one could
expect it of you. But even you, Walter, should have found a diamond
lead in the first place. Against H.H., always lead diamonds. It's a
golden rule. It's elementary. Even you...'

'I was leading diamonds, young man, while you were still in your crib!' cried the Walrus, outraged by Colin's facetious manner. 'If I had wanted a club, I should have signaled...'

'With the two, I suppose,' interrupted the Corgi, determined to have the last snap.

The Hog was enjoying himself. At the Griffins he would never have got away with that last hand. But it would take that absurd Walrus years to grasp the implications of his diamonds technique. With a wink in the direction of his victim, he told an admiring kibitzer: 'He's not quite with it, you know.'

'... young puppy... impertinence... a sixteen count...' the Walrus was muttering angrily.

The Hog beamed with approval at the looks of dislike exchanged between his opponents. They reflected a slate of perfect misunderstanding, and he resolved to lose no time in exploiting it.

The Corgi made a partscore. Then the Hog dealt:

```
              ♠ 7 6
              ♡ A 8
              ◇ 9 4
              ♣ Q J 10 9 8 3 2
♠ K Q 10 9 3         N
♡ 4 3 2        W          E
◇ A Q 7 2           S
♣ A
```

| West | North | East | South |
|------|-------|------|-------|
| W.W. | R.R. | C.C. | H.H. |
|      |       |      | 1◇ |
| 1♠ | 2♣ | pass | 3NT |
| dbl | all pass | | |

Despite the traffic, the sound of W.W.'s double must have carried easily across St. James's Street. Walter the Walrus was six foot one and a man of importance, who had inherited wisely and invested fortunately, and he did not like to be trifled with.

His opening lead was the ♠K. Colin produced the two and H.H. followed with the eight. W.W. knew all about the Bath Coup, and treating with contempt the Hog's opening bid, he switched promptly to the $\Diamond 2$. Dummy's nine, the Corgi's ten and the Hog's king made up the trick. Walter looked at it carefully and noted the contents.

Next came a small club. As he gathered the trick to his ample bosom, Walter's attention was riveted to his partner's $\heartsuit 5$. So! Partner had no clubs. Therefore H.H. had started with five. What, then, of his opening diamond bid? Surely it was not genuine. But was it completely spurious? All that could be said for certain was that partner had the jack, since it had taken the king to beat the ten. Beyond that all was problematical. The Hog's diamond holding could be the bare king or $\Diamond$Kx or $\Diamond$Kxx or $\Diamond$K8xx.

Determined to make sure of breaking the contract without running the least risk, the Walrus led his $\Diamond 7$ to partner's jack. Alas, against all reason and expectation, it was H.H., not partner, who produced that card. Instead of losing four diamond tricks, the Hog won two and lost none. A minute or so later he took the heart finesse, which he could by then well afford, to collect eleven tricks.

This was the full deal:

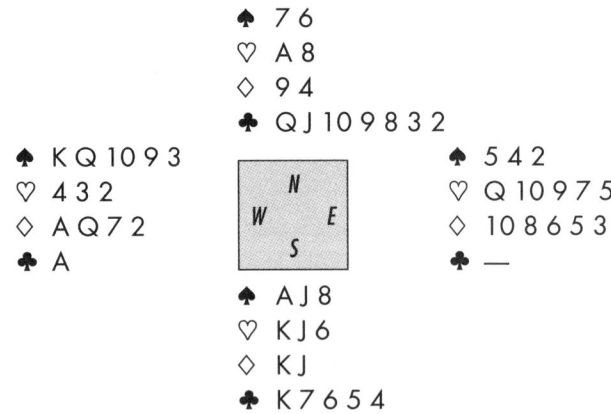

'I forgot to mention, Walter,' observed the Corgi, 'that it is not enough to *lead* diamonds. They are not all the same. Some are better than others.'

## Papa Cuts In

Two players joined the table, S.B., the Professor of Bio-Sophistry from Ghana and Themistocles Papadopoulos, our ancient and honored Griffin. The Walrus and the Corgi cut out.

'Sorry to lose you two,' remarked H.H. with feeling.

'I can well believe it,' said Colin 'but those whom the gods wish to keep asunder, let no man join together.'

Yet again the Hog cut the Rabbit. 'I marvel at your luck. How do you contrive to cut me so often?' asked H.H.

The Rabbit, who dealt, was too busy counting to reply. He opened 3NT. I was sitting between him and the Greek and these were their two hands.

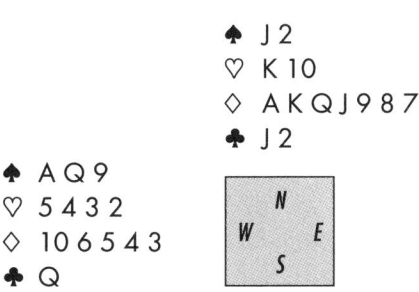

♠ J 2
♡ K 10
◇ A K Q J 9 8 7
♣ J 2

♠ A Q 9
♡ 5 4 3 2
◇ 10 6 5 4 3
♣ Q

'What do you understand by that bid?' inquired the Secretary Bird

'Normal Acol. Solid minor and a couple of hopes outside,' replied H.H., and as soon as S.B. passed, he bid 6◇.

'And what is that, if I may ask?' This time the question was put to the Rabbit.

R.R. had no idea. One never knew why the Hog did things. But he had to say something and after some thought he replied: 'Well, it's not in the book, but I think that partner knows my suit is diamonds and wants to play the hand himself. He does it better than I do, you see,' he added ruefully.

'How many points?' asked the Walrus, who was kibitzing. Nobody heard him and all passed. Papa was too cunning to expose himself to some deep first-round finesse by doubling, but as befits a man with a certain trump trick, he led his ace and continued with the ♠9 to dummy's jack. Two rounds of diamonds followed. When S.B. showed out, Papa looked jubilantly at the Hog.

The deal was:

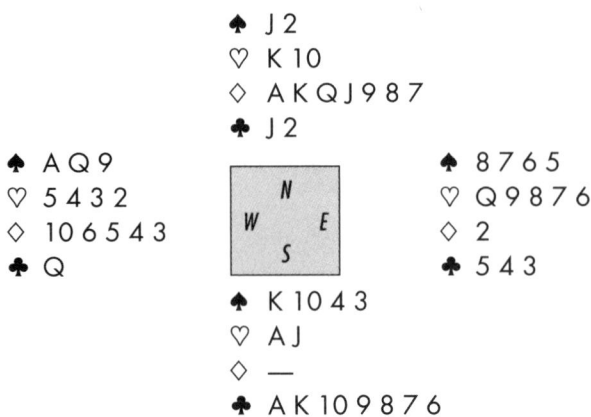

```
            ♠ J 2
            ♡ K 10
            ◇ A K Q J 9 8 7
            ♣ J 2
♠ A Q 9                       ♠ 8 7 6 5
♡ 5 4 3 2         N           ♡ Q 9 8 7 6
◇ 10 6 5 4 3   W     E        ◇ 2
♣ Q               S           ♣ 5 4 3
            ♠ K 10 4 3
            ♡ A J
            ◇ —
            ♣ A K 10 9 8 7 6
```

The Hog crossed to his hand with a club and cashed the ♠K, discarding a club from dummy. Next came a club, which he ruffed. Papa threw a heart. Playing smoothly and confidently, like a man without a care in the world, H.H. led dummy's ♡10 and finessed. When his jack held, he bestowed a pitying look on the Greek. Ruffing a second club in dummy he came back to his hand by overtaking the ♡K with the ace and with a contemptuous gesture tabled his cards.

The position was:

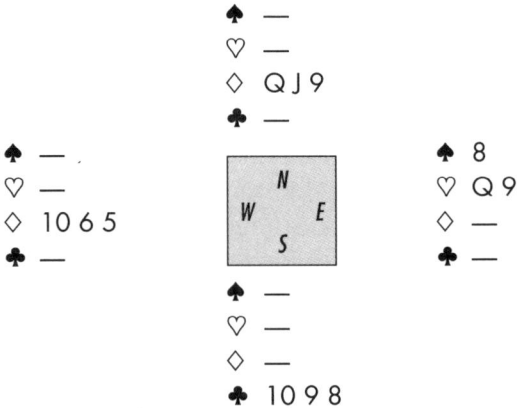

```
            ♠ —
            ♡ —
            ◇ Q J 9
            ♣ —
♠ —                           ♠ 8
♡ —              N            ♡ Q 9
◇ 10 6 5      W     E         ◇ —
♣ —              S            ♣ —
            ♠ —
            ♡ —
            ◇ —
            ♣ 10 9 8
```

and the lead was with declarer.

'Why didn't you cover the ten of hearts?' asked Papa.

'Why did you lead the ace of spades?' demanded S.B.

The Hog said reproachfully to the Rabbit: 'I bid six diamonds so that the opening lead should run up to my king of spades. Surely you know me too well to imagine that I could have had some other motive?'

# A Top for South-West

Barely ten days had elapsed since the Gala Individual held at the Unicorn to raise funds for Caccippuma — the Cash and Credits Cooperative for the Initiation of Primitive Peoples into the Use of Modern Arms. Donor of the first prize was a distinguished transatlantic member, head of Outer Space Development Inc., of New York, New York. He had presented a ten thousand acre estate on the moon — 'quiet, secluded, unspoilt by man, superbly situated between the Sea of Tribulation and the Lake of Calamity,' in the words of the brochure.

The Rueful Rabbit, who had started the Individual at 100-1, with no takers, was the winner. As his contribution to a lofty cause, the Rabbit had donated a case of Krug '59 to the player with the best slam record. The Hideous Hog, an easy winner, contributed, in turn, an autographed picture of himself as a prize for the competitor who scored the greatest number of cold bottoms.

'There is not a particle of skill in this Individual nonsense. It is sheer, unadulterated luck,' protested the embittered Greek when the Hog's picture was formally presented to him. 'Every player in the room set out to fix me and all won hands down.'

'Oh! Come, come,' jeered the Hog. 'The champagne I happened to win is an ephemeral trifle. Once drunk 'tis soon forgotten. But the picture of a master is a source of inspiration which lives forever. Indeed, Papa, you are to be envied.'

Thinking back on the Individual, I could not suppress a twinge of sympathy for Papa who played so well and fared so badly. After the Hog, he is easily the most skillful of the Griffins. Yet like other great technicians of my acquaintance, who always do the right thing, he does it invariably at the wrong time. The stars were not propitious to him that night. Maybe the cards were not shuffled as thoroughly as they should have been; maybe it was no more than a coincidence. Whatever it was, unusually big hands were out and the intrepid Hog shot his way into one slam after another.

## STRETCHING A POINT

On the first of these Walter the Walrus was his partner. Strange faces — two of the many which appeared from nowhere to grace the Gala — sat on either side of him. Walter opened 2NT and raised the Hog's 3♠ to four. Thinking no doubt of the Krug, the Hideous Hog bid a confident 6♠. These were the four hands:

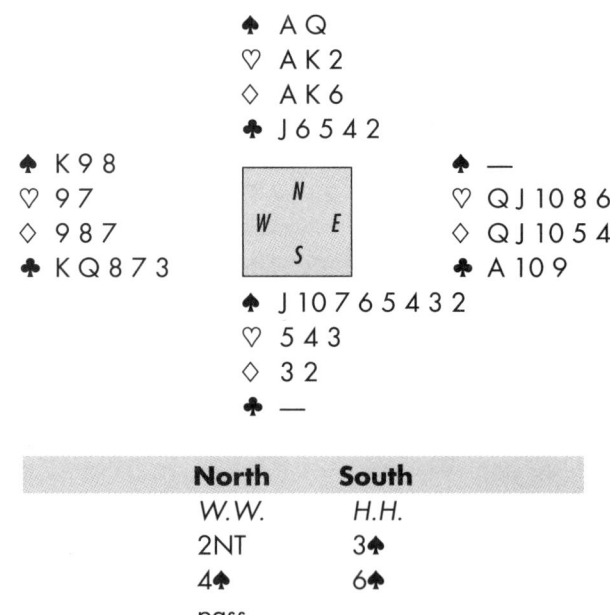

| | North | South |
|---|---|---|
| | W.W. | H.H. |
| | 2NT | 3♠ |
| | 4♠ | 6♠ |
| | pass | |

'You owe me a trump, Walter,' said the Hog severely when dummy went down. It was good tactics, for if the slam failed the Walrus would certainly bring up the question of points and the Hog's count was comparatively low.

The first Strange Face, sitting West, led the ♣K and it looked to the kibitzers as if the slam would depend on one of two things: catching the king of trumps or a 4-4 club break that would allow declarer to dispose of his losing heart. That was what I heard Oscar the Owl whisper to Peregrine the Penguin.

The Hog ruffed the opening club and finessed the spade. Dummy's queen held, but East, the second Strange Face, showed out.

'So much for catching the king of trumps,' murmured Oscar.

H.H. ruffed a second club, crossed to dummy with a diamond and ruffed a club again. Returning to dummy with his second diamond the Hog trumped a fourth club.

As East threw a diamond, Oscar and Peregrine sagely shook their heads, as if to say: 'Unlucky hand. Nothing works.'

The Hog now entered dummy with the ♡A and ruffed a diamond. Then came the ♡K. With three cards left this was the position:

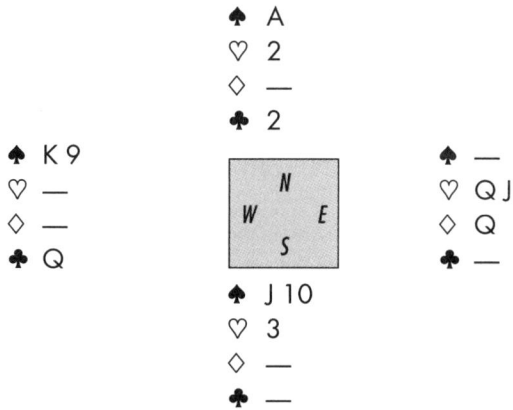

```
                  ♠ A
                  ♡ 2
                  ◇ —
                  ♣ 2
   ♠ K 9                          ♠ —
   ♡ —         ┌─────────┐        ♡ Q J
   ◇ —         │    N    │        ◇ Q
   ♣ Q         │  W   E  │        ♣ —
               │    S    │
               └─────────┘
                  ♠ J 10
                  ♡ 3
                  ◇ —
                  ♣ —
```

When the Hog played dummy's ♡2 West could ruff his partner's trick, of course, but since it would do him no good, he discarded his ♣Q. East led a red card, having no other, and H.H. ruffed with the ten, leaving West with the choice of underruffing or having his king smothered by the ace. Either way, the Hideous Hog was home.

The Walrus, heaving heavily from side to side, was about to say something. The Hog forestalled him: 'I didn't quite have the regulation point count,' he admitted handsomely, 'but with a ten-card suit, you know, one must stretch things a little.'

## ENTRIES GALORE

A few hands later Walter the Walrus was on the Hog's right. Papa was his left-hand opponent and the Rueful Rabbit was his partner. I was sitting between Papa and R.R., whose hands were:

```
                    ♠ 6 5 4
                    ♡ 5 4 3
                    ◇ K J 3 2
                    ♣ K 8 7
        ♠ K Q J
        ♡ Q J 8 7          N
        ◇ Q 9 7 6      W        E
        ♣ 5 4              S
```

The Hog opened with 2♣, and, after a while, R.R. replied with 2NT. This H.H. converted briskly into 6♣.

'I am a little weak in middle cards, perhaps, but with nine points I could hardly make a negative response,' explained the Rabbit apologetically.

'Which nine points?' inquired the Walrus who could only see seven. The Rabbit blinked. He nearly said something, but blinked again instead.

'Thank you, partner,' said the Hideous Hog mellifluously. Papa, who had placed the ♠K on the table, looked up suspiciously, sensing something underhand behind the Hog's civility.

H.H. ducked the first spade, won the second with his ace and reeled off seven clubs with the speed of lightning.

I could follow Papa's anguished thoughts. What four cards should he keep to the end? His partner's discards were singularly unhelpful. After following to trumps once only, he parted with two spades, then with three hearts. The Greek cursed him for not letting go his diamonds, which were clearly useless, but cursing was no help. Papa's mind was focused on the Hog's last four cards. What could they be? The bidding and the play confirmed that he held the two red aces. Which were his other two cards? A heart and a diamond? Or no heart and two diamonds? Could one of the four missing cards be the ♠2, which was still missing? Papa could not be expected to guess. Neither could he be held responsible for his partner's uninformative discards. One thing was clear. Unless he kept his diamond holding intact, dummy's four diamonds would take the last four tricks.

While the Greek was parting reluctantly with his ♠J, I crossed softly to the other side of the table to peer into the hand of Walter the Walrus. This is how things looked from his angle:

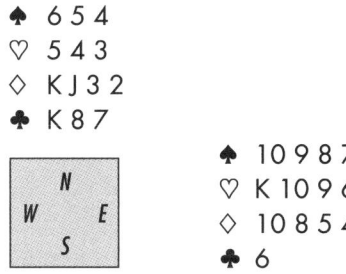

```
            ♠ 6 5 4
            ♡ 5 4 3
            ◇ K J 3 2
            ♣ K 8 7
                        ♠ 10 9 8 7
              N         ♡ K 10 9 6
           W     E      ◇ 10 8 5 4
              S         ♣ 6
```

Walter, too, knew from the bidding and the play that the Hog had seven clubs and the three other aces — eleven tricks in all, with dummy's ◇K. H.H. could not have the ◇Q, as well, for that would give him all thirteen tricks. Obviously, Papa had the ◇Q and obviously it was finessable. Worse still, it would come down. Therefore, come what may, he, Walter, must keep every one of his four diamonds. Papa's last spade discard shook him, but who was he to unravel the tortuous recesses of his partner's mind? If no more spades were out, the Greek was just the man to throw an honor and keep the two. This was the full deal:

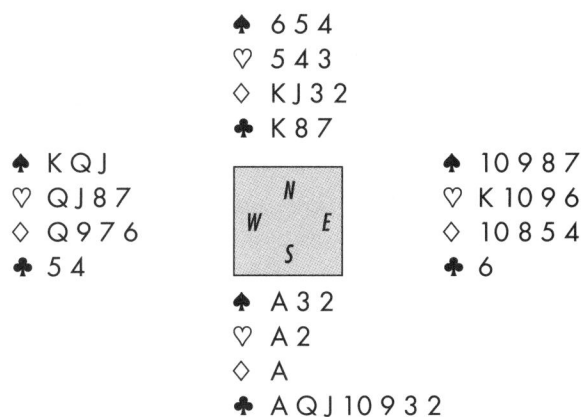

```
                ♠ 6 5 4
                ♡ 5 4 3
                ◇ K J 3 2
                ♣ K 8 7
  ♠ K Q J                      ♠ 10 9 8 7
  ♡ Q J 8 7        N           ♡ K 10 9 6
  ◇ Q 9 7 6     W     E        ◇ 10 8 5 4
  ♣ 5 4            S           ♣ 6
                ♠ A 3 2
                ♡ A 2
                ◇ A
                ♣ A Q J 10 9 3 2
```

Both defenders could see that declarer had three trump entries to dummy. That he would use them up, leaving the ◇K to pine away, uncashed, if he had no small diamond himself to get back to the table, was something which did not dawn on either of them. Both held on grimly to their diamonds, allowing the Hideous Hog to make the last four tricks with:

♠  2
♡  A 2
◇  A
♣  —

'Your diamonds made the hand,' said H.H. to the Rabbit. And baring his teeth in what was doubtless intended as a smile, he added with a sideways glance at Papa: 'A suit is neither good nor bad but thinking makes it so. Ha ha!'

By way of explanation to an admiring kibitzer, he added: 'Virgil, you know, greatest master of the Alexandrine...'

There was a venomous hiss from the Secretary Bird, who was walking past to take his place for the next round. 'If I had a low diamond,' jeered H.H, 'I was home on a finesse anyway. It was the fourteenth trick they were both after, not the twelfth. Ha ha!'

## Good Bidding by South/West

Another curious hand came up shortly before the end of the first session. H.H. was playing with that facetious young man, Colin the Corgi. His favorite opponents, Papa and S.B., the Emeritus Professor of Bio-Sophistry, were sitting East and West.

The Hog picked up the sort of hand which we have often enough at duplicate, but rarely, if ever, when we play for money.

♠ A K Q   ♡ —   ◇ A K Q 9 8 7   ♣ A 4 3 2

This was the bidding sequence:

| West | North | East | South |
|------|-------|------|-------|
| *Papa* | *C.C.* | *S.B.* | *H.H.* |
| | | | 2♣ |
| pass | 2♡ | pass | 3◇ |
| pass | 3♡ | pass | 4◇ |
| pass | 4♡ | pass | 4NT |
| pass | 5◇ | pass | 5NT |
| pass | 6♡ | pass | 7◇ |
| dbl | 7♡ | dbl | ? |

The Hideous Hog growled, chewing angrily at his cigar, for there was no mistaking the implications of those doubles. They were entirely unconnected with Theodore Lightner. In each case the doubler sat over declarer presumptive and possessed, without a doubt, a certain trick in the prospective trump suit.

The Hog's first impulse was to switch deftly to notrump, but a moment's reflection showed him that if both red suits were brittle, he could not hope to make thirteen tricks in notrump. He glowered and he snarled, but it did not help. Suddenly, there came a gleam into the small beady eyes and putting down the tattered remains of his Havana, the Hog called — or rather barked — 'Seven spades!'

His reasoning was simple enough. On the bidding, partner clearly had one diamond or none. He had not mentioned clubs. It followed that he might well have four spades. They might even be as good as ♠J10xx, and if so, his hearts could be set up, perhaps, by ruffing in the closed hand. It was, least, a chance. Bowing to an unkind fate in 7♡ or converting in desperation to 7NT offered no chance at all.

Papa led the ♣J, a cunning falsecard, and dummy came into view. This was the deal:

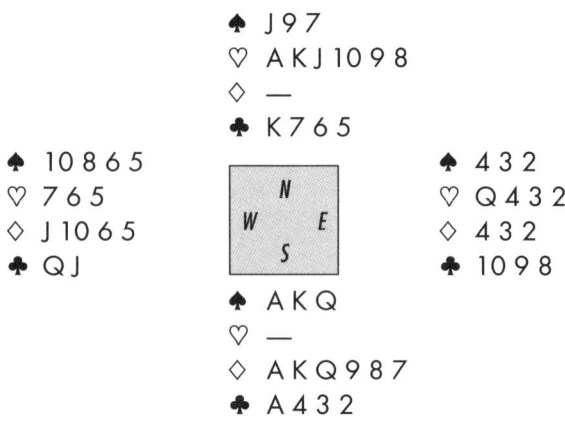

The Hog won in dummy, played off the ♡A and ♡K, discarding two clubs, crossed to his hand with the ♣A and cashed the three top diamonds. Then came another diamond, which he ruffed with dummy's ♠7. When the Secretary Bird failed to overruff, the Hog knew that he was home. He trumped a heart with the ♠Q and led another diamond, smirking sweetly at Papa, who, having nothing left but trumps, was forced to ruff. Dummy overruffed. Now came another heart from dummy and it was the Secretary Bird's turn to throw a trump.

The grand slam was made with the ♡AK, the ◊AKQ, the ♣AK and six trump tricks.

The Hideous Hog, who likes success to be spiced with a little ill-feeling, turned happily to his opponents: 'Considerate of you to warn me by doubling that the red suits would not break. But for that...'

'What made you double seven diamonds?' asked the Emeritus Professor angrily.

'We're playing for matchpoints,' retorted Papa vehemently, 'and an extra hundred might make a big difference. Since you evidently do not share this view, may I ask what made you double seven hearts?'

'A trump lead, which stood out a mile...' began the Emeritus Professor of Bio-Sophistry.

'Let us simply say,' interrupted Colin the Corgi, 'that we have witnessed a brilliant piece of cooperation between declarer and defense. No doubt, there is some valuable prize in this contest for the best South-West score. Or should it be for North-East?'

# B<sub>i</sub>ter B<sub>i</sub>t

*(A different story with this same title appears in* Murder in the Menagerie.*)*

Glass in hand, the Hog was still dwelling on the pleasurable experiences of the afternoon, chortling happily over Papa's discomfiture, when someone asked him to make up a table. H.H. was not keen. Who was kibitzing, he wanted to know. Eventually he allowed himself to be persuaded. I did not meet him again till the end of the session. Then, seeing him once more at grips with Papa, I strolled across. The Hog had just dealt at favorable vulnerability and soon he found himself in his favorite contract of 3NT.

```
                    ♠ J 7
                    ♡ A Q J 9 8 7
                    ◇ K 5
                    ♣ 6 5 4

                    ┌─────────┐
                    │    N    │
                    │  W   E  │
                    │    S    │
                    └─────────┘

                    ♠ K 9 8
                    ♡ 2
                    ◇ A 7 6
                    ♣ A Q J 10 9 8
```

| West | North | East | South |
|------|-------|------|-------|
| Papa | S.B. | W.W. | H.H. |
|      |       |      | 1♣ |
| 1◇ | 1♡ | pass | 3♣ |
| pass | 3♡ | pass | 3NT |
| all pass | | | |

Papa opened the ◇Q and was allowed to hold the first trick. Winning the diamond continuation with dummy's king, the Hog led a club and finessed the queen. The Walrus contributed the three and Papa the two. The Hog grunted meditatively. If W.W. had the ♣K, all was well. But if the missing clubs were split 3-1, Papa might be holding up the king. In that case, the clubs would yield five tricks only and it would be necessary to take the heart finesse. What should he do? Still undecided, the Hog led a heart. As the Greek came up with the ten, H.H. gave him a look of pity blended with malevolence. He went up with dummy's ace and led a club, saying nothing until the Walrus had followed suit. Then he cleared his throat.

'My friend,' he said addressing Papa, 'only this afternoon I had occasion to admonish you for falsecarding at every turn, often against yourself. Now you have done it again. But for that fatuous ten I might well have taken the heart finesse, for I didn't know then, as I do now, who had the king of clubs. After all, Walter might have had one club only. But that ten of hearts was too good to be true. Was I really meant to believe that six tricks would fall into my lap if only I took the trouble to finesse?'

As he spoke, the Hog played the ♣J, repeating the 'marked' finesse. Suddenly Papa whipped the king from his hand. With a triumphant look in his dark, liquid eyes, he seized the trick and shot a diamond across the table. These were the four hands:

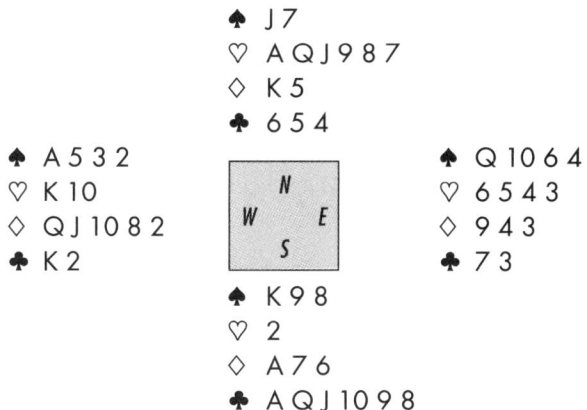

```
                    ♠ J 7
                    ♡ A Q J 9 8 7
                    ◇ K 5
                    ♣ 6 5 4
  ♠ A 5 3 2                              ♠ Q 10 6 4
  ♡ K 10            N                    ♡ 6 5 4 3
  ◇ Q J 10 8 2   W     E                 ◇ 9 4 3
  ♣ K 2             S                    ♣ 7 3
                    ♠ K 9 8
                    ♡ 2
                    ◇ A 7 6
                    ♣ A Q J 10 9 8
```

There was no longer a way of making more than eight tricks. Growling and snarling, the Hideous Hog had to concede defeat.

'The king of clubs would have dropped,' pointed out a kibitzer helpfully.

'The heart finesse was right, too,' added another.

'I only had two points,' declared Walter the Walrus. 'I expected a slam. How we beat the contract is something I shall never know.'

'Then let me tell you,' cried the victorious Greek. 'On the bidding, I rather expected a singleton heart and if H.H. had two, we couldn't beat the contract anyway. So I bared my king of clubs, as you saw, and that was half the battle. But it was the ten of hearts which won the day. So taken in was he by his own wisecrack, that business of my falsecarding with singletons, that he didn't allow for my play of a true card. It didn't dawn on him that I might have no other. There's a saying,' added, or rather declaimed, Papa, 'that he laughs best who laughs last. And that, let me tell you, is none other than Themistocles Papadopoulos!'

Brooding somberly over a cognac at the bar a little later, the Hog was saying: 'That odious exhibition of gloating. If I couldn't win gracefully, without bombast and boasting and all that vile vulgarity, I would sooner not win at all.'

He seemed to be taking it all very much to heart and four cognacs later I heard him murmur: 'He provoked me into a mistake.' Even when H.H. said it himself, it sounded profane.

'After all, you couldn't tell,' I said to comfort him.

Filling his glass, the Hideous Hog shook his head: 'There was really no excuse,' he whispered. 'If the heart finesse didn't work, the club finesse couldn't work either. He had to have at least one of the kings for his vulnerable overcall. Baring his king of clubs was good bridge. I might have made that play myself. I admit it. But that after all these years he should play a true card — it may not be downright unethical, but in my opinion it's sailing pretty close to the wind.'

## Enlisting T.T's Help

The next few deals were uneventful, but we all noticed how ostentatiously the Hog avoided saying anything offensive to his parter, T.T. did not hide his resentment.

Before long, Papa found himself once more in 4♡.

```
                    ♠ J 2
                    ♡ K 5
                    ◇ A Q J 10 8
                    ♣ 5 4 3 2
♠ K Q 10 9         ┌─────────┐
♡ 4 3 2           │    N    │
◇ 7               │  W   E  │
♣ A K 8 7 6       │    S    │
                    └─────────┘
```

| West | North | East | South |
|------|-------|------|-------|
| H.H. | W.W. | T.T. | Papa |
|      |       |      | 1♡ |
| 2♣ | 2◇ | pass | 3♡ |
| pass | 4♡ | all pass | |

The Hideous Hog led the ♣K, then the ♣A, to which the Toucan followed with the ten and nine, and Papa with the jack and queen. The Hog switched to the ♠K and the Greek, winning with the ace, forthwith returned the eight to the Hog's queen.

This was the decisive moment and we went over the inferences carefully that night when the hand came up for discussion over dinner. Oscar, who had been kibitzing at lower stakes that afternoon, put the questions.

'How many spades did you think he had?' he asked H.H.

'Two, of course,' replied the Hog. 'Obviously he was missing the queen of trumps. Otherwise he would have tried the diamonds first — or else, if he had the king, he would have simply drawn trumps and spread his hand.'

'Why, then, did he play back a spade?' persisted Oscar.

'To gain information,' explained H.H. 'Naturally, Papa knew that I knew he was looking for the queen of trumps and that I knew that he knew it. For all that, I might have given something away. Suppose, for instance, that I had a doubleton queen. Well, I might have led a third spade, because if he had to ruff in dummy he couldn't finesse and...'

'But surely,' broke in O.O., who was getting a little confused, 'if you had a doubleton queen the last thing you would try to do would be to stop him finessing. How else could you make your queen?'

'That's just it,' cried H.H., 'I would be protecting my queen by telling him that I had it so that he should think that I hadn't. And it would be quite safe, of course, since he wouldn't ruff in dummy anyway and he knew that I knew that he wouldn't.'

'And since you didn't have the queen,' said Oscar, 'you told him, I suppose, that Timothy had it, so that...'

'No, no, no,' broke in the Hideous Hog. 'Papa isn't taken in as easily as all that. Coming from me even the truth wouldn't necessarily deceive him. After all, I am an opponent. I am playing against him. But get the Toucan to tell him a lie and he wouldn't suspect a thing, for as you saw for yourselves, the Toucan is firmly on his side and though he does not know it, Papa does and acts accordingly, of course.'

'But how could you enlist Timothy's help?' inquired the Owl.

'With the eight of clubs,' replied H.H. 'The eight is quite an inconspicuous card, you know, and half the time, at least, T.T. wouldn't expect it to be master. After all, it isn't often that the ace, king, queen, jack, ten and nine are all swallowed up in the first two tricks. Expecting Papa to have some bigger and better club, the Toucan would ruff. And now,' went on the Hog, sweeping his arm towards the cognac, 'turn to Papa. He can finesse both ways, remember. Would he expect any sane defender to bare his queen just for the pleasure of ruffing his partner's trick? And mind you,' added H.H., 'even if by some mischance the

Toucan happened to remember that the eight was master and refrained from ruffing, nothing would be lost. The Greek would still be no wiser about the queen.'

'Yes, it seems like a chance to nothing,' agreed O.O., 'but what happened? Did he remember or did he ruff?'

'Both,' replied H.H. 'He remembered and ruffed.'

Full deal:

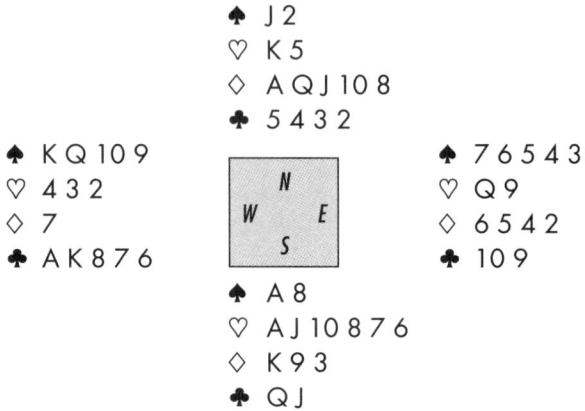

'And Papa finessed the wrong way?'

'Finessed?' thundered H.H. 'He didn't have to finesse. That sadist ruffed with the queen and as he did it, he beamed at me and said: 'I knew all along that you were staging another uppercut, but I didn't let you down this time, did I, H.H.?'

The Hog drained his glass and Oscar's and looked viciously at mine.

'I think that you demoralize that poor Toucan,' said the Owl severely. 'His friend the Rabbit complains that you don't even bother to be rude to him these days. That's hardly the way to get the best out of partners, you know.'

'I will try to be rude to him sometimes,' said the Hog, 'but honestly, Oscar, he doesn't deserve it.'

# Unnatural Alliance

Kibitzers gathered from the four corners of the room as word went round that the Hideous Hog had cut Papa the Greek. Things happened when these two natural enemies faced each other in unnatural alliance and no one wanted to miss a single word of abuse.

'Usual side bet, Papa?' asked S.B., the Emeritus Professor of Bio-Sophistry, who had cut the Rueful Rabbit.

'No, we'll give it a miss this time,' replied the Greek, looking H.H. firmly in the eye. 'I don't like to bet unless I play myself and I am hardly likely to do much of that this rubber.'

This was the first deal:

```
                  ♠ A 7 6
                  ♡ 6 5 4 3 2
                  ◇ A J 6
                  ♣ A 7
    ♠ K J 9                        ♠ Q 10 8
    ♡ K Q 9 7         N            ♡ A J 10 8
    ◇ K Q 10      W       E        ◇ 9 8 7
    ♣ Q 9 8          S             ♣ K J 10
                  ♠ 5 4 3 2
                  ♡ —
                  ◇ 5 4 3 2
                  ♣ 6 5 4 3 2
```

| West | North | East | South |
|------|-------|------|-------|
| R.R. | Papa | S.B. | H.H. |
|  | 1NT | pass | 2♠ |
| all pass | | | |

The auction, and more especially the Hog's call of 2♠, may appear somewhat unorthodox. But as H.H. later told an inquiring kibitzer, it was a routine sequence to which there could be no conceivable alternative.

'Any mathematician will tell you,' explained the Hog, 'that partner's thirteen point notrump, added to my zero, leaves opponents with a shade over twenty-seven points. Inevitably, the one notrump will be doubled and the resulting penalty can hardly be less than 800. A weakness takeout is, therefore, imperative and since two clubs would be interpreted as Stayman, the choice lies between two diamonds and two spades. The latter is preferable on account of its preemptive value and also because opponents are less likely to double a bid which, if made, will give the other side a game.

'Finally,' said H.H., 'though my hand is not rich in tenaces, it is always better that the opening lead should run up to the stronger player.'

The Hog's optimism proved justified, for no one doubled his 2♠. His confident tone, allied to his reputation, sufficed to deter the other side.

The Rabbit led the ♢K, which was allowed to win. No switch looked particularly attractive, but a heart seemed safe and R.R. continued with the ♡K, which the Hog ruffed. Crossing to dummy three times, once with the ♣A and twice with diamonds — taking the marked finesse — H.H. ruffed three more hearts in his hand. That came to seven tricks. Pointing to the ace of trumps as the eighth, the Hog graciously conceded the rest.

'I think that we could have made game in notrump,' ventured the Rabbit ruefully.

'Do not reproach yourself unduly,' the Hog reassured him, 'as you have just seen, we had a cheap save in spades.'

## A Certain Trump Trick

Papa dealt again, but the players did not notice it and the kibitzers did not seem to mind. At 60 up, the Greek had no hesitation in opening the bidding with 1♣. Tactically, with a partscore, substandard openings are sound enough. If partner has the cards, it makes little difference. But if opponents hold the balance of power, each in turn is inclined to suspect the other of stretching to save game, with the result that they sometimes fail to reach an easy game themselves. With the present opposition such possibilities were probabilities.

```
                    ♠ 7 5 4
                    ♡ 4 3
                    ◇ K J 10
                    ♣ A K 4 3 2
    ♠ 10 9 8                         ♠ K J
    ♡ 8 7 6 5 2       N             ♡ K J 9
    ◇ 2           W       E         ◇ 9 8 6 5 4 3
    ♣ J 7 6 5         S             ♣ Q 10
                    ♠ A Q 6 3 2
                    ♡ A Q 10
                    ◇ A Q 7
                    ♣ 9 8
```

| West | North | East | South |
|------|-------|------|-------|
| R.R. | Papa | S.B. | H.H. |
|      | 1♣ | 1◇ | 2♠ |
| pass | 3♣ | pass | 3◇ |
| pass | 3♠ | pass | 4NT |
| pass | 5◇ | pass | 5NT |
| pass | 6♣ | pass | 7◇ |
| all pass | | | |

The first three rounds of bidding were uneventful. Over Papa's 1♣, S.B. intervened with 1◇ and the Hog forced with 2♠. Opponents took no further part in the bidding and the Greek repeated his clubs. The Hog now bid the enemy suit, 3◇, and Papa signed off quietly in 3♠. Beginning to feel a little uncomfortable, he showed his ace over 4NT, but when H.H. went on to 5NT, Papa felt that he had done enough. Suppressing the existence of his two kings, the Greek's 6♣ bid was intended to banish forever all thoughts of a grand slam.

The six clubs bid had precisely the opposite effect on the Hog. Unable to visualize Papa's hand without a king in it, he assumed that the Greek was showing all four. Just as 5♣ over 4NT promises four aces or none, so an extension of the same principle could apply to kings. Surely there could be no other explanation for Papa's bid. By this time there was no doubt in the Hog's mind that the North-South hands would yield thirteen tricks. But what in? If Papa's clubs were solid, the hand should be played in notrump. If not, 7♠ might prove the better contract. Only Papa could know the answer and to put the picture clearly before him the Hog produced a master bid — 7◊, leaving it to Themistocles Papadopoulos to deliver the verdict at the seven-level.

Papa blinked. He blinked again. Then his eyes narrowed as the Machiavellian design behind the Hog's bidding sequence became apparent. Whatever he did, the Hog, as always, would play the hand, and if anything went wrong, and it could hardly do otherwise, Papa would be held responsible on account of his opening. It was a bitter thought but he was forced to admit that, once again, the Hideous Hog had endplayed him in the bidding. And then, suddenly, through black despair flashed the vision of escape, a dazzling exit-bid to which H.H. would have no answer. He would bid neither 7♠ nor 7NT. He would simply pass 7◊! Since he was bound to be abused anyway, at least he would have the satisfaction of deserving it — and of teaching that Hog a salutory lesson in the process.

The Secretary Bird passed, too, and a gasp went up from the serried ranks of the kibitzers. Not one of them had yet seen a grand slam played in a cuebid.

'I must say!' Walter the Walrus could be heard whispering across the room. 'Fancy not doubling with ten points and a certain trump trick too.'

S.B. hissed disdainfully. The gentle smirk, the superior smile on his thin bloodless lips told the world that he knew when he was on to a good thing and he had no intention of painting the beautiful lily.

The Rabbit led the ♡8 and the Hog, still hurling imprecations at Papa, won the trick with the ten. Not pausing a second in his tirade, he crossed to dummy with a club and took the marked finesse in hearts. After cashing the ace on which he threw one of dummy's spades, he went back to dummy with his second club and finessed against the ♠K. Scoring his seventh trick with the ♠A, the Hog sat back. Without another word of abuse, he proceeded to reel off six more tricks on a crossruff. Three times, when spades were led from the closed hand and ruffed in dummy, the Emeritus Professor underruffed. Three times, when clubs were led from dummy, the Hog overruffed the Professor.

'You see how wise our friend was not to double,' said the Hog, chuckling, to the Walrus. 'A certain trump trick does not always defeat a grand slam, you know — not when I am at the wheel, anyway.'

The Hog, who was now in magnanimous mood, had a kind word for Papa, too.

'Never mind, Themistocles,' he said, 'you meant well, I am sure, and maybe my bidding was a bit too advanced for you. Still, we reached the only makeable grand slam on the cards, so I... er... we did not do so badly.'

Papa gnashed his teeth. Never had he regretted making a grand slam so much.


# A PSYCHIC SUIT SIGNAL

It was some time before the conversation subsided and the kibitzers allowed the game to be resumed. Pleading that his legs were in a draft, the Emeritus Professor of Bio-Sophistry changed places with the Rabbit. As declarer on the hand which follows, R.R. is shown South in the diagram.

```
               ♠  4 3
               ♡  A K 3 2
               ◇  A 10
               ♣  K Q J 10 9

                     N
                W         E
                     S

               ♠  A 10 8
               ♡  9 8 4
               ◇  K J 9 8 7 6
               ♣  6
```

| West | North | East | South |
|------|-------|------|-------|
| H.H. | S.B. | Papa | R.R. |
| | 1♣ | pass | 1◇ |
| pass | 1♡ | pass | 2◇ |
| pass | 3◇ | pass | 3NT |
| all pass | | | |

The Hog led the ♠6 and Papa's king was allowed to win. The ♠9 came back and again the Rabbit ducked. Winning with the jack, the Hog carefully selected the ♠2 and placed it, with deliberation, in the centre of the table. The Rabbit did not pay much attention. As was so usual with him, he was wool-gathering. He took the third spade trick with

# Hideous Hog
# & Secretary Bird

his ace and led a diamond, absentmindedly. There was no malice in it, for his thoughts were far away. What, he wondered, had he done with that letter to his brother? He remembered distinctly not posting it and he couldn't think where else it might be.

Someone coughed. Someone else sneezed. 'Is it too late to look at the last trick?' asked the Rabbit, coming out of his reverie.

'Certainly,' replied S.B., who was a lawyer by instinct as well as by profession, and enjoyed suffering himself, so long as he could make others suffer, too, the full rigors of the law.

'Not at all, not at all,' declared the Hideous Hog. 'This is a friendly game, Professor, not a thieves' kitchen. Here you are, my dear R.R.,' and suiting his action to his words, the Hog stretched across the table to turn up obligingly the previous trick. Carefully he drew the cards. 'Your ace, dummy's little heart, Papa's little club and,' he went on, lingering over the words, 'my two of spades.'

The Secretary Bird hissed in protest. 'Ignore him,' cried Papa, looking at H.H. with loathing. The kibitzers exchanged significant glances. Why was H.H. so anxious to help the other side? Murmurs of disapproval could be heard all round the table.

'Do not distress yourselves,' said R.R. with dignity. 'I wouldn't dream of profiting by information to which I am not properly entitled. I can see now, since the trick has been turned, that the two of spades was an unmistakable suit preference signal showing the ace of clubs. As it happens, I can do better without touching clubs. The diamond finesse will see me home, and since H.H. has a lot of spades, Papa is likely to be longer in diamonds and therefore to have the queen. I was reading about it only the other day. The odds, I believe, are 112%. Anyway, it's all in Chapter XVIII. Of course,' went on R.R. 'I would have made doubly sure of leaving the clubs alone had I noticed that two, but since I was distrait I must pay for my carelessness. Sorry, partner. Here goes.' Stoically, the Rueful Rabbit led a club. This was the full deal:

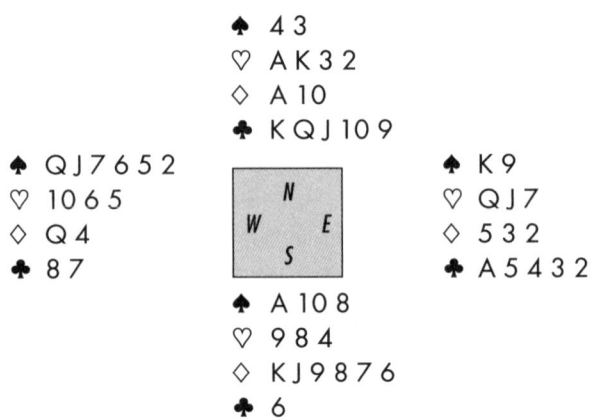

♠ 4 3
♡ A K 3 2
◇ A 10
♣ K Q J 10 9

♠ Q J 7 6 5 2
♡ 10 6 5
◇ Q 4
♣ 8 7

♠ K 9
♡ Q J 7
◇ 5 3 2
♣ A 5 4 3 2

♠ A 10 8
♡ 9 8 4
◇ K J 9 8 7 6
♣ 6

Papa came in with the ♣A, but since he had no more spades, the Rabbit made the rest of the tricks. Dropping the ◇Q came as a pleasant surprise, but it no longer mattered.

The Rabbit made a mental note to look up the chapter on suit preference signals. He had evidently misunderstood that piece on twos.

The Hideous Hog growled angrily. His psychic suit signal was the only defense against an unbreakable contract and it had failed because the woolly-minded Rabbit had been too proud to take advantage of it.

The Secretary Bird hissed. Turning up that trick was a breach of the laws which were, of course, the most important part of the game.

Papa smiled happily. The Hog, his partner, had been thwarted and his side had lost. He could sit back at last and enjoy a bad result.

# The Best Defense

*(The introduction and first deal in this story appeared in* Bridge in the Fourth Dimension, *but after that everything is unique.)*

'What a way to present a problem!' stormed the Hog, crumpling up in disgust Oscar's newspaper. 'South to make ten tricks against the best defense. And what sort of South, I should like to know, allows his opponents to put up the best defense?'

'Well...' began Oscar the Owl, our official kibitzer.

'On the contrary,' retorted the Hog warmly, 'East-West can only defend as well as South allows them to do. And if they put up the best defense it can only mean that South doesn't know his business. So why should anyone care how this ignoramus sets about making ten tricks?'

'But surely,' objected the Rueful Rabbit, 'that can't be right. I mean, when I'm East or West, I produce the worst defense no matter what South does, so it must work the other way, too. I mean...'

Oscar the Owl shook his head. 'You miss the point,' he told R.R. 'You do your best without malice aforethought. It's just that you have flair the other way. Now some defenders apply reason and...'

The Hideous Hog wasn't listening. With bold strokes of my fountain pen he was writing down a hand on the tablecloth.

```
            ♠ 7 5
            ♡ A 6 5
            ◇ K Q 10
            ♣ A K J 10 7

                  N
              W       E
                  S

            ♠ K 9 2
            ♡ J
            ◇ A J 9 4 3 2
            ♣ 8 4 3
```

| West | North | East | South |
|------|-------|------|-------|
| 1♠ | dbl | pass | 3◇ |
| pass | 4◇ | pass | 5◇ |
| all pass | | | |

'There you are,' said H.H. 'West opens a trump against five diamonds. Go ahead Oscar.'

'I draw trumps and I *don't* take the club finesse,' announced the Owl after due deliberation. 'If the finesse is right, I don't need it for I don't mind giving up the lead to West. He can't hurt me. But I want to keep East out, if possible, and I must give myself the chance of finding him with a doubleton queen.'

'Well, he hasn't,' said H.H., beaming malevolently at the Owl. 'East's queen is fully protected and you may rest assured that East — or any other nitwit, for that matter — will shoot a spade through your gizzard the moment he gains the lead. Yes, you can rely implicitly on the best defense.'

'If everything's wrong,' protested O.O., 'it would need a magician to make this contract.'

The Hog cast down modestly his thick red eyelashes. 'I made it, of course. Of course,' he repeated. 'But then I didn't allow East to put up the best defense.'

'How did you do it?' inquired the Rueful Rabbit, all agog.

'Quite simple,' replied the Hideous Hog, snarling prettily, 'and I'll show you how you, too, can do it. Suppose that the opening lead had been not a trump but a heart. The king to be precise. You would have ducked. Then you would have thrown a club on the ace of hearts and you would have ruffed the third club, setting up two clubs in dummy — and you would have kept East at arm's length all the time.

'Well, you do the same thing with a trump lead, because you expect West, on the bidding, to have the king of hearts. There's not much left for him to have anyway, but he's more likely to be missing a queen than a king. Now you all see it clearly, don't you?' asked the Hog, certain that no one could see anything.

His gaze swept round the table, but every glass was empty and with a dejected look he drained his own before continuing. 'At Trick 2 you lead a heart from dummy. West takes your jack with the king, but he can't hurt you and you have all the time in the world to set up the clubs.'

'You are assuming that West has the king and queen of hearts,' objected Oscar.

'Not at all,' replied the Hog. 'What's more he didn't.'

This was the deal:

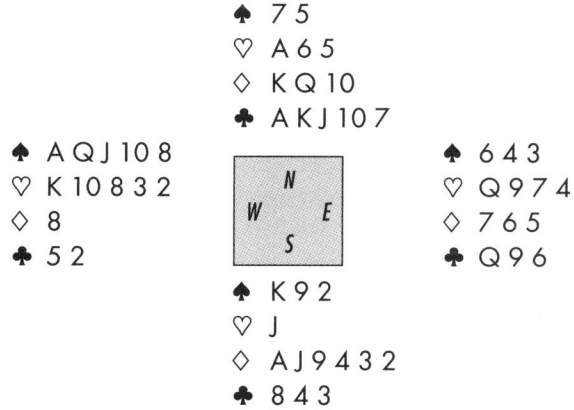

'Of course,' concluded H.H., 'East can break the contract by going up with the queen of hearts. But why should he do anything so eccentric? By taking into account that East is a rational human and not a cardinal point, declarer makes his five diamonds. And don't blame East. He did what anyone else would do — except someone writing about it afterwards. The best defense, you know, isn't clairvoyance.

# ALL ON A FINESSE

With a hearty tug at the tablecloth the Hog made room for another hand.

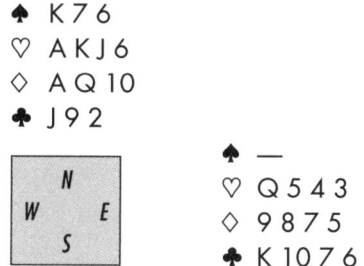

```
         ♠ K76
         ♡ AKJ6
         ◇ AQ10
         ♣ J92
                              ♠ —
                              ♡ Q543
                              ◇ 9875
                              ♣ K10764
```

| West | North | East | South |
|------|-------|------|-------|
|      |       |      | 1♠    |
| pass | 3♡    | pass | 3♠    |
| pass | 4♣    | pass | 5♣    |
| pass | 5◇    | pass | 5♠    |
| pass | 6♠    | all pass |    |

'You are East,' said the Hog, 'and partner leads the nine of hearts. Declarer goes up with dummy's ace, dropping the eight from his hand, and plays the two of clubs. His queen of clubs wins and now, at Trick 3, he leads a trump. Got it?'

It seemed simple so far. 'Partner,' went on H.H., 'goes up with the ace of trumps and continues with the seven of hearts. The king is played from dummy and the ten from the closed hand. Four cards have gone — two hearts, one club and a trump. Four good trumps come next. West follows all the way while the jack and six of hearts are thrown from dummy. With five cards left this is the position:

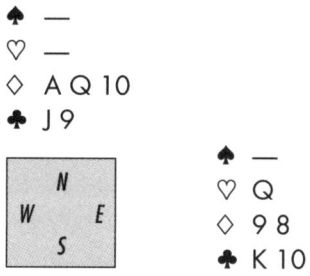

```
         ♠ —
         ♡ —
         ◇ AQ10
         ♣ J9
                              ♠ —
                              ♡ Q
                              ◇ 98
                              ♣ K10
```

'Having finished with trumps, declarer leads the jack of diamonds, overtakes with the queen in dummy and leads the jack of clubs. You cover and his ace wins. Now comes a diamond to the ace and the ten of diamonds. Yes, you can assume that declarer has the king of diamonds. Well, what do you throw, the queen of hearts or the ten of clubs?'

Oscar blinked inquiringly.

'Partner's been no help at all,' answered H.H. 'Having started with ♠A5432, he's had no opportunity to discard anything. He has shown the nine and seven of hearts and the two and four of diamonds. His clubs were the three and the five. Make what you like of it.'

'Unless declarer started with three clubs,' said the Owl, 'his finesse — the second time, when he played the jack — makes no sense. Presumably he was hoping to find West with the doubleton ten of clubs. Then...'

'And if he had three hearts,' broke in the Rabbit, 'he would have had to take the heart finesse willy-nilly.'

'So you throw the heart?' asked the Hog. The Rueful Rabbit twitched his left ear affirmatively.

'I keep the ten of clubs,' said O.O.

'So much for the best defense,' scoffed H.H., upsetting Oscar's coffee over dummy as he filled in the South and West hands.

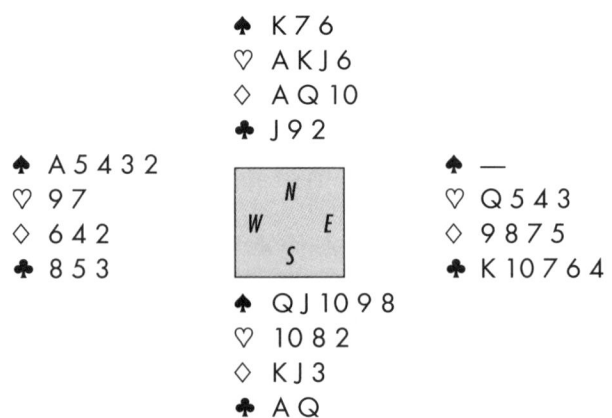

```
                    ♠ K 7 6
                    ♡ A K J 6
                    ◇ A Q 10
                    ♣ J 9 2
  ♠ A 5 4 3 2                        ♠ —
  ♡ 9 7              N               ♡ Q 5 4 3
  ◇ 6 4 2        W       E           ◇ 9 8 7 5
  ♣ 8 5 3            S               ♣ K 10 7 6 4
                    ♠ Q J 10 9 8
                    ♡ 10 8 2
                    ◇ K J 3
                    ♣ A Q
```

'The contract is unmakeable, as you can see, but declarer, a remarkably fine player, prevented you once again from putting up the best defense. On the opening lead of the nine of hearts I could see, I mean, he could see, that the finesse was doomed. So I... er... he relied on a pseudo-finesse in clubs to create an illusion. In fact, you might almost say,' went on the Hog, 'that you did put up the best defense — against the hand South should have held, as it were.'

## THE TRUTH IS SO DECEPTIVE

There was a virgin cloth on the next table and the Hideous Hog, needing more space, moved over. 'While you order some more cognac,' he told Oscar the Owl, 'I'll jot down a rather curious hand.'

H.H. wrote out the full deal, putting plates over the East-West hands. He was still writing when Walter the Walrus, S.B. and two other Griffins walked into the room.

'Just in time,' he called out to them. 'You can have our table. We've finished.' Then, with a friendly nod, he invited us to join him at the clean tablecloth.

'I was playing against our friend Themistocles Papadopoulos,' explained H.H. 'I want you to make three notrump — against the best defense, of course,' he added with a chuckle.

```
            ♠ 43
            ♡ 10 4
            ◇ A K 4
            ♣ Q J 10 9 6 3
                  N
              W       E
                  S
            ♠ A 5 2
            ♡ A 9 7 6
            ◇ 9 7 3
            ♣ A 8 2
```

| North | South |
|-------|-------|
|       | 1NT   |
| 3NT   | pass  |

'West leads the six of spades and East puts on the jack. Your turn, Oscar.'

'I play the five,' vouchsafed O.O., after a while.

R.R. nodded vigorously. 'Yes,' he said, 'to rectify the count.'

'Aren't you missing something, Oscar?' asked H.H., sneering delicately at the Rabbit. 'Since the vital club finesse must be taken into the West hand, a hold-up can surely serve no purpose.'

'And how can it help me to go up with the ace?' countered O.O.

'Because there's scope here for a pretty piece of deception,' replied H.H. 'Look at those cards,' he went on pointing to the plates over the East-West hands. 'East's jack at Trick 1 denies the ten. So West has it. And, of course, if East had the king he would have played it. So West has the king of spades, too. Now from a suit headed by the KQ10 he would have led the king, not the six. Ergo, as the ancient Romans used to say, West has the king and ten of spades and East has the queen, though West doesn't know it.

'Seeing declarer grab the first trick with the ace, a cultured West may be suspicious. After all, isn't it a classical piece of deception to win the first trick with the ace, holding AQx, when there's another suit wide open? Here it might well be hearts.'

The Rabbit's ears twitched nervously. 'No, no,' jeered the Hog 'no one is rectifying anything. The idea is to deter West from switching. If he controls the long suit — in this case he might have the king of clubs — West is intended to lead another spade, fondly imagining that his partner has the queen. Of course, Papa is very familiar with this stratagem.'

'In fact, going up with the ace of spades is a trap to make West suspect a trap that isn't there,' explained Oscar to the Rabbit, who still seemed perplexed.

'And did Papa switch to hearts, thinking that you had the ace and queen of spades?' asked R.R., suddenly seeing the light.

'Presumably, the king of clubs was offside,' ventured the Owl.

'It was,' agreed H.H., 'and West was certainly taken in. But you had better look at the full deal.'

The Hog removed the plates. 'Tell them' he said, turning to me with a knowing wink. A fortnight earlier I had watched this battle of wits between the Hog and Papa and I remembered the hand distinctly.

The ♠A won the first trick. Then came a diamond to dummy's ◇A and the ♣Q, which held the trick. When East followed to the jack, declarer heaved a sigh of relief. That was the climacteric of the hand.

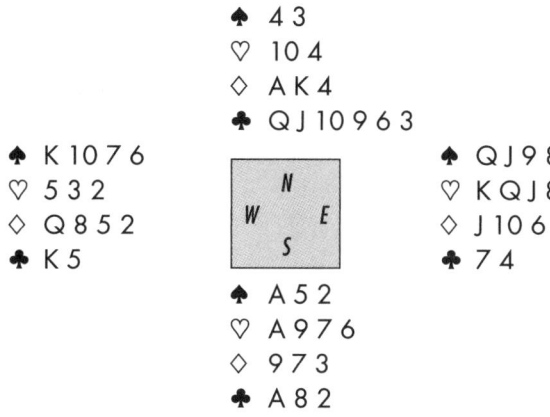

```
                    ♠ 4 3
                    ♡ 10 4
                    ◇ A K 4
                    ♣ Q J 10 9 6 3
  ♠ K 10 7 6              N            ♠ Q J 9 8
  ♡ 5 3 2            W         E       ♡ K Q J 8
  ◇ Q 8 5 2              S            ◇ J 10 6
  ♣ K 5                                ♣ 7 4
                    ♠ A 5 2
                    ♡ A 9 7 6
                    ◇ 9 7 3
                    ♣ A 8 2
```

Suddenly West produced the ♣K and before South could complete his first gasp, the ◇Q flashed across the table, killing dummy's beautiful clubs stone dead. For evermore the ace blocked the suit.

'Three down,' I told them as I came to this point in the story, 'and as you can see, the spades broke four-four and the contract is unbeatable.'

'Against the best defense,' put in H.H.

'So, for once, Papa outwitted you,' said the Rabbit gleefully.

'Undoubtedly,' agreed the Hog. He was laughing uproariously.

Readiness to admit defeat was singularly out of character. The Owl and the Rabbit looked at him with deep suspicion.

'What he hasn't told you,' said the Hog, wiping the tears from his eyes, 'is that Papa was declarer and I was West. Ha ha! Yes, he certainly deceived me. That's what's so funny. He banged that ace of spades so quickly, I felt sure he had the queen behind it. He might easily have had something like: ♠AQx(x) ♡Qxx ◇Jxx(x) ♣Axx, you know.'

'Then, surely, you were wrong to run a risk by holding up the king of clubs,' objected Oscar. 'All you had to do was to let partner take his two top hearts and wait for a spade to come to your king and ten.'

The Hog shook his head. 'East would never have returned a spade,' he said casting a pitying look around him. 'Just as I thought that Papa had the queen, so East must have felt doubly certain that he had the king. If I had it, I would have led a spade without a doubt. That's how it would have looked to East. Papa had deceived me and I, in turn, deceived my poor partner.'

'Who, then, deceived Papa, who paid for it all?' asked the Rueful Rabbit.

'He set in motion a train of deception which boomeranged on him,' explained O.O. 'If you are known to be a clever, devious player, like Papa, you can't afford to play true cards. If you have no others, it's bad luck and you go down...'

'Except, of course, against the best defense,' chipped in the Hideous Hog. 'Ha ha!'

# Practice for the Guardian Angel

For once the Hideous Hog saw eye to eye with Papa the Greek. Both had been wronged by fate and neither was disposed to forget or forgive.

We were sitting in the Unicorn bar, waiting for the results of the monthly Individual, and everyone had something bitter to say about the twists and quirks of matchpoint scoring. The Hog admitted somberly that he had probably won by the slimmest margin. Without going so far, Papa confided privately that he was no more than a top or two in front of the rest. Everyone had fixed him. The worst players in the room — and there were hardly any others — had performed superbly against him. Then, the moment they partnered him, they relapsed into lunacy laced liberally with masochism. Even his friend Karapet had let him down badly.

'No, no,' broke in the Free Armenian at this point in Papa's lamentations, 'it was your fault. Ask anyone. Show them the hand.' As he spoke, Karapet Djoulikyan passed round this diagram.

```
♠ 4 3                      ♠ A K 2
♡ A Q 9 8 7 6       N      ♡ 5 4 3
♦ K 10 4        W       E  ♦ A J 9 5 2
♣ A 4                S     ♣ 3 2
```

'The Rueful Rabbit, who was sitting North,' explained the Armenian, 'led the queen of clubs against Papa's four hearts. How should he have played the hand?'

'You missed a top?' inquired the Hog in surprise.

Ignoring him, Papa turned to Oscar the Owl, senior kibitzer at the Griffins. 'What would you do?' he asked.

O.O. blinked slowly, waiting hopefully for ideas. None intruded and at last he said: 'I lay down the ace of hearts. Then, if the king doesn't drop, I cross to dummy with a spade to lead another heart. It's a safety play...'

'But if North has the ♡KJx,' cut in Papa crisply, 'you lose two trumps and a club. Then you misguess the diamond and go down.'

'If everything is wrong,' retorted the Owl testily, 'and if one isn't allowed to find the queen of diamonds either, the contract's unmakeable, so what do you expect me to do?'

'To make it, of course, as I did,' declared Papa proudly. 'After putting down the ace of hearts, at Trick 2, you lead out the ace and king of spades and ruff a spade. Then you exit with a club — and you don't care who wins or what happens next. If a trump is led — by either defender — you lose one trump only. A diamond finds the queen for you and anything else gives you a ruff and discard. That's perfect technique and defenders have no answer to it,' concluded the Greek triumphantly.

'Yes,' said Karapet sadly, 'it was one of my coldest bottoms. Every other declarer in the room made thirteen tricks. Only my Papa confined himself to eleven.'

'And only your Papa could do it,' remarked the Hog good-humoredly. 'I remember the hand well. The ♡Kx are under the AQ and the ◇Q is bare. Ha! Ha!'

'That's duplicate for you,' cried Papa indignantly. 'The only declarer in the room to play correctly gets a bottom.'

Karapet sighed deeply. 'You forget that you were my partner, Papa,' he said reproachfully. 'You know that I am the unluckiest player North of the Equator — and on the Southern side, too, for that matter. Every card was bound to be wrong which means, at duplicate, that it would be right. Without a thought for me, you did nothing to guard against good fortune.'

The Owl hooted softly. 'It is sometimes better,' he murmured, 'to play badly than to play too well. At least, if things go wrong, you are in good company.'

# A DEDICATED RESULT-MERCHANT

'How did you fare on this one?' asked the Hideous Hog, thrusting a hand at the Greek.

|  | ♠ A K 2 |  |  | ♠ 4 3 |
|---|---|---|---|---|
|  | ♡ A K 2 | N |  | ♡ 5 4 3 |
|  | ◇ K | W    E |  | ◇ A Q 10 4 3 2 |
|  | ♣ K Q 10 5 4 2 | S |  | ♣ A 3 |

'One of my early boards,' replied Papa without much interest. 'I was in six notrump like everyone else, I suppose, so I put it down, tentatively, as an average.'

'Average!' repeated the Hog scornfully. 'You mean, no doubt, that you botched it up, Themistocles. How do you play it, Oscar? North leads the queen of spades against your six notrump.'

The Owl pondered. 'If the diamonds break three-three or if the clubs are split three-two or if the jack of diamonds comes down, I make thirteen tricks. If not, I make twelve. So what's the problem?'

'Play on,' insisted the Hog.

Oscar squared his rounded shoulders. 'At Trick 2, the king of diamonds. Then a club to the ace and the ace and queen of diamonds. Someone shows out?'

'North,' answered H.H. laconically.

'I play on the clubs,' went on O.O.

'North has a singleton,' said the Hog. 'South comes in with the jack of clubs and cashes the jack of diamonds. One down. Bad luck, Oscar.'

'Console yourself,' said Papa reassuringly. 'All the Wests must have suffered the same misfortune.'

'Except one,' snapped the Hideous Hog. 'For my part, I don't hold with misfortune. After taking the king of diamonds, at Trick 2, I ducked a club and as soon as South followed, I spread my cards. Nothing could go wrong. Papa himself couldn't fail...'

'How absurd!' interrupted the Greek vehemently. 'Every declarer in the room makes thirteen tricks while you think up a safety play for twelve. A few minutes ago you were ridiculing safety plays at duplicate. Now you turn a somersault. Why? I'll tell you. Because it so happens that both minors broke badly, quite against the odds, mind you, and all your life, my dear H.H., you have been a dedicated but unscrupulous result-merchant.'

'Certainly,' replied H.H. 'When the results bear out my expectations, I approve of them, and they usually conform, of course.

'On that last hand, on which you fixed poor Karapet, every West was bound to be in four hearts, so you certainly couldn't afford any high-falutin' safety plays. This time, as Oscar pointed out, it's long odds on making thirteen tricks and most declarers would, therefore, bid the grand slam. Since you stopped in six, just as I did, you couldn't avoid a poor result by making thirteen tricks. Your only hope of a good score was a bad break in both minors. Then the good bidders, who reached the grand slam, would go down, while the good card-players, whose partners bid badly and who, therefore, stayed in a small one, would gather the matchpoints.'

## A TEXTBOOK DOUBLE

'Yes, that was a tie for top for you, H.H.' said S.B., the Emeritus Professor of Bio-Sophistry 'but I did even better the other way. We got them one down doubled in seven clubs. It was our last board and I could see that our 200 was a cold top.'

'Doubled? Who? Why? How?' sceptical eyebrows went up round the table.

'My partner was the Rabbit,' explained the Secretary Bird. 'Sitting South, with Jxxx in both minors, he made what he described as a textbook double...'

'Textbook double? Who could have written such a crazy book?' I asked incredulously.

'You did, I believe,' replied S.B. 'The idea... er your idea, to be precise, is that no one but a lunatic would double a grand slam with a finessible trump honor. So the double protects the honor. It's an insurance that declarer won't guess right, since he won't suspect a lunatic...'

'Talking of lunatics,' broke in the Hog, 'I had that spade-heart freak with the Rabbit. R.R. dealt, sitting West, and opened four spades at favorable vulnerability and...'

'One of my tops,' cried Papa. 'My partner, too, opened four spades and I was wondering what to do with:

♠A  ♡QJ987  ◇AK  ♣AK765

when lo and behold, North came in with five hearts. I doubled, with baited breath, hardly believing my ears, and we collected 1400. Perfect defense, mind you. Just try making one more trick, H.H. I should like to see it.'

The Hog nodded. 'Just about average, I suppose,' he observed amicably. 'No doubt every West opened four spades and most Norths called five hearts. I doubled, as you did, but that wretched Rabbit, oozing fright from every pore, fled into five spades. What would you have done now, Themistocles?'

'And the Rabbit still breathes?' asked someone unbelievingly.

'Temporarily,' replied the Hog with an indulgent smile. 'Had I executed him on the spot, I should have been awarded an average and I needed better than that. It was obvious,' went on H.H. 'that the distribution was freakish, and no less clear that the penalty in five hearts doubled couldn't be less than 1100. At the vulnerability, even a small slam wouldn't, therefore, make up for it. Our only hope was a grand slam, so I bid seven spades and the Rabbit's guardian angel was given another chance to save his protegé.'

This was the full deal.

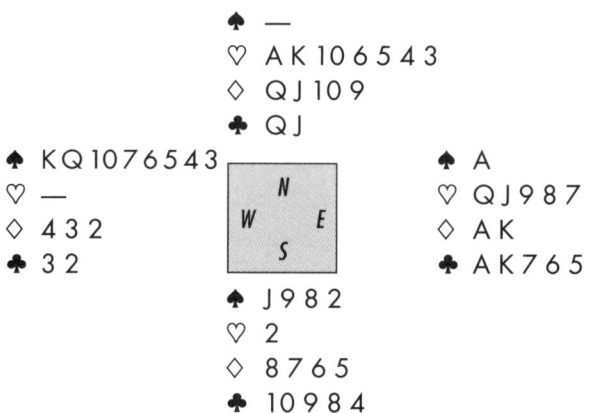

```
              ♠ —
              ♡ A K 10 6 5 4 3
              ◇ Q J 10 9
              ♣ Q J
♠ K Q 10 7 6 5 4 3            ♠ A
♡ —              N           ♡ Q J 9 8 7
◇ 4 3 2      W     E         ◇ A K
♣ 3 2              S         ♣ A K 7 6 5
              ♠ J 9 8 2
              ♡ 2
              ◇ 8 7 6 5
              ♣ 10 9 8 4
```

'But for the 4-0 trump break,' remarked O.O., 'he might have set up dummy's long club and made the contract.'

'He did make it,' said H.H.

'But there's a certain trump loser,' objected the Owl.

'The Rabbit doesn't go in for such niceties,' explained the Hog, 'and he didn't think of anything so advanced as setting up dummy's fifth club. To use his own expression, he made the contract on a crossruff.'

'With a singleton trump on the table?' asked someone.

'And why not?' retorted H.H. 'After all, he wasn't playing for overtricks. Knowing nothing about the 4-0 trump break — I doubt if he's discovered it yet — he counted twelve tricks. So he only needed one ruff in dummy. The play was quite simple. He ruffed the heart lead and crossed to dummy with his two ace-kings to ruff the rest of the hearts. That left him with ♠KQ10 and the ♢4. He ruffed the diamond with the ace and a club with the ten of spades, and when he came to add the tricks the total came to thirteen.'

'That guardian angel certainly gets plenty of practice,' said the Owl, nodding to himself wisely.

# How Are Your Reflexes?

Meditatively stroking his chin, Oscar the Owl repeated to himself *sotto voce*: 'West leads the five of clubs and South to lose against any defense.'

'What's it all about?' asked the Toucan, breaking in on the Owl's soliloquy.

'It's a new type of problem' explained O.O., pointing to a diagram in the evening paper. 'I have to work out the contract and to plan declarer's misplay.'

♠ A 4 3
♡ 8 7
◇ Q J 10 9
♣ A 9 8 2

♠ 7 6 5
♡ A K Q J 10 9
◇ A 2
♣ Q 10

T.T. looked at the hand critically. There seemed to be no good reason why anyone should go down in anything.

'Could it be four spades or something odd, after a psychic opening, perhaps?'

'No, no,' replied Oscar, 'everything must be reasonable. No psychics, no lunatics.'

'Oh, so it's not the Rabbit,' said T.T. with relief, but the solution still eluded him.

As we pondered, the Hideous Hog and Walter the Walrus joined us in the bar.

'Curious,' said W.W., poring over the problem, 'all in all, the North-South hands add up to a full-blooded thirty points — not enough for a slam but far too much not to make game. So how does one lose it? There must be a coup. Perhaps declarer should smother dummy or endplay himself or...'

The Hog looked at him with the scorn he usually reserved for partners.

'Allow me to help you, Walter,' he said with a gentle sneer. 'We might be hard put to it to lose five tricks in notrump. So let's try four hearts. We are told that West leads the five of clubs. We'll call the cards in turn, you and I, trick by trick. You go first.'

'The two,' called the Walrus.

H.H. bowed low to the Owl. 'You have your solution,' he announced. 'Walter has smothered his dummy, broken his contract and solved the problem for you — though unintentionally, I fear, so he cannot really claim the credit for it.'

'It will be interesting to see the full deal in tomorrow's paper,' observed Timothy the Toucan.

'Why?' asked the Hog. 'The problem is to lose the contract and Walter's way is surely the best. Just give East the king of clubs, and the rest of the distribution doesn't matter. He wins the first trick — the king of clubs could even be a singleton — and returns a spade, driving out dummy's ace before the diamonds are set up. As happens so often, declarer butchers his contract at Trick 1. The defense isn't called upon to do anything.'

'I didn't have to play that two,' protested the Walrus. 'I spoke too quickly. I... er... didn't mean...'

'On the contrary,' retorted the Hog, 'you did mean and you had to play the two of clubs. That's just it, don't you see. It looked right. It felt right, and most of the time it would have been right, too. Playing low from dummy was an automatic reflex, an inner compulsion to do the right thing even though it was wrong.'

'But surely...' began T.T.

'Yes, surely...' echoed W.W.

'Not at all,' declared H.H., rejecting the arguments which were about to be put forward. 'Why do you make the game so difficult? Most of the mistakes at bridge are obvious ones — as soon as you spot them, that is. Oscar's problem is no exception, but it points a moral. People who make the right play automatically, without malice aforethought, often live to regret it. Conversely, a well-planned absurdity may succeed because no one allows for it. Now here are a couple of hands to illustrate both sides of the medal.

```
        ♠ A 10                        ♠ Q 7 5
        ♡ A Q 2          N            ♡ J 10
        ◇ A K         W     E         ◇ Q J 10 9 8 7 6
        ♣ A J 9 8 7 2    S            ♣ 10
```

| West | East |
|------|------|
|      | 3◇   |
| 3NT  | pass |

'It's your turn, Timothy, to call the cards. You are West. North leads the six of spades against your three notrump. You play dummy's seven of spades and South covers with the eight of spades. Go on from there.'

The Toucan bounced up and down in his armchair. The rhythmic movement helped him to think. 'Trick 1 — ten of spades. Tricks 2 and 3 — ace and king of diamonds. Trick 4 — queen of hearts. T.T. looked up expectantly.

'Go on,' said the Hog, 'all follow and you've made four tricks. Only five more to go.'

'I, er... no, I don't. I...'

'It doesn't matter what you don't do,' interrupted H.H. brutally. 'You did your best to kill the hand at Trick 1, just as Walter did on the previous deal and for exactly the same reason. An inner voice told you not to waste the ace of spades on the eight when the ten would do. Now you can't get at dummy's diamonds and you'll need a lot of luck in the black suits to get home, but there are no miracles, not even small ones, so down you go.'

The Walrus opened his mouth. He was probably about to say something, but the Hog stopped him in time. 'No, Walter,' he told him firmly, 'we are no longer trying to lose the contract, so your contribution is unlikely to be helpful.'

'What should I have done?' asked T.T. meekly.

'You should have won the first trick with the ace of spades, not with the ten,' said H.H. 'Then, after cashing the ace and king of diamonds you should have played back that ten, hoping to find North with the king. A heart, a spade or a low club return from him would let you into dummy and a high club would allow you to make five club tricks. The whole thing is just like taking a simple finesse. You play for a particular card to be well-placed. That's all.'

'A fifty-fifty chance,' boomed the Walrus, who fancied himself as a mathematician.

'If the six of spades is a true lead it's nearer a hundred per cent,' replied the Hog 'and even if it isn't, it's still the best chance.'

'And did you in fact win the eight with the ace?' asked the Toucan admiringly.

'Certainly,' replied the Hog. 'Who do you take me for? I mean, that's what I should have done had I been West. As it happens, I was East.'


## PAPA'S GOOD LUCK

We registered the surprise expected of us and H.H. explained.

'I was playing with Papa. He's enjoying a good run just at present and cuts me at least half the time. Mind you, I don't object. One has to work out one's bad luck somehow and if I didn't cut Papa I'd break a leg or something. It would come to the same thing in the end. Anyway, I opened three diamonds, Papa bid three notrump and when North doubled, I retreated into four diamonds. After all, why should he play every hand? But just because he'd been dummy twice or three times already that rubber, Themistocles lost his temper. At the top of his voice he bellowed seven diamonds, and before North and South had finished doubling, he redoubled. If he couldn't play the hand, he was going to make me pay for it. I had half a mind to convert to seven notrump just to see him squirm, but one mustn't be uncharitable, not at £2 a 100.

'Hardly a good contract,' observed the Toucan, 'looking at the four hands.'

'Nine points short,' noted the Walrus, disapprovingly. 'What did it cost?'

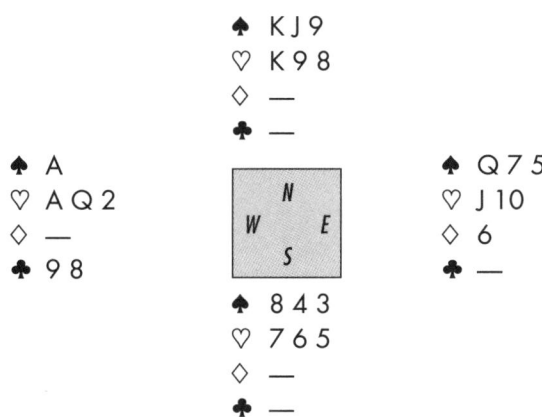

```
              ♠ K J 9 6 2
              ♡ K 9 8
              ◇ 5
              ♣ K Q 6 5
♠ A 10                              ♠ Q 7 5
♡ A Q 2          N                 ♡ J 10
◇ A K        W       E             ◇ Q J 10 9 8 7 6
♣ A J 9 8 7 2    S                 ♣ 10
              ♠ 8 4 3
              ♡ 7 6 5 4 3
              ◇ 4 3 2
              ♣ 4 3
```

| West | North | East | South |
|------|-------|------|-------|
| *Papa* | | *H.H.* | |
| | | 3◇ | pass |
| 3NT | dbl | 4◇ | pass |
| 7◇ | dbl | pass | pass |
| redbl | all pass | | |

'The four of clubs was led,' said the Hog ignoring the question. 'I won with the ace and ruffed a club. Returning to dummy with the ace of trumps, I ruffed a second club. Then I repeated the process — a trump to the king and another club ruff, setting up two long clubs in dummy. There was still a trump out, so I drew it, throwing the ten of spades from the table and leaving this position:

```
              ♠ K J 9
              ♡ K 9 8
              ◇ —
              ♣ —
♠ A                                ♠ Q 7 5
♡ A Q 2          N                 ♡ J 10
◇ —          W       E             ◇ 6
♣ 9 8            S                 ♣ —
              ♠ 8 4 3
              ♡ 7 6 5
              ◇ —
              ♣ —
```

'I crossed to dummy with a heart and cashed the two clubs. On the penultimate club I threw my remaining heart while North let go a spade, keeping doubleton kings in both suits. The last club was a killer. If he parted with a heart I would ruff the two and set up the queen. So he bared his king of spades and my queen brought home the grand slam.'

'Poor Papa,' said someone, 'how it must have hurt him. If you'd had any regard for his feelings you'd have gone down.'

'Perhaps I played too quickly,' conceded the Hog graciously. Already he was writing down another hand.

## WRONG VIEWS

♠ 10 4 3
♡ 9 8 5 3
◇ 8 7 6 3
♣ J 4

|   | N |   |
|---|---|---|
| W |   | E |
|   | S |   |

♠ A 9 5
♡ K 4 2
◇ Q 5
♣ A K Q 6 2

| West | North | East | South |
|------|-------|------|-------|
| 1◇ | pass | 1♠ | 1NT |
| all pass | | | |

'West leads the king of diamonds, doesn't like his partner's two and switches to the two of spades on which East plays the king. How do you propose to make seven tricks?'

'There's no future in ducking,' observed Oscar philosophically. 'A diamond would come back bringing down the queen and, well, it wouldn't be so good.'

'If we cash all our clubs,' broke in the Toucan hopefully, 'something may happen. It often does, you know, when people cash things against me.'

W. W. wasn't impressed. 'I cross to dummy with my jack of clubs and lead a heart. If East has the ace, I'm home. It's rather like the last hand the first time round...'

'Almost identical,' agreed the Hideous Hog, 'the only point of difference is that on that occasion we had every reason to expect the king to be on the right side of the ace, whereas this time we know — *we know*,' repeated the Hog, accentuating the words, 'that it's on the wrong side.'

The Walrus wheezed. The Toucan gulped.

'What! You can't see it?' exclaimed the Hog. 'Then shut your eyes, look at West's hand and think of the bidding. What did he intend to rebid over partner's response of one spade? He wasn't strong enough to reverse into two hearts or he wouldn't have passed. A raise in spades? Hardly. East has shown four or more and looking across the table we can see six our way. Clubs can be ruled out, too. It's our suit. No, clearly he intended to rebid one notrump and to do that he would need fourteen-fifteen points. Well, count them. In spades, two — no more, for he would have led the queen, not the two, from ♠QJ2. Eight points are hidden from view in diamonds. Give West the lot, bringing his total to ten. Now you see why he must have the ace of hearts. Without it, he would be short of the barest minimum for his one notrump rebid.'

'You needn't look at me as if it's my fault!' cried the Walrus. 'If West has the ace of hearts it's no use playing East for it. I agree. But what do you expect me to do about it?'

'To play West for it, of course,' snapped back the Hog contemptuously.

'How?' cried T.T. and W.W. Two minor kibitzers gurgled sympathetically.

'At Trick 3,' replied H.H., 'you play the king of hearts — from your hand, just like that, expecting it to hold.'

'Why should it?' asked T.T. incredulously.

'Absurd,' agreed W.W.

'Certainly,' admitted H.H. 'so much so, in fact, that no one will suspect you of doing it. And now put yourself in West's place. He is a reasonable man and expects you to be reasonable, too, and to lead out an unsupported king isn't reasonable. So he will assume instinctively that you have the queen of hearts as well.'

'But why shouldn't he take it just the same?' objected Oscar. 'His ace will only make once.'

The Hog shook his head. 'West doesn't know that your queen of diamonds will drop or that his partner has the jack of spades or how the clubs are divided. So what should he lead if he goes up with the ace of hearts? No prospect pleases. He would much rather that you played away from something, if only your imaginary queen of hearts. Can you really blame him for ducking? Look at his hand.'

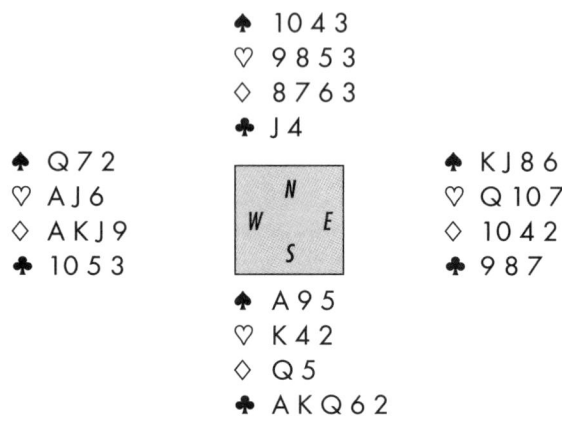

```
                   ♠ 10 4 3
                   ♡ 9 8 5 3
                   ◇ 8 7 6 3
                   ♣ J 4
  ♠ Q 7 2              N              ♠ K J 8 6
  ♡ A J 6                             ♡ Q 10 7
  ◇ A K J 9        W       E          ◇ 10 4 2
  ♣ 10 5 3             S              ♣ 9 8 7
                   ♠ A 9 5
                   ♡ K 4 2
                   ◇ Q 5
                   ♣ A K Q 6 2
```

'I should never have thought of playing it that way,' admitted the Toucan 'but of course it's easy enough for West to take a wrong view.'

'Everyone does that at times,' agreed the Walrus.

'Almost everyone,' corrected the Hog.

# A Nine-Letter Word

'When I retire,' announced the Hideous Hog, 'I'll write a book on logistics, and I'll expose ruthlessly all those charlatans,' his eyes swept defiantly round the Griffins bar, 'who prate about right and wrong, as if anyone could tell which is which without knowing how long it took to do it.'

Glass after glass, the Hog had been expounding the art of counting the hand. 'Anyone,' he said, 'can count up to thirteen when only three or four cards are left to play — present company excepted, of course,' he added, bowing politely to the Rabbit, 'and a good player can often get a count half-way through, but it takes an artist to do so at Trick 1.'

As H.H. raised his glass, the Toucan nipped in quickly and he had uttered the best part of a syllable before the Hog could stop him. 'Irrelevant,' snapped H.H. 'Where was I now, when you interrupted me? Ah, yes, logistics. As I was saying, the time taken to find a bid may be more important than the bid itself, and the same is truer still of card play. Before counting the hand, count the seconds. Tune in to the vibrations, measure the peevish frowns, the vacant looks, the pregnant pauses and you'll soon have a picture of what's going on.' The Hog passed a diagram across the table.

```
                    ♠ J 10 2
                    ♡ Q 9 8 7
                    ◇ A K
                    ♣ A K 4 3
    ♠ K 7
    ♡ K                    ┌─────────┐
    ◇ Q J 9 8 7           │    N    │
    ♣ Q 10 9 8 7        W │         │ E
                          │    S    │
                          └─────────┘
```

| West | North | East | South |
|------|-------|------|-------|
|      |       |      | 1♡    |
| pass | 3♣    | pass | 3♡    |
| pass | 4◇    | pass | 4♠    |
| pass | 4NT   | pass | 5♡    |
| pass | 6♡    | all pass |   |

'You are West, Oscar,' he said turning to the Owl. 'You lead the queen of diamonds to dummy's king and declarer leads the two of spades, playing the queen from his hand. East contributes the six. Now then, what are your chances of breaking the contract? Tell us all about it.'

'How long did it take declarer to decide on his play?' asked O.O. The Hog's homily had not been lost on him.

'No time at all,' replied H.H., nodding approvingly at the question.

Oscar looked wise, but he seemed loath to commit himself and Timothy the Toucan was the first to hazard an opinion. 'I expect to make both my kings,' he declared. 'South can't tell that my king of hearts is bare, so he's bound to finesse. After taking the king of spades I lead another diamond *a tempo* and sit back in comfort.'

O.O.'s amber eyes blinked. He knew that there must be a catch somewhere and he would have liked dearly to lead out his lone king of hearts. It would be so spectacular — if only he could find some likely excuse.

'And now,' resumed the Hog, 'suppose that before playing to the first trick declarer goes into a huddle, purses his lips, screws his eyes and goes through all the motions of a man in deep thought. Then he makes the same play, the two of spades to his queen. What now?'

No one spoke, so H.H. prompted. 'You are exactly where you were before. The only difference is that you've had plenty of time to work things out and you know that declarer gave the matter much thought before leading that spade. Well then, what is it all about?'

'It's pretty obvious,' ventured the Toucan, 'that the contract, as seen from South's seat, depends on one of two finesses, so...'

'So the trump finesse is taken first. Surely,' insisted H.H., 'it's unnatural to do otherwise. Why, then, did declarer start with the spade?'

The Rueful Rabbit, who had been engrossed in a crossword puzzle, looked up for the first time. 'Maybe he just wanted to know who had the king of spades,' he suggested.

'Why?' demanded the Hog.

'One just likes to know things,' replied R.R. 'Why should one always look for ulterior motives? ...er, can you think of a word of nine letters beginning with 'm' and ending in a consonant or a vowel?'

'What a lucky analysis!' snorted the Hog. 'Purely by accident, as usual, he's hit upon the truth — half of it, anyway. South's play does show that he badly wants to know who has the king of spades and that he can't wait. He wants the answer *immediately*. Does that suggest anything?'

The Toucan and the Owl nodded understandingly. 'All right, since you can't see it, I'll tell you,' said the Hog with a scornful look. 'If declarer loses a spade, he can't afford to lose a trump, too, so his only hope will be to lead out the ace boldly, praying for the king to drop, and as you can see, his prayer will be answered. If, however, the spade finesse succeeds, he will be able to afford a safety play, a low heart towards the queen, ensuring the contract against a three-nil trump break. Now you can see why he must know about the king of spades before touching trumps.'

'So he's got you either way! How very clever,' cried T.T. 'Who was South?'

'Our old friend, Themistocles Papadopoulos,' answered the Hog, 'and it was good play, I agree, but it would have been better still had it not taken him so long to think of it. I was West, you know, and I might well have gone up with the king of spades if I had to play quickly. But while he was thinking I had plenty of time to count his hand, the part that mattered, anyway, and I was ready for him.'

The Hog showed us the deal in full:

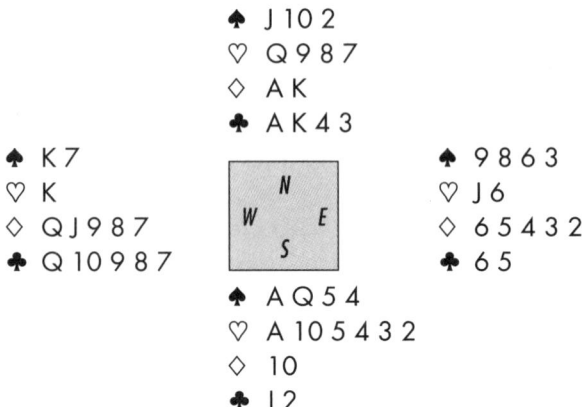

♠ J 10 2
♡ Q 9 8 7
◇ A K
♣ A K 4 3

♠ K 7
♡ K
◇ Q J 9 8 7
♣ Q 10 9 8 7

♠ 9 8 6 3
♡ J 6
◇ 6 5 4 3 2
♣ 6 5

♠ A Q 5 4
♡ A 10 5 4 3 2
◇ 10
♣ J 2

'A pause would have given the show away,' went on H.H., 'but I needed no more time for reflection as I played low to that queen of spades, allowing Papa at Trick 2 to make his safety play in trumps. He could afford it once he 'knew' that the spade was right and it would have been quite a coup, mark you, had East turned up with ♡KJ6. Poor Papa! He looked so unconcerned when I made my king of hearts, even when he discovered that it was bare and would have dropped. He didn't look so pleased later,' chuckled H.H., 'when I produced the king of spades. He couldn't believe I had it. Ha ha!'

'So in a manner of speaking,' observed the Toucan, 'you broke the slam by making two singleton kings, one that was and one that wasn't.'

'How many esses in mendacity?' asked the Rabbit, looking up momentarily from his crossword.

# A SAFETY BID

The Hideous Hog measured the madeira with a practiced eye. With just over half a bottle to go there was enough for a short, snappy hand. 'Here's one I had a couple of days ago,' he began, passing round a bit of paper.

♠ K 10 8 7 6   ♡ A J 5   ◇ 10 6   ♣ A 4 3

'That's North, and North-South alone are vulnerable. Over one spade South forces with three hearts and West barges in with five clubs. Your turn.'

The Owl hooted softly. 'I agree,' said the Toucan.

'That's just what I expected you to do,' sneered the Hog, 'so while you sit on the fence, I'll make the next bid for you, five hearts. East passes and, after mature reflection, partner calls six spades. No sound from West and it's your turn once more.' The Hog looked inquiringly at the Owl, then at the Toucan.

'Enough's as good as a feast,' said T.T.

'And yet...' began O.O.

'Precisely,' agreed H.H., 'if partner expects to make twelve tricks you have the thirteenth, the ace of clubs.'

'What if South has a void?' objected T.T.

'Impossible,' declared the Hog. 'With a void South would have called six clubs, not six spades. He took his time, don't forget, so he isn't likely to have overlooked the cheaper, more informative cuebid. Neither need you be ashamed of your hand. The point count is low, but you have controls, an excellent fit, and every card works. Even the jack of hearts looks important. So you should take the plunge, shouldn't you?'

O.O. and T.T. nodded cordially.

'Kindly bid,' commanded the Hog, who didn't like equivocation.

'All right, seven hearts,' obeyed the Toucan reluctantly.

'No,' Oscar shook his head. 'Partner has shown a super-fit in spades and we don't really know much about his hearts. I call seven spades.'

'Not much of a suit,' protested the Toucan.

'Partner may have four hearts only,' countered the Owl.

The ball went back and forth across the table. It was a long rally and little was left in the bottle by the time the Hog was called upon to mediate.

'It's a draw,' he declared 'for you are both right, which means, of course, that you are both wrong. South must have outstanding support for spades. I agree. But it's obviously a freakish hand and if he has long hearts, too, West may have a void. He will double for a heart lead and it will be too late to go back and...'

'Yes, yes,' broke in the Toucan excitedly, 'that why my seven hearts...'

'Your seven hearts,' retorted H.H., 'will come badly unstuck if South has four hearts only and East turns up with five.'

'I did not want to bid seven of anything,' protested the Toucan. 'It's a case of tails they win and heads we lose.'

'To win whichever way the coin comes down,' replied H.H., 'North should bid seven clubs. Let South choose the trump suit. If it's hearts and East, with a void in spades, doubles for a lead, North can still convert to seven spades.'

'And what if that, too, is doubled?' asked O.O. 'Isn't West the most likely player at the table to have a void?'

'True,' agreed the Hog, 'but even if both defenders have voids, there will still be time for seven notrump. It's a pity to forgo the ruffing value, especially in spades, but in an emergency notrump may provide a way of escape. First, however, let's wait for those Lightner doubles. There may not be any.'

'And I suppose,' asked Oscar, his heart-shaped face registering incredulity, 'that North took all this into account at the time and duly called seven clubs.'

'Certainly,' said the Hog.

'And what did South bid?' persisted Oscar.

'Seven hearts,' replied the Hog.

'Who was your partner?' asked the Toucan.

'The Walrus,' answered the Hog. He seemed to enjoy the soaring eyebrows and gasps of astonishment which rippled through the bar.

'Weren't you afraid,' asked Oscar, 'that you'd be left to play the hand in seven clubs?'

The Hog greeted this with a loud guffaw. 'You are confusing me with Papa and that's actionable, or should be anyway,' he told Oscar, wagging at him playfully a fat, pink forefinger. 'Papa sat North and the Corgi was his partner. I was West and the Walrus, as I've just told you, was East.' The Hideous Hog filled in the four hands, then the bidding sequence, ending with a flourish as he marked a cross to indicate the final double.

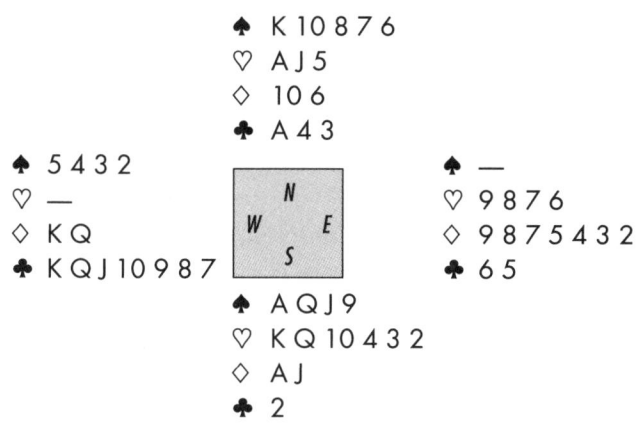

♠ K 10 8 7 6
♡ A J 5
♦ 10 6
♣ A 4 3

♠ 5 4 3 2
♡ —
♦ K Q
♣ K Q J 10 9 8 7

♠ —
♡ 9 8 7 6
♦ 9 8 7 5 4 3 2
♣ 6 5

♠ A Q J 9
♡ K Q 10 4 3 2
♦ A J
♣ 2

| West | North | East | South |
|------|-------|------|-------|
| H.H. | Papa | W.W. | C.C. |
|      | 1♠    | pass | 3♡    |
| 5♣   | 5♡    | pass | 6♠    |
| pass | 7♣    | pass | 7♡    |
| dbl  | all pass |   |       |

'What on earth made you double?' asked the Toucan in bewilderment. 'It's your own lead and, anyway, you can't ruff trumps can you?'

'Precisely,' agreed H.H., 'but I was pretty sure from the bidding that the Walrus had no spades. He could just have one, I suppose, but it was a chance well worth taking. Besides you should have seen that Walrus. He had been looking utterly bored throughout the auction — until Colin called seven hearts. Then he came to. The glazed look was already fading from his eye. Another minute and he would have shown his spade void by doubling. Papa would have switched to seven spades and if I doubled that he would have retreated into seven notrump — unhappily, no doubt, but he would have made it just the same. So, you see, to stop that double I had to do it myself. It was a safety bid. There was no other way.'

The Hog chortled as he came to the denouement. 'Everyone looked at me suspiciously. They knew I was up to something, but they couldn't think what it was. Both Colin and Papa reasoned that if I had a certain trump trick, I obviously wouldn't double. So I was probably trying to make them switch. Therefore they wouldn't. Ha ha! And it was all because they took so long over their excellent bidding sequence. Why, I knew what they had before they knew it themselves, for as they thought and thought, I had all the time in the world to read their hands, to measure their vibrations, beat by beat, just like a metronome, recording...'

'I've got it!' cried the Rabbit exultantly. 'That nine-letter word beginning with 'm'. Metronome, of course!'

# The Rabbit Takes the Biscuit

'They tend to go to his head,' said Oscar the Owl, our Senior Kibitzer at the Griffins.

Peregrine the Penguin, his opposite number at the Unicorn, nodded.

'And yet, to be fair to him,' resumed O.O., 'he only munches them to give him something to think about while he is playing.'

We were talking about the Rueful Rabbit and his habit of nibbling chocolate and almond biscuits during the play of the hand.

A chocolate and almond grand slam had come up recently while the Rueful Rabbit was playing with the Hideous Hog against Karapet, the Free Armenian, and Walter the Walrus. This was the deal:

Both Vul.
Dealer East

```
                    ♠ A 10 9 4
                    ♡ A K J 7
                    ◇ 7 6 3
                    ♣ J 2
  ♠ 8 6                              ♠ K Q J
  ♡ 2              N                 ♡ 6 5 4 3
  ◇ 9 8 5 4 2    W   E               ◇ A K Q J 10
  ♣ 9 8 7 6 5      S                 ♣ 3
                    ♠ 7 5 3 2
                    ♡ Q 10 9 8
                    ◇ —
                    ♣ A K Q 10 4
```

| West | North | East | South |
|------|-------|------|-------|
| *Karapet* | *R.R.* | *W.W.* | *H.H.* |
| | | 1◇ | 2♣ |
| 2◇ | 3◇ | 4◇ | pass |
| pass | 5◇ | pass | 5♡ |
| 6◇ | 6♡ | pass | pass |
| 7◇ | pass | pass | 7♡ |
| pass | pass | dbl | redbl |
| all pass | | | |

The bidding calls, perhaps, for a few words of explanation. Engrossed in wiping specks of chocolate from his fingers, the Rabbit missed the opening bid. Opposite a call of 2♣ he felt that he had something big to offer and that only 3◊, the enemy's suit, could convey the full measure of his strength.

With nothing to spare for his overcall, the Hog passed the barrage bid of 4◊, and after a reflective nibble, the Rabbit persisted with 5◊. Come what may, he was determined to find a fit, yet understandably reluctant to suggest a suit himself. Reaching 6♡ presented no problem, but the grand slam would have surely been missed had Karapet not decided to sacrifice. Over his seven diamonds R.R. made a forcing pass and now, with a void in diamonds, H.H. had no qualms in soaring to seven hearts. He had no precise information about his partner's hand and he suspected that partner had even less, but the Rabbit's excited state, the nervous twitching of his left ear, the tense, quickened crunching of biscuits, all proclaimed a galaxy of high cards.

In righteous wrath, the Walrus doubled. He did not like people to take liberties, and knowing that he had 16 points — he had checked them carefully — he wasn't going to allow anyone to flaunt grand slams before him with impunity on a brazen 24. The Hog's redouble was a matter of simple arithmetic. Since W.W. had not doubled 6♡, he, the Hog, could surely make seven.

The play presented no problems. Ruffing the opening diamond in his hand, H.H. crossed to dummy with a club to the jack and ruffed a second diamond. Overtaking a trump on the table he ruffed dummy's last diamond and it only remained to reenter dummy with a spade and draw trumps. The clubs provided the rest of the tricks, the grand total being made up of: dummy's four trumps, three ruffs in the closed hand, five clubs and the ♠A.

'Your diamond lead gave it to him,' complained W.W. in injured tones. 'Without it he would be short of an entry for a dummy reversal.'

'But you doubled, Walter,' said the Hog, gloating happily. 'A Lightner double, surely, calling for the lead of the first suit bid by dummy, and dummy... ha ha!... had bid only diamonds... Ha ha ha!'

# The Judo System

*(The second deal appears in* Bridge in the Fifth Dimension.*)*

The Rueful Rabbit and Timothy the Toucan were deep in conference when I joined them at the bar of the Griffins.

'We are perfecting a system,' explained the Rabbit.

'An artificial one?' I asked apprehensively.

'No, no,' replied the Toucan. 'It is not artificial, neither is it natural. It's sort of surrealist. Not that I really know what that means,' he added hastily, 'but you don't have to. That's the main part of the system.'

'Very well put, Timothy,' said the Rabbit approvingly. 'You see,' he went on, 'it's a defensive system, a form of Judo, combining Papa's methods with the Hog's. What put us on to it was that hand they had the other day, the one H.H. has been gloating about ever since.'

The Rabbit produced a bit of paper with the familiar diagram. Someone must have set out the hands for him, because he was quite incapable of remembering the cards in his own hand even while he was playing it. Besides, each one had exactly thirteen cards.

'I was playing with the Hog,' he told us, covering up the hands of South and East, 'and Timothy was Papa's partner.'

                              ♠ 10 2
                              ♡ K 8 3 2
                              ◇ A K 5 4 3
                              ♣ J 2
        ♠ A 8 7 4
        ♡ J 10
        ◇ 10 7 2
        ♣ A 10 8 7

| West | North | East | South |
|------|-------|------|-------|
| H.H. | T.T. | R.R. | Papa |
| | | | 1♣ |
| pass | 1◇ | pass | 2NT |
| pass | 3NT | all pass | |

'The Hog led the four of spades to the ten, jack and queen. At Trick 2,' went on R.R., 'Papa crossed to dummy with a diamond and played the jack of clubs. I followed with the six and Papa with the three. And what do you suppose happened next?' asked the Rabbit, turning to the Owl and the Penguin who had strolled across to join us and were looking at the hands.

Oscar the Owl blinked.

'Quite so,' said Peregrine the Penguin.

A low hissing sound proclaimed the approach of the Emeritus Professor of Bio-Sophistry, known at the Griffins as the Secretary Bird on account of his appearance. With him was Walter the Walrus. 'I duck,' boomed W.W., taking the hand in at a glance.

'I win and lead the jack of hearts,' said S.B. with a confident glint in his pince-nez. 'Declarer is marked with the king of spades, but he is unlikely to have the nine since he played dummy's ten at Trick 1. So I want to put partner in to lead his nine through the king in the closed hand. Obviously, a heart switch is better than a diamond. If declarer has the ace, it won't cost a trick.'

'You're both wrong,' purred the Rabbit. 'Papa would have made his contract against either of you. The Hog was far more cunning. He pounced on the club with his ace and pushed the ace of spades right under Papa's nose. "Drop that king, Themistocles," he said, and Papa did just that.'

The Rabbit uncovered the other two hands to show the deal in full.

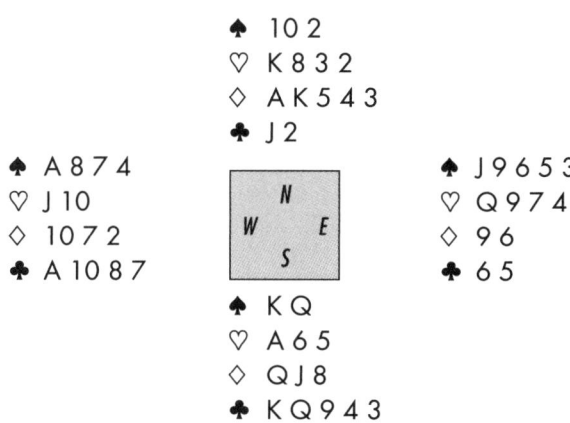

```
              ♠ 10 2
              ♡ K 8 3 2
              ◇ A K 5 4 3
              ♣ J 2
♠ A 8 7 4            N         ♠ J 9 6 5 3
♡ J 10          W         E    ♡ Q 9 7 4
◇ 10 7 2            S         ◇ 9 6
♣ A 10 8 7                    ♣ 6 5
              ♠ K Q
              ♡ A 6 5
              ◇ Q J 8
              ♣ K Q 9 4 3
```

'How could he possibly tell?' asked the Walrus incredulously.

'Just guessing. Bound to come off sometimes,' hissed the Secretary Bird contemptuously.

'On the contrary,' replied the Rabbit. 'H.H. explained in detail how he came to be so clever. It all started with Papa winning the first trick with the queen. Why not the king? The queen was such a false true card, if you see what I mean. The king would conceal the queen because East, and that's me, of course, would still play the jack from queen-jack. But I'd put up the king if I had it. Why, then, was Papa so revealing about his spade holding? Because he wanted everyone to know that he had both honors. It's what politicians call 'leaking information.' That crafty Papa wanted to stop the Hog from leading another spade, if he got in. And that could only mean that his king would drop, for otherwise he wouldn't mind the suit being led, would he? Even Timothy and I could see that. It followed that Papa had started with the king-queen of spades bare. The Hog saw it at once and banged down the ace. Very simple really, but it only goes to show...'

'And that's what gave us the idea of the Judo system,' broke in the Toucan excitedly.

'The system only works against good players,' pursued the Rabbit. 'This is how...'

'We want three more to make me up,' called the Hideous Hog, putting his head round the door, and we all trooped into the cardroom before the Rabbit could explain his system.

Going by results, a Judo hand came up that same afternoon. Papa, who was declarer on the deal, showed it to us at dinner. He began by quizzing the Walrus.

♠ 10 9 8
♡ 6 5
◇ A K 10 8 6
♣ A Q 3

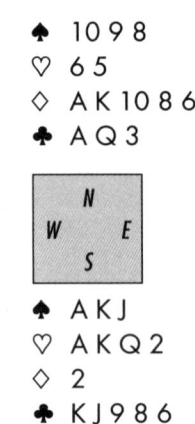

♠ A K J
♡ A K Q 2
◇ 2
♣ K J 9 8 6

North was a Simple Soul who played straight down the middle. This was the auction.

| West | North | East | South |
|------|-------|------|-------|
| T.T. | S.S. | R.R. | Papa |
|      |       |      | 1♣ |
| pass | 1◇ | pass | 2♡ |
| pass | 3♣ | pass | 3NT |
| pass | 4◇ | pass | 4♠ |
| pass | 5◇ | pass | 5NT |
| pass | 7♣ | all pass | |

The Toucan led the ♡10 on which the Rabbit played the ♡J. 'How do you go on?' asked Papa.

'Nothing to it,' replied the Walrus. 'I've twelve tricks on top. A heart ruff in dummy makes it thirteen.'

'Didn't you notice East's jack of hearts on West's ten?' asked Papa. 'Think how foolish you would look in a grand slam if your second heart was ruffed!'

'Have it your way,' said W.W., heaving himself towards the madeira. 'I'll ruff out the diamonds instead. Just as good. Two to the ace, then...'

'One moment,' interrupted the Greek, 'to set up a diamond you need a four-three break and the trumps mustn't be four-one. If East has a singleton heart, as his jack indicates, is all this likely?'

'Very well,' agreed the Walrus good-naturedly, 'I'll finesse the spade. If East is short in hearts, he's the more likely candidate for the queen of spades. I suppose you thought of something better.'

'Naturally,' replied Papa. 'The point you missed is that if East has the queen of spades you don't need the finesse for there's a certain double squeeze! But you must give yourself that extra chance of picking up a doubleton queen with West.

'Follow me,' commanded Papa. 'After taking ten top tricks, that is, five trumps, three hearts and the ace and king of spades, dummy is left with ◊AK10 while in the closed hand you have the jack of spades, the two of hearts and the two of diamonds. West has to keep a heart and East can't let go his queen of spades, so neither can hold on to three diamonds.'

'You did that?' asked the Walrus, deeply impressed.

'Certainly,' replied Papa.

'And you made seven clubs?' persisted W.W.

'I thought you were a student of technique,' replied the Greek with hauteur. 'Going by results, well...' Then, having filled in the East-West hands, he went on: 'One doesn't plan the play on the assumption that opponents are lunatics, so the actual result is hardly relevant.'

This was the complete deal:

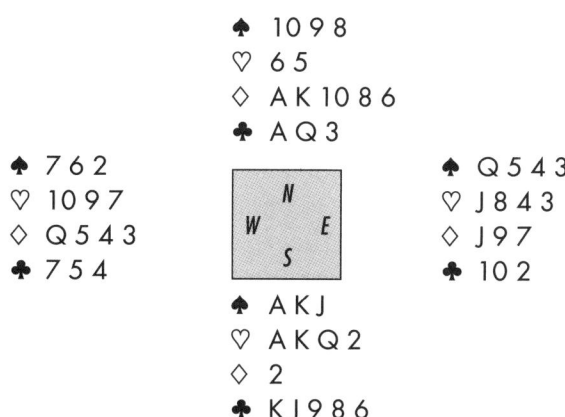

```
              ♠ 10 9 8
              ♡ 6 5
              ◊ A K 10 8 6
              ♣ A Q 3
  ♠ 7 6 2          N          ♠ Q 5 4 3
  ♡ 10 9 7      W     E       ♡ J 8 4 3
  ◊ Q 5 4 3        S          ◊ J 9 7
  ♣ 7 5 4                     ♣ 10 2
              ♠ A K J
              ♡ A K Q 2
              ◊ 2
              ♣ K J 9 8 6
```

'So I missed the point, did I?' bellowed the Walrus. 'I made the contract in three different ways while you found the one clever way to lose it.'

'You've nothing to be proud of,' retorted the Greek scornfully. 'Anyone can make that sort of contract, but it takes a good player to lose it, and your technique, my friend, is just not up to it.' And with that Papa drained defiantly his empty glass.

Later that night I asked the Rabbit: 'What made you play your jack of hearts on Timothy's ten? Just carelessness?'

'Of course not,' replied the Rabbit indignantly. 'It's our Judo system, based on turning an opponent's strength against himself. You see, to an expert every card means something different, even tens and jacks and things. He can unearth a hidden meaning under every pip. So he should be highly flummox-prone, if you see what I mean. Yet it's no use falsecarding the ordinary way, because if it's sensible, it will have a meaning, too, and he'll see through it. So we've decided, whenever possible, to play completely pointless cards leaving declarer to find a message in them. The better he is, the more significant will be the message and the more will he be flummoxed. And it all costs nothing, of course, for Timothy doesn't worry overmuch about all those little cards and neither do I, so we can't flummox each other, can we?'

## An Utterly Useless Card

One of the side-effects of the Judo system claimed the Hog himself as a victim a few days later. The Walrus, sitting North, opened 1NT and the Hog promptly bid 6♠.

♠ 10 9 7
♡ A K Q
◇ A 8
♣ 7 6 5 4 3

♠ A K Q J 4 3
♡ J 10 9
◇ 7 6 5 4
♣ —

The Rabbit led the ♠2 and H.H. began the countdown. With the ten top tricks he needed two diamond ruffs, in dummy, to bring the total to twelve. There could be little doubt, however, that as soon as he lost the lead in diamonds, the defense would play another trump cutting down dummy's ruffing value to one. What could be done about it?

After scowling at each player in turn, and at one or two of the kibitzers, H.H. won the trump lead with dummy's ten and ruffed a club in the closed hand. Then he entered dummy three times with hearts to ruff three more clubs. On the fourth club, R.R. threw the ◊J.

Had the clubs broken 4-4, H.H. would have made his contract with four club ruffs in his hand, three trump tricks in dummy, three top hearts, the ◊A and a long club. As it was, he had to rely on a complete dummy reversal. At the ninth trick the Hog went over to the ◊A, the Rabbit following with the ten and the Toucan with the king. Then he ruffed dummy's last club with his last trump, the ♠A.

The Rabbit's left ear twitched nervously. Shaking his head in perplexity, he muttered to himself inaudibly. What was the correct Judo discard on that fifth club? Was there, in fact, a flummox card to play? His fourth heart was utterly useless, so he had to keep it. He had parted already with his two best diamonds. To throw the third would be too passive for Judo. Suddenly, half-way through a sigh, R.R. found the answer and with a jaunty air he flicked his little trump under the Hog's ace. The three-card end position was:

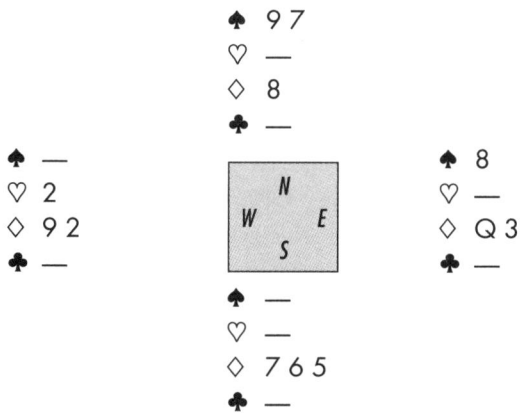

The Hog led a diamond, hoping and expecting to endplay the Toucan. He did not know, of course, that T.T. had thrown his ◊K on the ace without malice aforethought, as his only opportunity on the hand to follow the system. The Rabbit's ◊9 won the eleventh trick and now the thirteenth heart pierced dummy's ♠97.

'You should have drawn that trump,' spluttered the irate Walrus. 'Why is it that you all make mistakes when you play with me?'

The Hog ignored him. 'I demand to know why you underruffed,' he barked at the Rabbit. 'You could have discarded that fatuous heart. Didn't you know spades were trumps? Have you no sense of responsibility towards your opponents?'

'It was the Judo card,' explained the Rabbit proudly. 'You see, if we play the right card it's no good, because you do that, too, and your right cards are more right than ours, but if we play wrong cards they are more right — that is, less wrong — well, anyway you know what I mean...'

# H.H. v. H.H.

'I often wish,' said the Hideous Hog as he joined us at the Griffins bar, 'that I could play against myself. It would be such a good game, you know, though of course I couldn't afford high stakes. Why, it would cost me a fortune.'

Oscar the Owl, our Senior Kibitzer, motioned to the barman. There was no doubt that the Hog was anxious to recount his triumphs, but as H.H. was the first to admit, he was sensitive and moody by nature, and he found it dispiriting to sit at a cold, bare table. Oscar hastened to put the matter right.

'I've given up non-sparkling beverages for Lent,' said the Hog.

'But it's not Lent,' objected the Toucan, who had a factual approach to life.

'However,' went on the Hog, ignoring the interruption, 'I'll be glad to join you in a bottle of Krug. The '62 is, I believe, Peregrine's favorite.' H.H. smiled at the Penguin and with a commanding gesture dismissed the barman. Before anyone could say a word he had jotted down a hand and was in full spate.

'I'm going to show you the full deal,' he told us, 'because as you will soon see for yourselves, declarer and defenders alike could play on double dummy lines. But let's see first whether you would rather be South or West, and just to help you decide, I'll give you the bidding.'

The Hog passed round this diagram.

Both Vul.
Dealer South

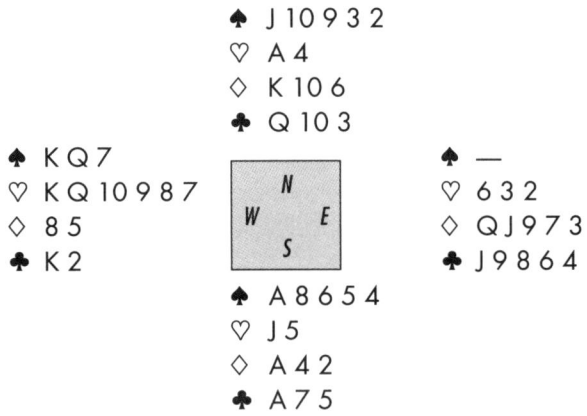

♠ J 10 9 3 2
♡ A 4
◇ K 10 6
♣ Q 10 3

♠ K Q 7
♡ K Q 10 9 8 7
◇ 8 5
♣ K 2

♠ —
♡ 6 3 2
◇ Q J 9 7 3
♣ J 9 8 6 4

♠ A 8 6 5 4
♡ J 5
◇ A 4 2
♣ A 7 5

| West | North | East | South |
|------|-------|------|-------|
|      |       |      | 1♠    |
| 2♡   | 3♠    | pass | 4♠    |
| dbl  | all pass |   |       |

The opening lead was the ♡K.

'South appears to have five losers,' observed O.O. 'Two trumps and one trick in each of the other suits.'

'Seems a bit hopeless,' ventured the Toucan, bouncing gently on his high stool.

The Hog turned to Colin the Corgi, the facetious young man from Oxbridge.

'Quite right,' agreed C.C., 'and therefore I'll back South, for as there would be nothing clever in breaking the contract, I assume that you were South, H.H., and made it, and as you know, I like to be on the winning side. Gloat and the world gloats with you. Moan and you moan alone.'

'Since there would be nothing clever in breaking the contract,' retorted H.H., 'perhaps you would be good enough to do it. I'll be South as I was this afternoon. I hope that you agree with the lead.'

The Corgi nodded.

'I win, noting East's deuce, and I lead a diamond to my ace, then another towards the table,' announced the Hog. 'Observe that already I know a lot about the distribution. West must have six hearts for his bid, but not seven, for with a doubleton East would have started a high-low signal. To have doubled me, Themistocles, who was West, of course, must be credited with the three outstanding trumps, ♠KQ7. That leaves him with four cards in the minors. I played the diamonds as I did in case he had a singleton, but anyway he followed and I was in dummy with the king of diamonds. At Trick 4 I led a heart. Pray proceed.'

The Hog put down an empty glass and picked up his own.

'Whatever I do will cost a trick,' said C.C., 'but had I not seen all the hands, I should have looked on a third heart as the least of all evils.'

'Very well,' resumed the Hog, 'I throw dummy's little diamond and ruff in my hand. I now know, of course, that you have two clubs, for if you had a third diamond you would have led it. You will note that one of my five losers has evaporated. Watch another vanish. At Trick 6, I lead a spade towards dummy. East shows out, confirming my diagnosis. You are in with one of your trump honors.'

'Second throw-in,' observed P.P.

'I return a low club,' murmured C.C. Weakly.

'I go up with dummy's queen of clubs, cash the ace of clubs and we come to this five-card end position' said the Hog.

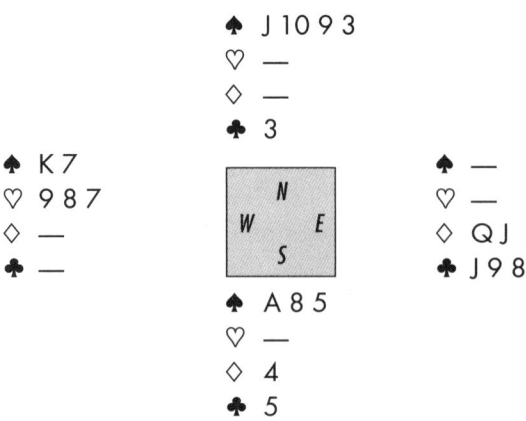

♠ J 10 9 3
♡ —
◇ —
♣ 3

♠ K 7
♡ 9 8 7
◇ —
♣ —

♠ —
♡ —
◇ Q J
♣ J 9 8

♠ A 8 5
♡ —
◇ 4
♣ 5

'I lead my ace of spades and another trump to your king and...'

'Third throw-in,' remarked O.O. P.P. concurred, nodding gravely.

'Precisely,' agreed the Hog. 'You have to lead a heart. I throw dummy's club, ruff with my last trump and it's all over. Let me tell you,' added H.H., smiling indulgently, 'that Papa did better than that. At least he gave himself a chance, which is more than you did.'

We held on to our glasses, saying nothing.

'I can see that you are all impatient to know how Papa defended,' continued the Hog. 'Very well, I'll tell you. He could see well enough what was coming, so when I threw him in with a heart, at Trick 3, he boldly led the king of spades. Though it cost a trick, it gained two, for he was no longer obliged to give me a ruff and discard and what's more, he now had an exit card, for the next throw-in. When I returned a trump to his queen, after taking my ace, he could lead the seven of spades in perfect safety.'

'I get it,' broke in Timothy the Toucan, bouncing vigorously. 'Though you were only going to lose one trump trick, you could no longer get rid of your club and diamond losers, and Papa had taken two tricks already.'

'But surely,' objected Oscar, 'you could still throw him in with the king of clubs. He would have to lead a heart and ...'

'You're doing Papa an injustice,' replied the Hog. 'Of course, I played my ace of clubs, but again Papa could see what was coming and he threw his king on the ace. No, there was no longer any way of endplaying him.'

'And so...' prompted Peregrine.

'And so,' continued the Hog, 'I endplayed East instead with a diamond, leaving him the choice of leading into dummy's ♣Q10 or returning another diamond and presenting me with a ruff and discard.'

'But didn't you just tell us,' said the Corgi, 'that if you had to play against yourself, you would lose a fortune? Does that mean that had you been West, as well as South, you couldn't have made four spades?'

'I wouldn't have given myself the chance,' declared the Hog. 'I would have broken the contract by...'

'But you have just proved that it can't be broken,' protested the Owl.

'Not by other Wests,' admitted the Hideous Hog, 'but then no other West is H.H.'

'Like Colin,' explained the Hog, 'I would have given South a ruff and discard when I was thrown in the first time with the queen of hearts. Then, when I was thrown in the second time with one of my trump honors, I should have given him another ruff and discard. He would have still had a losing club in each hand, of course, so he would throw me in a third time with my second spade honor and I would again play a heart, presenting declarer with yet another ruff and discard.'

'What's so clever about that?' asked the Penguin. 'Can't he now get rid of that club?'

'Try it,' advised H.H. 'After three rounds of trumps, a diamond ruff and a club ruff, only one trump remains in each hand to deal with two losers — two clubs in dummy, a club and a diamond in the closed hand or vice versa, if you prefer it.'

The Owl hooted softly. 'Curious hand,' he observed, 'South makes his contract by endplaying West three times and West breaks it by conceding three times a ruff and discard.'

'Mind you,' said the Hog, 'Papa didn't play so badly, when all is said and done. Unfortunately for him, he had endplayed himself before Trick 1 by that double of his. Coming on top of the three hearts bid, it pinpointed every card. As West, I shouldn't have had the temerity to double myself as South. But then,' sighed H.H., 'arrogance has always been Papa's undoing.'

The bottle was empty. 'Bring me some paper,' the Hog called to the barman. It was a purely tactical move. A book was within easy reach and in the usual way H.H. would have written down the next hand on the flyleaf. But champagne always made him thirsty and the company needed a reminder.

'Thank you,' said the Hog, tearing a sheet from the barman's pad. 'These gentlemen would like, I think...' he broke off in mid-sentence to draw the familiar diagram, leaving the Penguin in charge of the catering.

'I wonder,' mused H.H., 'which hand to give you, West's or South's. The play is interesting for both sides.'

'Give us your hand,' urged the Corgi, 'so that you can tell us afterwards how clever we might have been had we been you.'

'There,' said H.H., passing round this hand:

Both Vul.
Dealer South

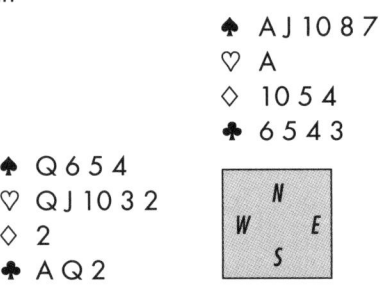

```
                    ♠ A J 10 8 7
                    ♡ A
                    ◇ 10 5 4
                    ♣ 6 5 4 3
     ♠ Q 6 5 4
     ♡ Q J 10 3 2       N
     ◇ 2            W        E
     ♣ A Q 2            S
```

| West | North | East | South |
|------|-------|------|-------|
|      |       |      | 1◇ |
| 1♡ | 1♠ | pass | 2♣ |
| pass | 2♠ | pass | 2NT |
| pass | 3♣ | pass | 3NT |
| all pass |  |  |  |

'Sitting West,' said the Hog, 'you lead the queen of hearts to dummy's bare ace. The seven of spades is led at Trick 2. East plays the deuce and declarer the nine of spades. Your turn, my friends.'

'It looks to me,' said the Owl, after due reflection, 'as if declarer's spade holding is K9. He was unlucky to be deprived of a vital entry to those spades at Trick 1 and now hopes, no doubt, to lose his nine to my queen. Later, overtaking his king of spades with dummy's ace, he would score four spade tricks.'

Peregrine the Penguin flapped an approving flipper. 'Yes,' he nodded, 'that fits in nicely with the bidding. South can't have three spades or he would have called three spades over North's three clubs and he must have the king, for with the ♠Kx alone, East would have obviously gone up with the king at Trick 2.'

'Will you be so good as to play?' insisted H.H.

'I duck,' O.O. and P.P. spoke together.

'I go up with the queen of spades, of course,' declared the Rueful Rabbit, who had joined us a few minutes earlier.

'Why?' demanded the Hog.

'Because everyone is so certain that it's wrong,' explained the Rabbit. 'Declarer, too, must see how wrong it is and naturally he wouldn't expect West to do anything so bad, would he? So he doesn't really expect him to play the queen at all, and if declarer doesn't expect me to do something, well, it must be right not not to do it, if you see what I mean. It's quite simple really.'

The Hideous Hog filled in the other hands and showed us the full deal:

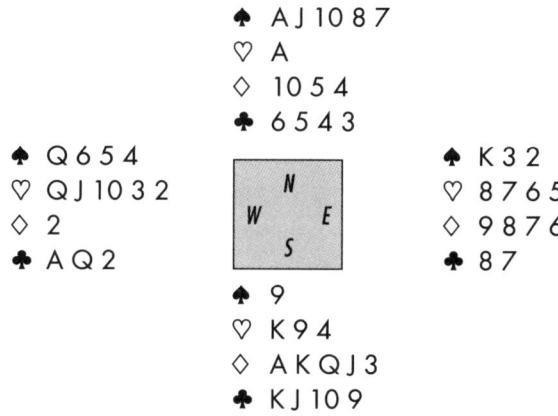

'But this is nothing more than a confidence trick,' exclaimed the Owl. 'If West takes the trick you haven't a hope.'

'Sheer hocus pocus,' protested the Penguin indignantly. 'You are not playing double dummy this time, so how do you know that West has not both spade honors, the ♠KQx or ♠KQxx, for that matter? On the bidding...'

'That's just it,' broke in the Hog, 'on the bidding, West should, as you say, have the ♠KQx, in which case he wouldn't dream of going up with an honor. Not knowing, as you now do, that my spade is a singleton, he would naturally duck to prevent me from finessing next time and bringing in four spade tricks. But let me assure you,' went on the Hog, 'that even if holding, say, ♠KQxx, West decided to take my nine, I would still make my contract.'

'Of course,' said the Rabbit.

'Impossible,' declared the Toucan, 'you have only eight tricks.'

'True,' agreed H.H., 'but by not taking one of them I would come to two others. After winning that spade at Trick 2, West no doubt would clear his hearts. I would win and play my diamonds, taking care to cross to dummy with the ten of diamonds, just to show that I had an entry, in case anyone overlooked it. I wouldn't touch the ace of spades, of course, confirming the impression that I had a second spade in my hand and could get at the ace any time I liked.

'Now turn to the end-position. After two hearts, one spade and five diamonds, we should be down to five cards. West would have to keep his second spade honor guarded. Naturally. And if he bared his ace of clubs, I would knock it out, letting him take two hearts, but claiming the last two tricks. So he would keep the ♣AQ and by now he would have room for only one heart and I would throw him in with it.'

'He might get suspicious,' objected P.P.

'Certainly,' agreed the Hog, 'but he would come under pressure from my third diamond onwards and once he threw a heart, it would be too late for suspicion.'

'And none of this would have happened, of course,' observed the Corgi, 'had you been West as well as South.'

'True,' admitted the Hog. 'As West I wouldn't have bid one heart. Then as South I wouldn't have played for a pseudo hold-up or a pseudo-squeeze either. I should have looked for my ninth trick to the clubs, a better than even-money chance.

'But, of course, after that butt-in, I could be pretty certain that West had both the missing honors in spades or in clubs, if not in both suits. So, you see, once again our friend Papa, who was West as you must have guessed, contrived to hold himself up, as it were, before play started. Perhaps the Greeks have no word for "Pass".'

The Hog looked at the bottle. 'Empty,' he said. 'Very empty! It's time we went in to dinner.' And in a confidential voice he added: 'If I manage to keep my end up at this game it isn't only because I play... er... rather well, but above all because I pass so well — and very, very often.'

# The Treble Cross

'So there, not one of them will get it right,' chuckled the Hideous Hog. He had been invited to set a couple of problems for our quarterly journal, the *Griffins Chronicle*, and he was looking more than usually smug.

'Difficult, are they?' inquired Oscar the Owl, our Senior Kibitzer.

'Impossible,' replied H.H. with quiet satisfaction.

'Yes, yes,' chipped in the Rueful Rabbit eagerly. 'I've often found that the best problems are like that. They say: "Make six spades against any defense." Well I can't, not against any defense, but it's fun trying.'

As the Hog's scowl turned into a snarl, the Rabbit's voice faded away.

'May we see this impossible problem?' asked O.O. The Hog handed him with a flourish a piece of paper.

```
                    ♠ J 4
                    ♡ K 7 6 2
                    ◇ K J 3
                    ♣ A J 10 8
  ♠ 10 8 7 3                        ♠ A K Q 2
  ♡ 5 3            ┌─────────┐      ♡ J 10 9 8
  ◇ 9 8 7 6        │    N    │      ◇ 5 4 2
  ♣ 7 4 2          │  W   E  │      ♣ Q 3
                   │    S    │
                   └─────────┘
                    ♠ 9 6 5
                    ♡ A Q 4
                    ◇ A Q 10
                    ♣ K 9 6 5
```

| North | South |
|-------|-------|
|       | 1♣    |
| 1♡    | 1NT[1] |
| 3NT   | pass  |

1. 15-16 HCP.

West leads the ♠3. How should East plan the defense?

At the bottom of the page we read: A bottle of Krug '64 will be awarded to the first competitor who sends in three correct solutions.

Twice the Owl blinked. Then he blinked again, more slowly and frowned, coming near to not looking inscrutable.

'Three solutions?' he repeated in puzzled tones. 'But how many solutions can there be?'

'As many as there are declarers, of course,' replied the Hog. 'It's all a question of judgment and psychology.'

Timothy the Toucan bounced unsteadily on his high stool by the bar. The Rabbit's ears twitched nervously. Hastily he jotted down some figures, checked them carefully on the fingers of both hands, and put the question: 'Surely if South's one notrump rebid shows fifteen-sixteen, West has nothing, if that?'

The Hog nodded.

'I presume,' ventured the Owl, 'that every competitor can pick his own declarer. Well then,' he went on as H.H. grunted in agreement, 'let's start with Walter the Walrus. How do you suggest that East should plan his defense against W.W.?'

'Easy,' replied the Hog. 'He cashes the three top spades and switches to the jack of hearts. The Walrus assumes, of course, that East has no more spades, duly finesses clubs into East's hand and lives unhappily for ever after.'

'Very clever,' said the Toucan. 'I think I'll have that for two of my solutions. Mind you, I'm not really good at finessing anyway, I am better at conceding losers to rectify the count and to, er, well...'

The Hog turned on him a withering look and T.T. duly withered.

'Let's now try another declarer,' went on H.H. 'Your turn, Oscar. How would you plan the defense against that Secretary Bird?'

The Owl hooted non-committally.

'Why not do the same as before?' asked the Rabbit.

'Because,' replied the Hog, 'the Secretary Bird wouldn't lose sight of the two of spades. He would want to know where it was. West, who led the three, would be following upwards to the top spades, proclaiming unmistakably a four-card suit. So the Emeritus Professor would realize that you had the two and were concealing it with malice aforethought, and he would guess the reason for the malice. No, that play would be too crude. Your best bet against S.B. would be to continue with the fourth spade and to hope for the best. And you would be likely to get it, too, for he could see that you and your partner couldn't have more

than twelve points between you, so if you showed up with ten — the
♠AKQ and the ♡J — he probably wouldn't place you with the queen
of clubs as well.'

'Yes, I like that,' said the Toucan approvingly, 'and if nobody
minds, I'll change my first two solutions for two of these.'

## THE THIRD MAN

'What about the third solution?' inquired Oscar. 'We've had a poorish
player as declarer and one who is, I suppose, somewhat above average.
Let's try a good one, say Colin the Corgi. How do you plan the defense
against him, H.H.?'

Thoughtfully the Hog took a last puff at the Toucan's cigar and
stubbed it out. 'Yes,' he agreed, 'Colin is a good player. He would
spot at once that the two of spades was missing, but if we played out
our spades, as we did against S.B., he would wonder why we allowed
him so obligingly to count our hand, and he would come up with the
right answer. There could be but one reason for exhibiting all those
high cards — to throw a smoke screen round the queen of clubs. So he
would finesse the right way. No, against the Corgi we must be more
subtle. We win the first trick with the king of spades and switch at
once to the jack of hearts, conveying the impression that the spades will
break four-four and that we are looking for the fifth trick. That way,
at last, we give nothing away.'

'What happened when the hand was actually played?' asked O.O.
'Who was declarer? Who sat East?'

'Papa was declarer and I was East,' replied the Hog with his most
engaging leer.

'The Greek is a fine player,' said the Owl, 'so I suppose you adopted
against him the same line of play as against Colin and...'

'No, no,' interjected the Hog, 'I followed the first variation, the
three top spades, then the jack of hearts.'

'But surely,' protested the Owl, 'that was the right psychological
approach against W.W., a poor player, who would miss the two of
spades and...'

Raising imperiously, a fat, pink forefinger, the Hog stopped him.
'Of course,' he explained, 'Papa knew my spade holding exactly and
he knew that I knew that he knew that the contract depended on his

finding the queen of clubs. Take that as read. Why, then, should I flaunt before him ten of the missing high card points? Why...'

'You've told us already,' broke in the Rabbit. 'So that he shouldn't think that you could have the queen of clubs as well as everything else. That's why, against Colin...'

'Ah! But Papa is much cleverer than Colin,' retorted the Hog, 'and he would ask himself at once: would I really show him that I was unlikely to have the queen of clubs, if I had it? Wouldn't that be altogether too disingenuous? No, Papa would be far more inclined to suspect that I was trying to deceive him by telling him the truth, a straightforward double cross, if you see what I mean.'

'If he is as subtle as that, what can you do?' asked the Toucan, looking thoroughly non-plussed.

'Quite simple,' replied the Hog. 'I was one move ahead of him all the time, so I applied a treble cross. I told him a lie to make him think that I was telling the truth to deceive him...'

'Sorry to interrupt,' broke in the Rabbit, 'but isn't that a quadruple cross, or even...?'

'A vicious circle?' ventured T.T.

'Let's have a look at the next problem,' said the Owl, firmly stretching out his hand.


## Papa's Cold Bottom

The Hog passed round his second problem.

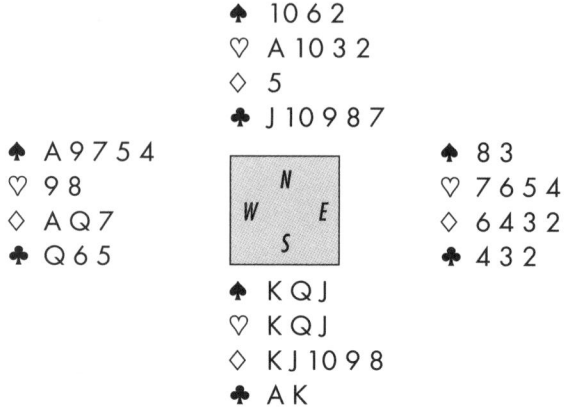

```
              ♠ 10 6 2
              ♡ A 10 3 2
              ◇ 5
              ♣ J 10 9 8 7
♠ A 9 7 5 4                   ♠ 8 3
♡ 9 8              N          ♡ 7 6 5 4
◇ A Q 7      W         E      ◇ 6 4 3 2
♣ Q 6 5           S          ♣ 4 3 2
              ♠ K Q J
              ♡ K Q J
              ◇ K J 10 9 8
              ♣ A K
```

| West | North | East | South |
|------|-------|------|-------|
| 1♠ | pass | pass | dbl |
| pass | 2♣ | pass | 3NT |
| all pass | | | |

West leads the ♠5. How should declarer plan the play?

The Rabbit was the first to speak. 'I just take my nine tricks,' he announced simply, 'two spades, four hearts, two clubs and one diamond.'

'The only snag,' pointed out H.H. 'is that before you come to that diamond, West will collect five tricks, three spades and two diamonds. Any ideas, Oscar?'

The Owl's heart-shaped face remained expressionless.

'If only we had another entry in dummy, we could have a go at those clubs,' suggested the Rabbit hopefully.

'Quite so,' agreed the Hideous Hog, 'and that is the crux of the hand. You must conjure up an additional entry in dummy. So after winning the first trick, you cash the ace and king of clubs and play the hearts, overtaking the jack of hearts with the ace and discarding a spade honor on the ten of hearts. You continue with the jack of clubs, throwing on it your last spade honor. West is helpless. He cannot clear his spades without providing you with an entry in dummy through the ten of spades and so allowing you to bring in the clubs. And if he doesn't set up his spades, he gives you time to develop a ninth trick in diamonds. Heads he loses, tails you win.'

'Very elegant,' conceded the Owl. 'And is that how declarer played?'

'You really did that?' asked Timothy the Toucan, lost in admiration. 'I am sure no one else would have thought of it.'

The Hog shook his head. 'You seem to be laboring under a misapprehension,' he observed. 'Certainly the hand was played as I have just told you and I haven't changed a pip in the North-South hands. But I happened to be West, not South, with Colin the Corgi as my partner. Declarer was none other than Papa and his play deserved, no doubt, a better fate. The fact remains that when this board came up in a pairs event, he scored the roundest and coldest of bottoms. Most Souths were in three notrump and all made it, except Papa. The fact is that for the purpose of my little competition I have altered the East-West hands slightly. This was the original version:

```
    ♠ A 9 7 5 4 3              ♠ 8
    ♡ 9              N          ♡ 8 7 6 5 4
    ◇ A 7 6      W       E      ◇ Q 4 3 2
    ♣ Q 6 5          S          ♣ 4 3 2
```

'Of course,' pursued the Hog, 'I was deeply impressed by Papa's spectacular unblocking play, so when I came in with the queen of clubs, I exited with a little diamond. Colin ducked and Papa won with the eight of diamonds. He continued with the king of diamonds, a good card, but not good enough. I went up with the ace of diamonds, cashed the ace of spades and led another diamond to Colin's queen. He had a heart to cash, so that was that.

'The best part about it,' chortled the Hog, 'was that all the other unsophisticated Souths played in palooka fashion, cashed the hearts, finessed the diamond and made nine tricks. Only Papa, who played so much better than anyone else, managed to go down. Ha ha!'

The Hog laughed happily as he recalled Papa's discomfiture. Next to winning himself, his greatest pleasure was to see Papa lose.

'It's an amusing hand,' agreed the Owl, 'but how can you use it in your competition? It doesn't matter about R.R. and T.T., for they do not go in for these things...'

'We do, it's only that we don't send in our solutions. We're too unlucky,' explained the Rabbit.

'...but Papa,' went on Oscar, 'might recognize the hand, which would give him an advantage.'

'Come, come, Oscar,' replied the Hog with a meaningful smile. 'Do you really fancy Papa's chances? Need I remind you that the Competition Editor's decision is final?'

'Surely,' cried the Rabbit, deeply shocked, 'you wouldn't take advantage of your position by discriminating against Papa if he sent in the winning solution? That would be most improper. You surely wouldn't, I mean, you couldn't, you er...'

'No, no, of course not,' declared the Hog with quiet dignity. 'I would always maintain the most scrupulous impartiality. But I don't suppose for a moment that Themistocles will enter my competition. He is a cynic, I fear, and is inclined to ascribe the lowest motives to all his friends, yes, even to me, incredible though it may seem, so I don't somehow think that you need worry overmuch about Papa.'

# Upholding the Law

Not long after the card committee's decision to introduce the Monster Points scheme, chance brought together four of the best players at the Griffins. Papa cut that facetious young man, Colin the Corgi. The Hog's partner was the distinguished lawyer and Emeritus Professor of Bio-Sophistry, known on account of his appearance as the Secretary Bird.

There was nothing unusual about the first few hands of the rubber. The Hog went down two or three times in 3NT. Then he made 3NT. Then, through a misunderstanding, the bidding stopped in 2NT and the Hog scored eight tricks. With opponents game and 70, Papa dealt and in sheer desperation opened 3♠ on:

♠ J 10 9 8 5 4   ♡ 6 5   ◊ J 10 8   ♣ J 10

The Professor said nothing and Colin raised to 6♠, which became the final contract. Much to Papa's relief no one doubled.

As the Professor led the ♠7, Colin the Corgi began to table his hand, slowly, card by card. First came the ♠2 and ♠3. 'That,' he said cheerfully, 'should be adequate trump support for I have every other card in the deck. Look!' One by one he put down the ♡A, the ◊A and the ♣A, then the ♡K. 'More treasures to come,' he said pleasantly, but by now Papa's patience was exhausted and he flicked the two of spades testily to the centre of the table. The Hog played the ♠Q and just as Papa was about to follow from the closed hand, the rest of dummy came into view. The last two cards were the ♠A and ♠K. This was the deal in full:

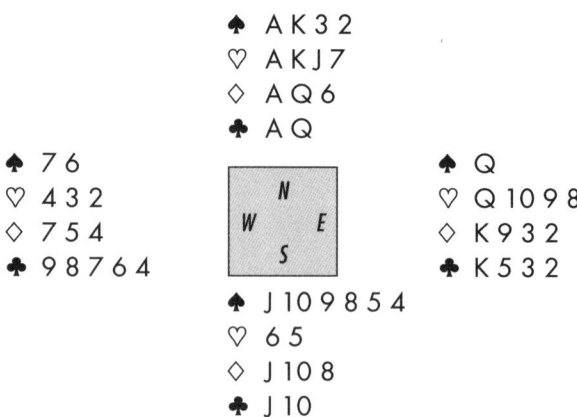

♠ A K 3 2
♡ A K J 7
◇ A Q 6
♣ A Q

♠ 7 6
♡ 4 3 2
◇ 7 5 4
♣ 9 8 7 6 4

♠ Q
♡ Q 10 9 8
◇ K 9 3 2
♣ K 5 3 2

♠ J 10 9 8 5 4
♡ 6 5
◇ J 10 8
♣ J 10

'You might wait...' began C.C.

'Oh!' exclaimed the Greek, hastily propelling the ♠2 back towards dummy.

'That card has been played,' announced S.B., pursing his thin bloodless lips.

'But I was only joking,' protested the Corgi.

'Very funny,' rejoined S.B. in icy tones, 'but the law states clearly that a card once played may be withdrawn only to comply with a penalty or to correct an illegal play. Section 47.'

'But I hadn't really played anything,' pleaded Papa.

'Declarer plays a card from dummy by moving it towards the center of the table,' pursued the Secretary Bird inexorably. 'Section 45.'

The Hog now joined in the discussion. 'Wouldn't it be in keeping with the spirit of the laws, partner, if we allowed Themistocles to — er — substitute, to replace, as it were...'

The Secretary Bird's Adam's apple throbbed dangerously. Uncrossing his long, wiry legs, he hissed angrily and was about to make some withering retort when Papa threw the ♠4 defiantly on the table.

'It's all yours,' he said contemptuously, pushing the trick towards H.H. The Professor's legalistic pedantry was bad enough, but to be proffered favors by the Hog was insufferable.

Sullenly the Hog gathered the trick, won so unexpectedly by his singleton queen, and continued with the ◇2.

Papa went up with the ◇J, and when it held the trick, a light came into his eyes. Surely S.B. would have covered had he been dealt the ◇K. And if the Hog had the king, why had he led a diamond? There could be only one explanation, that whatever the Hog led would cost a trick, and that meant that he had the ♡Q and the ♣K as well, all of which would account for his sudden interest in the spirit of the Laws.

The corners of his lips curving upwards in a triumphant smile, the Greek swished the ♠A excitedly on the table, then the ◊A, then the ♣A. Four trumps followed in quick succession and as the last touched down, this was the position:

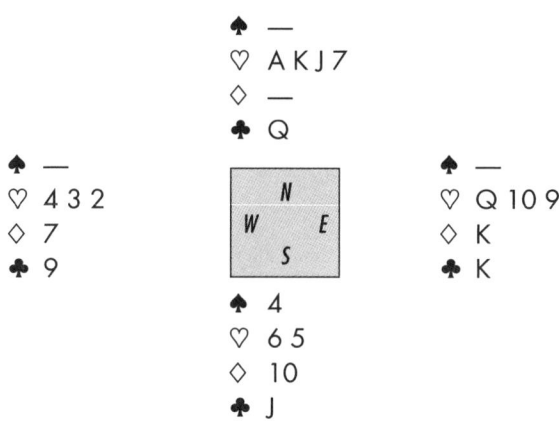

```
              ♠ —
              ♡ A K J 7
              ◊ —
              ♣ Q
  ♠ —                        ♠ —
  ♡ 4 3 2      ┌─────────┐   ♡ Q 10 9
  ◊ 7          │    N    │   ◊ K
  ♣ 9          │ W     E │   ♣ K
               │    S    │
               └─────────┘
              ♠ 4
              ♡ 6 5
              ◊ 10
              ♣ J
```

Discarding with a flourish dummy's ♣Q, the Greek looked exultantly at the Hog. With a snarl H.H. let go the ◊K. The ◊10 followed, squeezing him in hearts and clubs.

'Curious hand,' observed Oscar the Owl. 'Left to himself, declarer would never make his contract. He tries to ruff out the queen of hearts, fails, tries in turn one finesse after another in the minors and fails again. Every card is wrong.'

'No, no,' corrected Papa, 'the queen of spades is right, very much so. What is that splendid law, Professor? What section did you say it was?'

'Congratulations, partner,' cried the Hog bitterly, 'no other player in the world has been known to execute a progressive squeeze at Trick 1.'

The Secretary Bird hissed venomously, glaring first at Papa, then at the Hog. He couldn't be sure for the moment which of them he hated more.

Meanwhile, S.B.'s performance has taken him to the head of the Monster Points table and a leading bookmaker has made him favorite in the race to be the first Life Monster.

# Monsters in the Menagerie

The Monster Points Committee had carefully studied the evidence. All the accused were found guilty and it only remained to pass sentence.

'Suicide is one and indivisible,' argued Oscar the Owl, our Senior Kibitzer. 'The fact that partner may be a willing accomplice does not diminish the gravity of the offense and should not, therefore, affect the punishment.'

Peregrine the Penguin shook his small round head in disagreement. 'Just as there are degrees of murder,' he insisted, 'so there are degrees of suicide. A defender who commits *felo de se*, throwing the contract single-handed, must not be confused with one who merely aids and abets or conspires with partner, so to speak, to er...'

'To murder each other,' interposed the Hideous Hog, finishing the Penguin's sentence. 'And yet,' went on H.H., puffing thoughtfully at O.O.'s cigar, 'it isn't as simple as that. A sharp distinction, I feel, should be drawn between suicide in any form, unilateral or caused by the finest partnership misunderstanding, and artistic homicide in which the victim shows no initiative, but merely obliges by graciously putting his head in the noose. Why should he enjoy all the limelight if the credit belongs to his executioner? By all means punish the sinners sternly,' concluded the Hog, 'but give just praise to those who led them into temptation.'

There were three cases before the committee. The award of the first Monster Point went to Timothy the Toucan, who sat West on this hand:

North-South Vul.
Dealer West

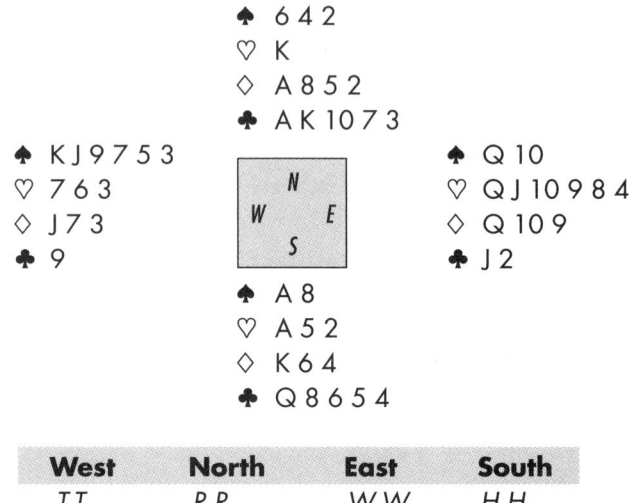

```
                    ♠ 6 4 2
                    ♡ K
                    ◇ A 8 5 2
                    ♣ A K 10 7 3
   ♠ K J 9 7 5 3                      ♠ Q 10
   ♡ 7 6 3            N               ♡ Q J 10 9 8 4
   ◇ J 7 3        W       E           ◇ Q 10 9
   ♣ 9                S               ♣ J 2
                    ♠ A 8
                    ♡ A 5 2
                    ◇ K 6 4
                    ♣ Q 8 6 5 4
```

| West | North | East | South |
|------|-------|------|-------|
| T.T. | R.R. | W.W. | H.H. |
| 3♠ | 4♣ | pass | 6NT |
| all pass | | | |

The bidding was simple and straightforward. After the Rueful Rabbit's 4♣, it was no longer possible to stop in game. 5♣ would be too ambitious, since the Rabbit rarely made eleven tricks, while 4NT he would read as Blackwood. The slam, therefore, presented the lesser risk — provided that it was played by the right hand.

The Toucan led the ♡6, and as dummy went down, the Hog grunted approvingly. He could see eleven tricks, more than he usually required for a slam. The lead, too, looked promising. If the ♡6 was the top of nothing, the Walrus would have to guard the heart suit all on his own, while the Toucan would have to look after the spades. It followed that in the endgame neither defender would be able to keep three diamonds.

The first step was to rectify the count for a squeeze, so at Trick 2 the Hog led the ♠2, allowing the ten to hold the trick. Walter the Walrus returned the ♡Q to the Hog's ace and this is where Timothy the Toucan earned his Monster Point. With cold deliberation he played the ♡7. It wasn't sabotage. Still less was it carelessness. The Toucan was simply obeying the dictates of MUD, a conventional sequence in which the middle card is led from a holding of three small, the top card being played next and the bottom card last. Middle, up, down, the first letters making up MUD. Having just mastered the convention — of which W.W. was wholly innocent — T.T. was happy to find so soon an opportunity of putting it into practice. It was, in fact, the one redeeming feature of a deal which held for him no other interest. But observe the difference that the ♡7 made in the four-card endgame. When the last club was led from dummy, this was the position:

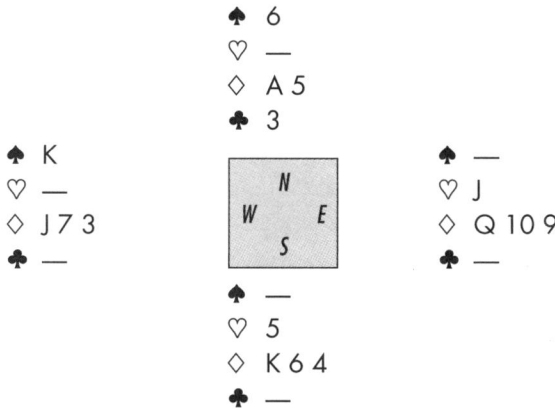

Since H.H. still retained the ♡5, the Walrus had to cling on to the ♡J and to let go a diamond. The Hog now threw a heart and T.T. was squeezed in spades and diamonds.

'Why did you do it to me? What made you throw away your seven of hearts?' demanded the outraged Walrus. 'But for that, I would have kept the diamonds, leaving you with the best spade and the master heart. Quisling!'

'MUD,' murmured the Toucan feebly.

'A secret convention, undisclosed even to partner. Very improper,' mocked the Hideous Hog.

'It only goes to show,' observed the Owl sagely, 'that it's better to know too little than too much. It comes to the same thing in the end, but it's less humiliating.'

# A KILLING LEAD

On the next case submitted to us, the Greek and Karapet, the Free Armenian, claimed Monster Points against each other. Both being parties to the dispute it fell to the Hog, who was declarer, to present the hand to the committee. He invited us from the first to treat it as a double dummy problem.

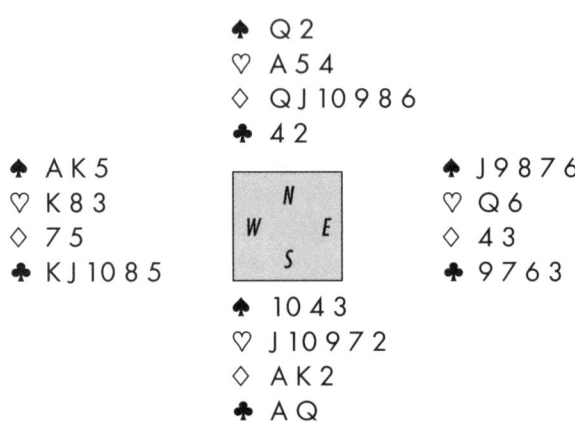

```
                    ♠ Q 2
                    ♡ A 5 4
                    ◇ Q J 10 9 8 6
                    ♣ 4 2
    ♠ A K 5                             ♠ J 9 8 7 6
    ♡ K 8 3            N                ♡ Q 6
    ◇ 7 5         W         E           ◇ 4 3
    ♣ K J 10 8 5          S             ♣ 9 7 6 3
                    ♠ 10 4 3
                    ♡ J 10 9 7 2
                    ◇ A K 2
                    ♣ A Q
```

| West | North | East | South |
|------|-------|------|-------|
| Papa | R.R. | Karapet | H.H. |
| 1♣ | pass | pass | dbl |
| pass | 1◇ | pass | 1♡ |
| pass | 2♡ | pass | 4♡ |
| all pass | | | |

'You will agree, gentlemen,' began the Hog with his most engaging leer, 'that either on a spade or on a trump lead — and the latter was the case here — four hearts can't be made. How, then, do you suppose that I made all thirteen tricks?'

'On a trump lead?' inquired the Owl incredulously.

Putting down my glass and smacking his lips as he picked up the Penguin's, the Hideous Hog nodded in assent. Each of us had a shot, but we soon gave up.

'The solution to the problem,' explained H.H., 'lies in the infinite subtlety of Themistocles Papadopoulos, so clever, so resourceful that he can find a way to falsecard with a singleton. Papa sensed that a trump would be the best lead and to confuse me as much as possible, he picked with superb cunning the eight of hearts, a most deceptive card. It worked wonders — against Karapet. I played low from dummy, and seeing no reason to waste a perfectly good queen, Karapet played low, too. I won with the ten of hearts, cashed the two top diamonds and continued with the jack of hearts.

'Turn to Papa. He 'knew' that I had the queen of hearts, so unless he covered the jack, I would simply pick up his king of hearts on the next trick and run the diamonds. If he covered, the day might still be saved. All depended on the two of hearts. Had it been played to the first trick? If so, I couldn't get to dummy with the five of hearts and the diamonds would be dead. That's what he thought, though he won't admit it, of course. He pretends that he expected me to make a mistake. I might not know, he says, that his last trump was lower than dummy's five of hearts. It simply didn't dawn on him that I had the last diamond. Poor Karapet had followed with the four of diamonds before playing the three, but if Papa noticed it, he dismissed it as routine deception, the sort he would practice himself. He preferred to believe me and surely I wouldn't have laid down the ace and king if I had another diamond. Besides, how could he gain by holding up his king of hearts? Ha ha!'

Absent-mindedly the Hog raised his own glass. 'Imagine the cries of anguish,' he continued, chortling gleefully, 'when the queen of hearts suddenly fell on the king, right under my ace!

'The rest was automatic. I played off the hearts, then the diamonds, leaving myself with the ace and queen of clubs and dummy with the queen of spades and a club. Papa was helpless.

'I must say,' concluded H.H., 'that Karapet took it very well. He put it all down to the ancient curse on his house which had always made the Djoulikyans the unluckiest family on their side of Mount Ararat — and on the other side, too, of course.'


## Unusual Trump Break

It was the last of the three hands brought before the Monster Points Committee which made the Hog coin that phrase about artistic homicide. The fact that he was himself the artist was, needless to say, purely incidental.

Neither Vul.
Dealer South

```
                    ♠ 7 6 4
                    ♡ J 5 4
                    ◇ A K J 7
                    ♣ Q 8 3
     ♠ Q J 10 9                    ♠ A 8 5 3
     ♡ K Q           ┌─────────┐   ♡ A 3 2
     ◇ 10 9 8 6      │    N    │   ◇ 5 4 3
     ♣ 10 9 6        │ W     E │   ♣ 7 5 2
                     │    S    │
                     └─────────┘
                    ♠ K 2
                    ♡ 10 9 8 7 6
                    ◇ Q 2
                    ♣ A K J 4
```

| West | North | East | South |
|------|-------|------|-------|
| S.B. | R.R. | W.W. | H.H. |
|      |      |      | 1♡ |
| pass | 2◇ | pass | 2♡ |
| pass | 4♡ | all pass | |

The contract was a poor one and the Hog was the first to admit that his
partner had bid badly.  Yet what else was the Rabbit to do?  With 14
points — 11 in top cards and 3 more which he was instructed to add
when the Hog would play the hand — he could hardly stop under game.

Sitting West, the Emeritus Professor of Bio-Sophistry, known on
account of his strange habits and appearance as the Secretary Bird, led
the ♠Q.  Winning with the ace, the Walrus played back a spade to the
king.  The Hog's problem was to avoid, somehow, the loss of three
trump tricks.  Should he play low towards dummy in the hope that with
♡Q32, the Secretary Bird would go up with the queen?  If he fell for
it, the ♡Q would crash with the king, but it was a remote possibility.
And why, anyway, should the Walrus turn up with the ♡A and ♡K, as
well as the ♠A?  No, there was no reasonable way to play the trumps
for the loss of only two tricks.  That being the case, H.H. didn't play
trumps.  He played instead the ◇Q, crossed to dummy with the ace and
continued with the king on which he threw a club from the closed hand.
Then he led the ◇J.  Walter the Walrus was not the type to let declarer
get rid of another winner with impunity, so he promptly ruffed with the

♡2, an eminently expendable card. The Hog overruffed and now the five outstanding trumps happily broke 2-2, and all was well.

The Secretary Bird hissed venomously and the wild tufts of hair over his ears bristled with anger.

The Walrus didn't notice it. 'An uninspired lead, I am afraid partner,' he said with an accusing look. 'Had you led a trump — and the bidding called for it, you know — we could have taken three trump tricks and a spade before he could get at those diamonds.'

'A monstrous situation,' said the Hideous Hog, winking merrily at the kibitzers. 'The ace of trumps didn't take a trick, as it were. Most unlucky. Doesn't often happen, even to Karapet.'

# Stayman — the Hog Variation

'Partnership understanding! What does it mean?' asked the Hideous Hog rhetorically, putting down my glass and picking up Oscar's. 'It's really a question of semantics. The usual idea is that each player, in turn, knows what his partner means, draws the inferences and plays accordingly. That works well enough when Benito Garozzo faces Giorgio Belladonna, but what happens when one's sitting opposite the Rueful Rabbit or Walter the Walrus or Timothy the Toucan? In the first place they wouldn't know what you meant, and couldn't draw the right inferences if they did. So why tell them anything?

'When I speak of partnership understanding,' went on H.H., 'I mean something very different. Now take the Rabbit. He tells me what he has and I tell him what to do with it. Once I've got that message across, we've achieved perfect understanding.'

We had been discussing two-way Stayman, an adaptation of the original convention devised by H.H. for use with some of his less gifted partners. This is how it works.

When the Hog opens 1NT and partner bids 2♣, a rebid in a major is two-way. The Hog either has it or he hasn't. Partner can raise it to the three-level, but no more and must pass the Hog's next bid.

The advantages of this method are considerable. If the two clubs bidder has the major shown by H.H., the suit will have stoppers in notrump. If he hasn't, opponents won't know whether to lead it or not. After all, H.H. isn't debarred from having a suit just because he has bid it. So they must guess.

'I can see one snag,' objected Oscar the Owl, our Senior Kibitzer. 'Suppose you open one notrump and bid two spades in response to the Rabbit's two clubs. Now, though he may be worth four spades, he can only bid three spades.'

'And how is R.R. to know,' countered the Hog, 'whether he is worth three spades or four spades? No, no, two-way Stayman is foolproof, almost Rabbit-proof.'

This was the hand which gave rise to the discussion:

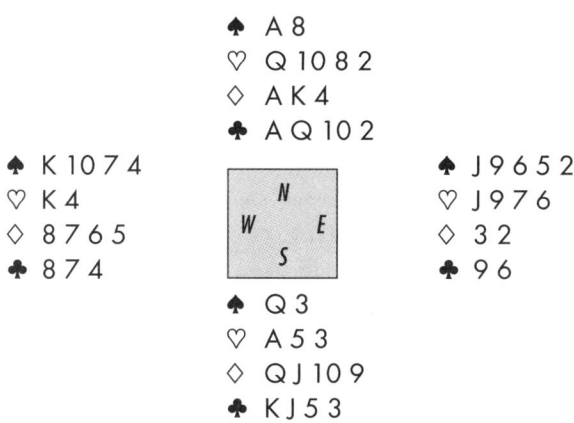

♠ A 8
♡ Q 10 8 2
◇ A K 4
♣ A Q 10 2

♠ K 10 7 4
♡ K 4
◇ 8 7 6 5
♣ 8 7 4

♠ J 9 6 5 2
♡ J 9 7 6
◇ 3 2
♣ 9 6

♠ Q 3
♡ A 5 3
◇ Q J 10 9
♣ K J 5 3

| West | North | East | South |
|------|-------|------|-------|
| Papa | R.R. | Karapet | H.H. |
|  |  |  | 1NT |
| pass | 2♣ | pass | 2♠ |
| pass | 4NT | pass | 6NT |
| all pass |  |  |  |

Of course, with the 4-4 fit, 6♣ would have been a better contract, but the Hog liked to get notrump in first, in case of an accident.

Suspicious of the 2♠ bid, Papa nearly led a spade. That would have been a triumph for the convention, presenting declarer with the contract at Trick 1. The Greek thought better of it, however, and picked on the ◇8, which gave nothing away, leaving H.H. with ten top tricks and the need to develop two more.

The Hog began by cashing three diamonds and three clubs, but nothing interesting happened and the decisive moment could be postponed no longer. So, leaving two winners uncashed and with communications still open, H.H. laid down the ♡A.

The danger signal flashed through Papa's mind. He could see just what would happen. The Hog would take his fourth diamond and the ♣K, and now, with spades only in his hand, Papa would be thrown in with the ♡K. Promptly, the Greek jettisoned the king on the ace. It was safe enough, for Karapet was marked with the ♡J. Had the Hog had it, he would have surely taken the finesse.

The queen of hearts wouldn't give H.H. his twelfth trick and meanwhile the endplay had been averted.

There was a price to pay. The spectacular unblocking play gave away the position of the ♠K, for without it the Greek would have been in no trouble.

Making the most of the information, the Hog cashed the ♣K and discarded dummy's ♠8 on his fourth diamond. With four cards remaining, H.H. spread his hand. If Karapet retained two spades and two hearts, H.H. would simply concede a heart. If the Armenian kept one spade and three hearts, the Hog would cash the ♠A and exit with a low heart, endplaying Karapet in hearts.

'Could we have got there without two-way Stayman?' asked the Rueful Rabbit.

# Beware of Extra Chances

'Those who can, play. Those who can't, count,' said the Hideous Hog with aplomb, sipping thoughtfully his Taylor '27.

'Percentages! Mathematicians!' he went on contemptuously. 'Look at the forest, not the trees! You can keep all your extra 2% chances. Why, they won't buy you a magnum of iced water at the end of the year. It's doing opponents out of their 100% chances that brings in the money — or the matchpoints, if you happen to care for them.'

We had been mulling over a few hands during dinner at the Griffins and as we passed round the port, the Hog began to expound one of his favorite theories — the iniquity of science in general and of mathematics in particular.

'And let's not have any of that other nonsense about meeting invariably with the best defense and making the contract regardless of the distribution,' continued H.H., warming to the subject. 'That's all very well when you're solving double-dummy problems in your bath. Once the cardinal points take on flesh and blood, there's no such thing as perfection. The best percentage chance is often a slip by the other side. As for esoteric distributions, why worry about them? If you make all your makeable contracts against likely distributions and the second-best defense, you will be doing pretty well. You won't always play against me you know,' he added modestly, measuring the decanter with a practiced eye.

Whoever did the talking wouldn't get much of what was left. Realizing that it was a listener's market, the Hog turned to Oscar the Owl, our Senior Kibitzer. 'Tell them about that five diamond contract,' he suggested. 'It's a good example.'

O.O. cleared his throat. He liked recounting hands. As for the port, someone would surely order another bottle, even if he had to do it himself.

'I will mention no names,' began O.O., 'for I don't want to prejudice you. Take the South seat:

East-West Vul.
Dealer North

```
                    ♠ A 3
                    ♡ 5 2
                    ◇ A 10 3
                    ♣ K Q J 10 9 2

                        N
                    W       E
                        S

                    ♠ 2
                    ♡ A Q 6 3
                    ◇ K 8 7 6 5 2
                    ♣ 8 4
```

| West | North | East | South |
|------|-------|------|-------|
|      | 1♣    | pass | 1◇    |
| 2♠   | 3◇    | 3♠   | 4◇    |
| 4♠   | 5♣    | pass | 5◇    |
| dbl  | all pass |   |       |

'West leads king of spades. You rise with dummy's ace of spades and
lead the three of diamonds, intending to insert the five of diamonds if
East plays the four of diamonds.'

'Why?' asked Timothy the Toucan.

'Just in case East has all four trumps, but has omitted, carelessly,
to play the nine of diamonds,' explained O.O. 'It's an extra chance,
costing nothing and declarer doesn't mind losing the lead to West. If
he wins the trick, he can do no harm. South will win the next one and
drive out the ace of clubs. Two rounds of trumps, ending in dummy,
will then ensure the contract.'

'And did East produce the four of diamonds?' inquired T.T.

'No, he played the nine of diamonds,' replied O.O., 'so declarer
went up with the king of diamonds and West dropped the queen. What
next?'

Fearing a catch, no one said anything, and the Owl continued.

'If West had a doubleton queen-jack of diamonds there was no
problem. So declarer set out to cope with a three-one break.

'His plan was to take a second round of trumps, in case they split
two-two — playing dummy's ace of diamonds either way — and to

clear the clubs.  If trumps broke nicely, he would make twelve tricks.  If West showed out on the second round, he would ruff dummy's second spade and still be fairly happy, so long as West had the ace of clubs, which was likely enough on the bidding.  The contract would hinge on finding East with three clubs.

'So, at Trick 3, declarer continued with the two of diamonds.  West followed with the four of diamonds.'

The Owl paused.  The Rabbit and the Toucan exchanged meaningful looks.  'I somehow think,' ventured R.R. smiling broadly, 'that West was our friend Papa.  With the queen and four of diamonds he couldn't resist the temptation to drop that queen.  Mind you, it can't cost anything, for it's due to come down the next time anyway.'

'Well, then,' persisted O.O., 'how many tricks will declarer make?'

'Twelve,' replied R.R. and T.T. in unison.

'The ace of diamonds picks up East's jack of diamonds,' explained the Rabbit, 'a club drives...'

'You definitely play the ace of diamonds?' asked O.O.

'Naturally.' It was the Toucan's turn to speak. 'Even if East were not marked with the jack of diamonds, it would be folly to take the chance, for should he come in and lead a heart before the clubs were cleared, a cold contract would be defeated.'

R.R. nodded vigorously in agreement while the Owl filled in the East-West hands.

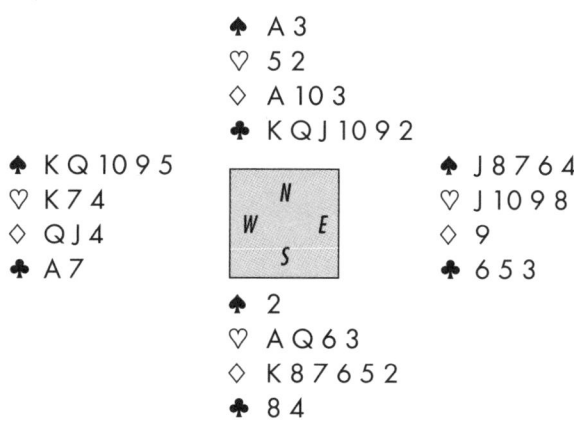

```
                    ♠ A 3
                    ♡ 5 2
                    ◇ A 10 3
                    ♣ K Q J 10 9 2
  ♠ K Q 10 9 5          N          ♠ J 8 7 6 4
  ♡ K 7 4           W       E      ♡ J 10 9 8
  ◇ Q J 4               S          ◇ 9
  ♣ A 7                            ♣ 6 5 3
                    ♠ 2
                    ♡ A Q 6 3
                    ◇ K 8 7 6 5 2
                    ♣ 8 4
```

After ordering another bottle, O.O. sat back to dot the 'i's and cross the 't's.

'As you can see, the contract is really unbeatable. If West follows low to the king of diamonds, declarer drives out the ace of clubs, crosses to the ace of diamonds and leads clubs till West ruffs. The ten of diamonds remains as a certain entry to dummy. Somehow, declarer had to be induced to cash both the king and ace of diamonds before touching clubs. That puts West in control.'

'A very pretty piece of deception that queen of diamonds. So pretty, H.H., that you would have fallen for it yourself,' suggested T.T.

'What!' cried the Hog. 'Do you take me for Papa? Can't you see that he lost the unlosable contract — or rather he gave me the chance to sink it for him — at Trick 2, when he led that three of diamonds?'

'Against any likely distribution, a club at Trick 2 would ensure the contract, and it's the likely distributions that matter.

'I admit,' concluded the Hog magnanimously, 'that after that little slip at Trick 2, poor Papa shouldn't be judged too harshly for being taken in by my queen of diamonds. It was sheer bad luck to have me sitting West. After all, there are lots and lots of Wests, but only one me. The percentage...'

# Papa Seizes His Only Chance

As always, when the Hideous Hog and Papa the Greek faced each other, kibitzers gathered from far and wide to watch the duel.

'All I ask you,' Papa was heard saying to Karapet who was to be his partner, 'is to defend soundly. No pyrotechnics. Nothing clever. Leave him to me. I know his style.'

In the other corner, the Hog was instructing the Rabbit. 'Be conservative when you're going to be declarer. People defend very well against you, as you know. Conversely, you can let yourself go a bit when I'm in the chair. My suits are longer than yours and people don't like doubling me. They're superstitious and fear that it will bring them bad luck.'

The first few hands were uneventful.  The Rueful Rabbit went two down in 1♠, but had 150 honors to make up for it.  The Hog made 2◇ and Papa explained that he could have made another trick on a trump squeeze, had the clubs broken 4-2, as they should have done.  Then this hand came along:

North-South Vul.

```
              ♠ 7 4 3 2
              ♡ 6 5 4 3
              ◇ A K 8
              ♣ K 6
  ♠ Q J 10          N
  ♡ A 8 2      W         E
  ◇ Q 9 4          S
  ♣ A 4 3 2
```

| West | North | East | South |
|------|-------|------|-------|
| Papa | R.R. | Karapet | H.H. |
| 1NT | pass | pass | 2♡ |
| pass | 4♡ | all pass | |

'A bit on the light side, your double raise, don't you think?' murmured Timothy the Toucan, who was sitting by his friend the Rabbit.

R.R. shook his head: 'Oh, no, I have sixteen points, you see — ten in high cards, one for the doubleton club, three for the Hog's skill and two more for my dummy play — when I'm dummy, that is.'

Papa led the ♠Q, which held the trick, and continued with the ♠J to the ace in the closed hand.  Karapet contributed the ♠8, then the ♠6.

At Trick 3, the Greek rose with the ♡A on the Hog's king and persisted with another spade.  The Free Armenian overtook with the ♠K and the Hog ruffed.  Two rounds of trumps came next.  Karapet discarded the ♣5 and ◇6.

With seven cards remaining, H.H. led the ♣7.  In a flash, Papa brought the ♣A down on the table and almost in the same movement detached the ♣2.  Before it left his hand, however, the Hog had time to throw dummy's king of clubs under his ace.

Slowly, the Greek replaced the ♣2 and leant back, looking thoughtfully at the ceiling.  I could hear the loud, rhythmic ticking of his brain as he appraised an unforeseen and unforeseeable situation.

His defense had been based on the assumption that the Hog had two clubs and no more. Otherwise he would have surely played clubs earlier, before drawing trumps. If Karapet had the ♣Q, going up with the ace would make no difference, but if H.H. had that queen, not going up with the ace would be fatal, for on the next round Papa would be thrown in and forced to lead away from his ◇Q or else to concede a ruff and discard.

Papa's defense was — or rather, was going to be — impeccable, and he was the first to admit it. But, as Brutus once observed, 'good reasons must of force give way to better.'

Why had the Hog suddenly jettisoned dummy's ♣K? There could only be one explanation for this spectacular unblocking play. He had ♣Q109(x) and feared that if Papa forced out his last trump — and he couldn't tell who had the thirteenth spade — he would be unable to get back to his hand to score the ♣Q. Jettisoning the ♣K created an entry and enabled him, at the same time, to finesse against the ♣J on the way back.

If H.H. had started with three diamonds and ♣Q107, there was nothing Papa could do, but if he had two diamonds only and ♣Q1097, he could be put to a guess, for he would then be in a position to take a ruffing finesse.

Seizing his only chance, Papa led the ◇9, an innocent-looking card, denying an honor. The subliminal suggestion was that if he hadn't the ◇Q, he must certainly have the ♣J to justify the barest weak, non-vulnerable 1NT.

The Hog could hardly wait to play low from dummy. This was the full deal:

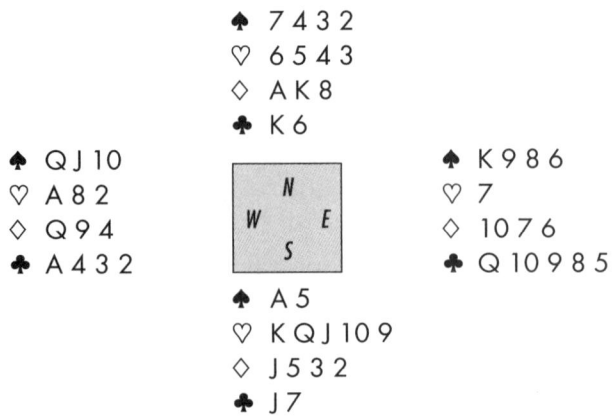

```
                    ♠ 7 4 3 2
                    ♡ 6 5 4 3
                    ◇ A K 8
                    ♣ K 6
    ♠ Q J 10                        ♠ K 9 8 6
    ♡ A 8 2           N             ♡ 7
    ◇ Q 9 4       W       E         ◇ 10 7 6
    ♣ A 4 3 2         S             ♣ Q 10 9 8 5
                    ♠ A 5
                    ♡ K Q J 10 9
                    ◇ J 5 3 2
                    ♣ J 7
```

After a loud guffaw, in which he invited the kibitzers to join, H.H. won the trick with the ◇J, cashed dummy's ◇A and ◇K, returned to his hand by ruffing a spade and scored his fourth diamond, discarding dummy's ♣6.

As he added up the score — his favorite pastime — the Hog could afford to be magnanimous.

'Never mind, Themistocles,' he said with a friendly leer, 'if I had the doubleton queen of clubs and no jack of diamonds, you would have been right to play as you did. Let's say that you took a 50-50 chance. You can hardly expect to do better than that against an... er... a more experienced player.'

# Mistaken Identity

'Playing too well can be expensive,' observed Oscar the Owl, our Senior Kibitzer at the Griffins.

'True,' agreed Peregrine the Penguin, his opposite number at the Unicorn, 'but if everyone plays too well it cancels out, so no one really loses.'

'Except the Rabbit, of course,' rejoined O.O. 'for he cancels himself out, as it were.'

These reflections were prompted by an unusual hand which gave rise to many flashes of brilliance, premeditated and otherwise.

North-South Vul. and 40; East-West 60
Dealer South

```
                    ♠ K Q J 6 3 2
                    ♡ 8 7 6
                    ◇ 10
                    ♣ A 5 2
   ♠ 9                                ♠ 10 8 7
   ♡ K Q J 10 9          N            ♡ 5 4 3 2
   ◇ K Q J         W          E       ◇ 3
   ♣ Q 7 6 3             S            ♣ K J 10 9 8
                    ♠ A 5 4
                    ♡ A
                    ◇ A 9 8 7 6 5 4 2
                    ♣ 4
```

| West | North | East | South |
|------|-------|------|-------|
| H.H. | Karapet | R.R. | Papa |
|      |       |      | 3◇ |
| 3♡ | 4◇ | 4♡ | 4♠ |
| pass | 5♣ | dbl | 5♡ |
| pass | 5♠ | pass | 5NT |
| pass | 6◇ | 6♡ | pass |
| pass | 6♠ | all pass | |

Papa readily agreed that his bidding sequence was impeccable. What's more, he had no fault to find with his partner, Karapet, the Free Armenian. Clearly, at unfavorable vulnerability, he wouldn't preempt without a strong hand and a good suit. And, in view of the partscore, he might have quite a bit extra. There was nothing wrong, therefore, in supporting him on a singleton.

Bristling with controls, Papa needed little enough for a slam and it cost nothing to bid 4♠ since the hand couldn't be played in less than 5◇ anyway. By the same token, Karapet took up no space in showing his ♣A. Diagnosing a singleton heart opposite, he rather liked his hand.

The Hog maintains that the only sound bid in the entire auction was his pass over Papa's 5♡. Admittedly, such subtleties, or any other kind for that matter, are wasted on the Rabbit, but to an intelligent partner the pass would convey the message: 'I am not looking for a sacrifice.' A double would have suggested the opposite.

Disdaining false modesty, the Greek explained in the post-mortem that his forcing pass over 6♥ was the most inspired bid of the sequence. He had demanded a grand slam if Karapet had two of the three top honors in diamonds. Despite the denial, Papa was still inviting a grand slam. Why? The unmistakable inference was that one of the two top honors would suffice.

The Armenian read the message. Papa had no losers outside trumps, but he needed the second-round control. Well, he, Karapet, had it — so long as the hand was played in spades. And why shouldn't it be once Papa had shown the ♠A? Moreover, since he was marked with one heart or none, he surely had two or three spades. Such was Karapet's reasoning.

## TRAPS FOR THE RABBIT

A group of distinguished kibitzers had gathered round the table. Among them were two Americans, paying their first visit to the Griffins.

The Hideous Hog led the ♥K and Papa sat back to examine his prospects. If the diamonds split 2-2, he could afford a 3-1 trump break. Conversely, if the trumps were 2-2 he could stand a 3-1 division in diamonds. If, however, both suits broke 3-1, he would face a well-nigh insuperable problem in setting up the diamonds and getting back to enjoy them. Against perfect defense there was no answer. On Papa's right, however, sat the Rueful Rabbit.

Crossing at Trick 2 to the ♠K, the Greek led the ♦10 to his ace and continued with another diamond, which he ruffed carefully with the ♠2. Surely, if R.R. had no diamond, he would pounce on it and then all would be well.

The Rabbit didn't even consider it. He had followed to the ♥K with the ♥5 and he now echoed with the ♥2.

'That must be the famous Hog, Hiram,' said one of the American visitors to the other.

The Rabbit's heart missed a beat, then another. His rosy cheeks turned to crimson and on to magenta. Never had he felt so flattered in all his life and he wondered what he had done to deserve it. In a daze he followed to the next trick, a spade to the ace in the closed hand, leaving this position:

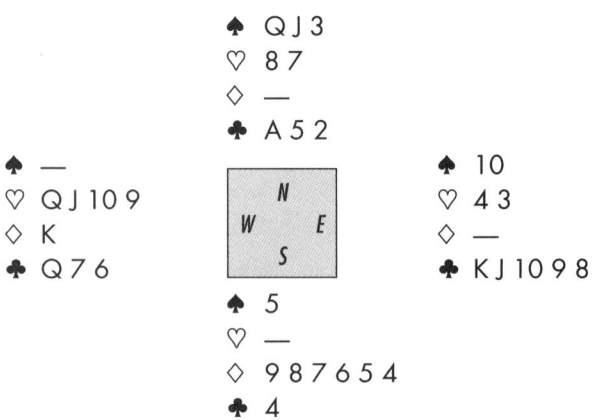

The ◊9, bringing down the ◊K, was ruffed with dummy's ♠3, giving the Rabbit another chance. If only he overruffed, the ♠5 would serve as an entry, and with no more trumps out, Papa would have five diamonds to cash.

Alas, R.R. didn't even glance at the ♠10.

With a surreptitious look at the Americans to observe the effect, he signaled loudly with the ♣J. As Papa reluctantly gathered the trick, the Rabbit stretched his hand for it.

'Our trick,' he murmured, 'the king of diamonds...'

'I happened to ruff it,' said Papa bitterly.

'Ruff it?' repeated the bemused Rabbit, 'but diamonds are trumps. I mean, one doesn't ruff trumps, does one?'

'Didn't you hear me bid six spades?' asked Karapet, interrupting a loud guffaw from the Hog.

'Of course I did,' replied R.R. indignantly. 'You both bid spades and every other suit, when it comes to that, but only after agreeing diamonds, so they were all cuebids and though it happens to me sometimes or to the Walrus, of course, experts don't play their slams in a cuebid do they?

'Sorry, partner,' added R.R. ruefully, 'but it is so very confusing when everyone bids everything.'

The diamonds were now dead and so was the slam.

'I figure that's not the Hog, Hiram,' said the first American.

'I guess not,' rejoined his companion.

# A Conventional Affair

'I agree with La Rochefoucald's maxim that we all enjoy the troubles of our neighbors,' said Oscar the Owl, thoughtfully dispatching an oyster, 'but we do not enjoy them in equal measure.'

Peregrine the Penguin raised an interrogative eyebrow.

'Some of us,' explained O.O., 'enjoy our neighbors' troubles more than others do.'

'Are you thinking of the Hog?' asked P.P., passing the Chablis.

'I am,' agreed the Owl. 'He savors far more keenly than most of us do the misfortunes of his fellowmen. And, of course, the misfortunes of some give him more pleasure than do those of others.'

'You mean Papa?' asked the Penguin.

'I do,' rejoined the Owl. 'Next to winning, his greatest pleasure is to see Papa lose.'

Our discussion over dinner was prompted by a rubber in which the Rueful Rabbit and his friend Timothy the Toucan faced Papa the Greek and Karapet Djoulikyan, the unluckiest player since Job — and before that, too, of course.

The Hideous Hog was the star kibitzer.

The Rabbit dealt the first hand.

```
                    ♠ K Q 10 8 6 5
                    ♡ K 10 3
                    ♢ 4 2
                    ♣ 10 9
   ♠ J 9 4                              ♠ 7 3
   ♡ Q J 8 6          N                 ♡ 9 5
   ♢ Q 9 5       W         E            ♢ 10 8 7 6
   ♣ K J 2           S                  ♣ Q 8 6 5 3
                    ♠ A 2
                    ♡ A 7 4 2
                    ♢ A K J 3
                    ♣ A 7 4
```

| West | North | East | South |
|------|-------|------|-------|
| Papa | T.T. | Karapet | R.R. |
| | | | 2NT |
| pass | 4♣ | pass | 4♢ |
| pass | 4♠ | pass | 5♡ |
| pass | 6♡ | pass | 7♣ |
| pass | 7♠ | pass | 7NT |
| all pass | | | |

Admittedly, the bidding sequence deviates from the strictly orthodox and requires, perhaps, a word or two by way of explanation.

The Toucan's 4♣ was Gerber, asking for aces. The Rabbit's 4♢ was a cuebid, agreeing clubs.

The Toucan assumed that just as 5♣ over a Blackwood 4NT shows four aces or none, so 4♢ had the same meaning in response to Gerber. Even so, however, he couldn't be certain of a slam and contented himself for the time being with a modest 4♠.

This the Rabbit took to be a cuebid, probably indicating a void, and his next move was to show the ♡A.

At this point the Toucan wasn't ashamed to show the ♡K, whereupon the Rabbit signed off in 7♣. What this meant the Toucan didn't profess to know, but it made no difference, for whatever it was, the hand wasn't going to be played in clubs.

Hearing 7♠ the Rabbit began to suspect that the Toucan had spades, as well as, or even instead of, clubs. His ruffing values being distinctly unimpressive, he quickly converted to 7NT.

Papa led the ♡J and as dummy went down the Rabbit surveyed his dubious prospects.

He could see eleven top tricks. The diamond finesse would yield the twelfth and the heart finesse would bring in the thirteenth. This would succeed if Papa's jack was a falsecard, or alternatively, if he had suddenly decided to take up Rusinow leads — one of two possibilities and therefore, in the Rabbit's estimation, a fifty-fifty chance.

The Rabbit began by reeling off six spades on which he shed two clubs, a diamond and a heart. Karapet discarded two clubs and two diamonds, while Papa, under pressure all the way, let go the ♣2, then the ♡6 and finally the ◊5.

Coming to hand with the ◊A, R.R. braced himself for the heart finesse. When dummy's ten held the trick, he gurgled contentedly and cashed the king.

This was the four-card end-position.

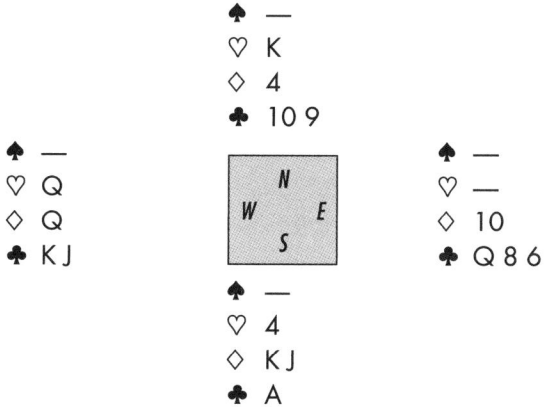

Clinging firmly to his clubs, Karapet parted with the ◊10.

The moment of truth had come. The fateful diamond finesse could be delayed no longer. When Karapet showed out the Rabbit shrugged his shoulders philosophically and going up with the king, murmured ruefully: 'One down.'

Since there was no possible way in which even the Rabbit could lose another trick, the grand slam was duly made.

Recriminations flowed thick and fast across the table.

'What an incredible lead! The only card in your hand to present them with the contract,' burst out Karapet. 'Couldn't you have picked one of the others?'

'Are you suggesting,' cried Papa, 'that I should have led a club from my tenace, a diamond from my queen or a spade into dummy's long suit? Or maybe you think that the best lead against a grand slam is the fourth highest of the longest suit?' Barely pausing for breath, Papa launched an immediate counterattack. 'But what has the lead to do with your failure to keep a diamond so as to put declarer to a guess instead of brutally exposing my queen?'

'You forced me to keep three clubs,' countered the Armenian. 'Why did you pick on the two of clubs as your first discard? Surely you could afford the jack. I would have...'

'The jack? With the ten on the table? Are you serious?' cried the indignant Greek. 'Don't you realize that if declarer had the ace and queen of clubs, as well he might on the bidding, throwing the jack would be tantamount to engineering a Vienna Coup against myself?'

The Hideous Hog was enjoying every minute of his neighbors' troubles.

'Evidently,' he chortled, 'you both defended and discarded very well. It was just that declarer happened to have the wrong cards. Very unlucky.'

Papa ignored him. 'I have always maintained and I affirm once again — people shouldn't be allowed to play conventions they don't understand.'

'I disagree,' rejoined the Hog. 'No convention is unfair if it's undisclosed to partner.'

# When Not to Double

Papa the Greek beamed appreciatively at the cluster of kibitzers who had gathered around to watch his duel with the Hideous Hog. He liked an audience. Not for him the flower born to blush unseen and waste its sweetness on the desert air. This was the first hand of the rubber, which I watched from a post of vantage between Timothy the Toucan, North, and Papa's partner, Charlie the Chimp, who was sitting East.

Neither Vul.
Dealer West

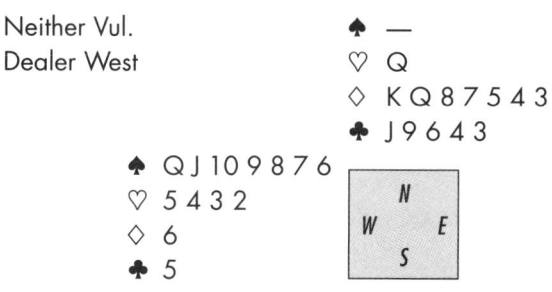

```
              ♠ —
              ♡ Q
              ◇ K Q 8 7 5 4 3
              ♣ J 9 6 4 3
♠ Q J 10 9 8 7 6
♡ 5 4 3 2              N
◇ 6                 W     E
♣ 5                   S
```

| West | North | East | South |
|------|-------|------|-------|
| Papa | T.T. | Ch.Ch. | H.H. |
| 3♠ | 3NT | 4♠ | 6♣ |
| all pass | | | |

Papa led the ♠Q and as dummy went down the Hog turned to the others. 'It's stifling,' he began. 'Do you mind if before we play on I get a drink? I just can't get hold of that wretched steward.'

'By all means,' agreed Papa with alacrity. 'I'll come with you. I could do with a cold lager myself.' Looking at each other suspiciously they left the table together.

The Toucan peered at the Chimp's hand and with a frightened look subsided in his chair. He didn't know what would happen, but it wouldn't be anything pleasant, and whatever it was, he would surely be blamed for it. Perhaps he should have passed, but then the Hog might have had the Chimp's hand and he would have been blamed even more. It was a hard life. A young trainee, anxious to learn the finer points of the game, turned to Charlie the Chimp. 'How is it, sir,' he asked, 'that you didn't double?'

With a superior smile, the Chimp explained: 'As you can see, the three notrump bid over three spades asks partner, conventionally, to bid a minor. Not knowing of the bad break, he has chosen the wrong one. If I were to double, warning opponents of their peril, they could switch to diamonds, which break perfectly, and instead of three trump tricks, I would be left with none. Declarer, of course, is marked on the bidding with the ace of diamonds. Observe this golden rule, my young friend,' added the Chimp sententiously, 'when opponents are where you want them, leave them there.'

Molly the Mule, conspicuous among the spectators in a primrose dress with a spray of orchids, greeted the Chimp's homily with a derisive snort. She was about to say something caustic and unpleasant, no doubt, when Papa and the Hog, with glasses in their hands, resumed their seats.

The Hog ruffed the ♣Q in dummy and continued with the ♣3. The Chimp played the two, the Hog the seven and the Greek the five. The position of every trump could now be deduced.

A second spade was ruffed in dummy and then came a diamond to the ace, another to the ◊K and the ◊Q. Papa, who followed once, threw two spades.

On the third round, the Hog also discarded a spade. A fourth diamond from dummy posed a problem for the Chimp. If, as seemed likely, Papa had seven spades, the Hog started with four and would now have one left. Unless the Chimp ruffed, he would promptly get rid of it. Admittedly, H.H. could overruff, but that would leave him with the king bare, so the Chimp's ♣AQ would still score two tricks. The Chimp ruffed with the eight. The Hog overruffed with the ten and continued with the ♡A, ♡K and ♡J. This was the deal in full:

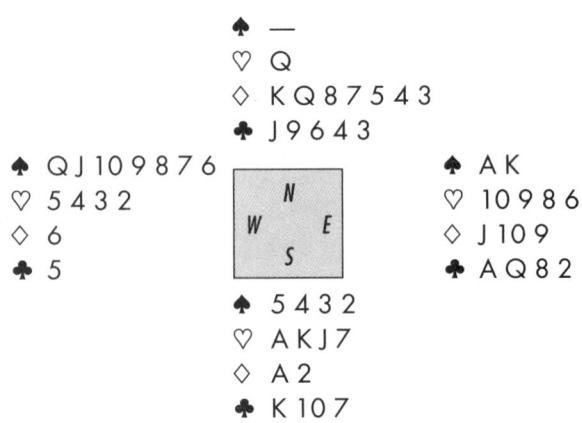

```
                    ♠ —
                    ♡ Q
                    ◊ K Q 8 7 5 4 3
                    ♣ J 9 6 4 3
♠ Q J 10 9 8 7 6           ┌─────────┐           ♠ A K
♡ 5 4 3 2                  │    N    │           ♡ 10 9 8 6
◊ 6                        │ W     E │           ◊ J 10 9
♣ 5                        │    S    │           ♣ A Q 8 2
                           └─────────┘
                    ♠ 5 4 3 2
                    ♡ A K J 7
                    ◊ A 2
                    ♣ K 10 7
```

At the eleventh trick the Hog led his last heart, ruffing it in dummy and leaving this position:

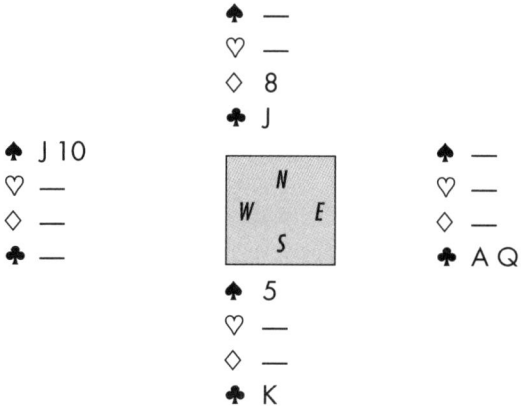

The lead of the ◇8 sealed the Chimp's fate. With the *coup en passant* the Hog had his twelfth trick.

Papa gnashed his teeth. Not only had the Hog brought off against him one of his unspeakable slams, but worse still, Papa hadn't been in the limelight from start to finish. Why, the kibitzers were more interested in the Toucan than they were in him!

'All you had to do was to go up with the ace of clubs and play another,' he cried indignantly to the Chimp. 'How many times did you think you'd make your ace?'

'Wouldn't it have been better, sir,' ventured the trainee kibitzer, 'if you hadn't ruffed at all? Then declarer couldn't have scored his trumps twice over, as it were and...'

'You showed admirable discretion, Charlie,' broke in Molly, matching her sarcasm with a contemptuous smile. 'If that's how you intended to defend, you were perfectly right not to double.'

# Papa Is Purely Incidental

A case of unusual complexity came up before our Monster Points Committee at a specially convened meeting last Thursday. There was no law, no rule, no precedent to guide us.

The bare facts were not in dispute.

Papa the Greek and Karapet the Free Armenian were pitted against the Rueful Rabbit and Timothy the Toucan. The Hideous Hog was kibitzing against Papa. Charlie the Chimp was, at the start, neutral, that is he was equally obnoxious to both sides. But as the cards were being dealt the Hog offered to back the Rabbit at £5 a 100 and the Chimp accepted with alacrity.

'How is it,' I asked H.H., 'that you go out of your way to back so weak a pair? Have you really such faith in the Rabbit's luck?'

The Hog shook his head. 'No,' he explained. 'It's true that R.R. has the most gifted Guardian Angel in the business. But there's more to it than that. It's precisely because they are so bad that I am backing them. That shows how little I think of Papa and it riles him, disturbs his concentration, and clouds his judgment, so when I cut against him, which I do every day, he starts with a sense of inferiority and plays worse than he need do.

'If you want to win,' declared the Hog, 'never show partner how little you respect his game. Never conceal from opponents how little you respect theirs.'

As we chatted, the play proceeded.

First Papa made game.  Then the tide began to flow the other way and three game hands later the Rabbit and the Toucan equalized.  And then came this deal:

Both Vul.
Dealer North

```
                    ♠ A 6 5
                    ♡ A 10 6
                    ◇ K 9 2
                    ♣ A K 9 8
```

```
                N
            W       E
                S
```

```
                    ♠ Q J 10 9 8 3
                    ♡ K 5
                    ◇ A 5
                    ♣ 5 4 2
```

| North | South |
|-------|-------|
| Karapet | Papa |
| 1♣ | 1♠ |
| 2NT | 5♠ |
| 6♠ | pass |

Bored by an auction in which he had no part, the Rabbit, sitting East, was peeping surreptitiously at an astrological chart on a coffee table beside him.  As he bent over, liqueur glass in hand, one of his cards slipped to the floor.  The players were too absorbed to notice it.  The Hog and the Chimp did and their eyes met.  Neither said a word.

T.T. led the ◇Q.

The contract appeared to hinge on the trump finesse, so winning in his hand the Greek ran the ♠Q.  The Rabbit showed out, discarding a diamond.  The jack followed.  The Toucan bounced, but didn't cover and this time R.R. threw a heart.

Papa surveyed his prospects.  If he lost a trick to the king of trumps, he would have to get rid somehow of his third club and the only hope would be a red-suit squeeze against West.  That meant finding him with the queen-jack of hearts and also with the ◇Q, ◇J and ◇10, too much to hope for.

More promising was the chance of a smother play to catch the ♠K. For that to succeed the Toucan's pattern would have to be 4=3=3=3, which would allow Papa to shorten his trumps twice. Then, when he and T.T. remained with two trumps each, he would cash the ♣AK and exit with another club. If the trick went to the Rabbit this would be the two-card end position:

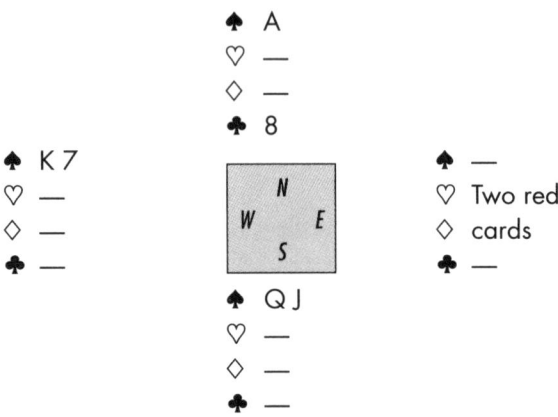

With the lead coming from East, West's king would be smothered.

Reputedly one of the most advanced plays in bridge, to a technician like Papa the mechanics of a smother play presented no problem. At Trick 4 he crossed to the ◊K and ruffed a diamond. Then came the ♡K and ♡A, followed by a heart ruff. Having shortened his trumps Papa proceeded to cash the ♣AK. The Rabbit followed with the jack and queen, and now came the moment of truth. Would he win the next trick with the ten?

R.R. had already detached a diamond, when the Hog holding up imperiously a fat, pink forefinger, stopped him.

'You've dropped a card. Allow me,' he said, and stooping, he picked up the ♣3.

Now the trick went to the Toucan's ten and the ♠7 to dummy's ace liberated the king. This was the deal:

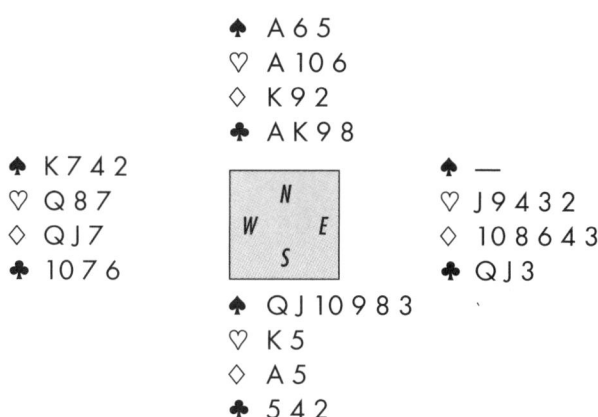

```
              ♠ A 6 5
              ♡ A 10 6
              ◇ K 9 2
              ♣ A K 9 8
♠ K 7 4 2                          ♠ —
♡ Q 8 7          N                 ♡ J 9 4 3 2
◇ Q J 7      W       E             ◇ 10 8 6 4 3
♣ 10 7 6         S                 ♣ Q J 3
              ♠ Q J 10 9 8 3
              ♡ K 5
              ◇ A 5
              ♣ 5 4 2
```

With loud supporting noises from the Chimp, Papa gave vent to his indignation.

By flawless technique he had brought off a brilliant smother play. Only a double-dummy defense could beat the slam and of that there was not the slightest danger — so long as the Rabbit was allowed to play with thirteen cards. To restrict him to twelve was a vile maneuver on the part of the Hog, who should have either spoken at once or kept quiet throughout.

Subversion of the natural course of justice, aggravated by grossly improper conduct — that was the charge brought jointly against H.H. by Papa and the Chimp.

That the Hog had done something wrong wasn't in doubt. He always did. But what was it? There is nothing in the laws to say that a kibitzer must or must not draw attention to a card on the floor. And if this is a matter for his discretion, what is to stop him from deciding at which point he should speak up?

The Hog submitted a two-pronged defense. Firstly, he pleaded that he was not aware of the card on the floor until the Rabbit was about to revoke. Secondly, he argued that his opponent was not Papa but the Chimp. He, too, had seen the Rabbit drop a card, but unlike H.H., he didn't realize that it had to be a club, for there was no room for T.T. to have more than three clubs.

'Getting a proper count on the carpet,' murmured the Owl softly.

Furthermore, went on H.H., the Chimp didn't appreciate the importance of the double jettison in clubs as the only defense against the intended smother play.

'My friend Themistocles,' declared the Hog, 'claims that he was robbed of the just reward of his skill — a baby smother play, by the way, if ever there was one. But it's my skill, not his, that would have gone unrewarded had the slam been made. I outplayed — I, er, showed a better sense of timing — than my opponent, the Chimp. It would have been indeed a gross miscarriage of justice had he won and had I lost. In all this,' concluded H.H., 'Papa is purely incidental.'

# Surprise, Surprise

Springing from nowhere, as is their wont, kibitzers quickly clustered round the table when the Hideous Hog and Colin the Corgi came up to face Papa and Karapet at our weekly duplicate.

On the first board Papa made 4♠. With nine trumps between the two hands the contract depended on not losing a trick to the queen and Papa took the right view. Then this hand came up:

Both Vul.
Dealer North

```
              ♠ K Q 10 4
              ♡ A 7 5 2
              ◇ K 9 2
              ♣ K Q
```

```
              ♠ A 5
              ♡ Q 10 9 8 6 4
              ◇ 8 7 6
              ♣ 5 2
```

| North | South |
|-------|-------|
| *Karapet* | *Papa* |
| 1NT | 4♡ |
| pass | |

The Hog, who was West, led the ♣J. Winning with the ace, the Corgi returned the three. The Greek came to his hand with the ♠A and led the ♡Q.

Sitting beside him, I tried to visualize the hand from his angle. He had three possible losers in diamonds and one more in trumps. One diamond could be parked on dummy's ♠Q, so it came to this: either the ◊A had to be on the right side of the king or else the trumps would have to be brought in without loss.

Should he, then, lay down the ace, hoping for a bare king, or lead the queen to pin East's singleton jack? The Greek was right, I thought, in choosing the latter. Other things being equal, it would be preferable to lose a trick to East than to West.

The ♡Q brought the jack from H.H. A moment's thought, a quick glance at the kibitzers, and with a flourish the Greek tabled his hand.

'I needn't dot the 'i's and cross the 't's,' he began, which meant, of course, that he was about to do so. 'The endplay against Colin, on my right, is automatic. I go up with dummy's ace and throw him in with the ♡K, leaving him to choose one of three ways in which to present me with the contract. He can lead a diamond, and if so, I only lose one diamond, no matter who has the ace. He can exit with a club, conceding a ruff and discard. Again, I only lose one diamond. Finally, he can lead a spade into dummy's tenace, allowing me to discard two diamonds. If anything isn't absolutely clear...'

'Oh, but it is,' broke in the Hog, tabling his hand. 'Two down.'

This was the deal in full:

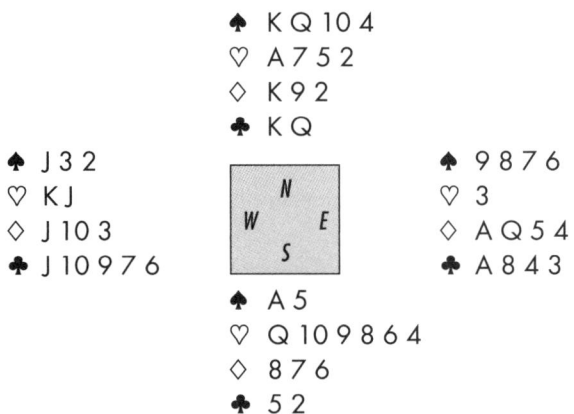

The kibitzers gasped. Papa looked incredulously at the ♡K.

Leering happily at the Greek, the Hog explained:

'The hand was an open book. If Papa started with seven hearts he had ten tricks, so I had to place him with six. With my jack of spades coming down, however, the addition would still come to ten, so it was painfully clear to me from the start that as the cards were, he couldn't find a way to go down. He needed help, a lot of help.'

'Had I covered the queen of hearts,' pursued H.H., 'Papa would have had no choice. Leaving the jack out, he would have played off the spades, intending, if the jack didn't fall, to exit with a trump. East might have the jack or else the ace of diamonds could be right. Unfortunately, as you can see, my jack of spades would come down, so relieving Papa of any further problem. How could I stop that happening? Only by setting up for him that splendid endplay which he has described so well.' The Hog paused to glance at the traveling scoresheet. 'Cheer up, Themistocles,' he said with a grin. 'It's not a cold bottom. You share it with pair 7.'

I looked over the Hog's shoulder. Only pair 13 had a plus on the East-West cards and that I knew to be the Rueful Rabbit and Walter the Walrus. I heard the full story later from Oscar the Owl, our Senior Kibitzer, who was in attendance at their table.

The Rabbit, sitting West, defended exactly as the Hog had done. Hearing that, I thought at first that he had mixed up the suits, exposed a card or revoked, perhaps, as he was apt to do from time to time. But, no, he had, apparently, played coolly and carefully. For once the Rabbit knew precisely what he was doing.

The key to his play, explained O.O., was to be found in what had happened on the previous board. Like Papa and Karapet, Charlie the Chimp and Timothy the Toucan reached the eminently reasonable contract of 4♠. The Chimp, declarer, had the ♠KJ1084 with ♠A962 in dummy. He led the king. The Rabbit, who was mumbling to himself, muttered something about a short French spider and followed with the three, the Walrus with the five. The Chimp continued with the jack. The Rabbit frowned, pursed his lips, and following slowly with the seven, asked: 'How many 'r's in arraign?'

The Chimp ran the jack, losing to W.W.'s bare queen.

'What on earth did you have to think about?' he cried angrily turning to R.R.

'Seven letters and the clue was 'indict the short French spider' and...' began the Rabbit, when suddenly he realized what he had done. From pink his cheeks turned to crimson and with beads of perspiration forming on his forehead he dithered incoherently. 'I thought, I mean, I didn't think... take it back, please. I, er, we... do take it back.'

'If you insist,' quickly agreed the Chimp.

The Toucan wouldn't hear of it.

'I only had five points,' spluttered the Walrus, 'and if I take a trick they want it back. Bah!'

Oscar pointed out that it would be highly improper to alter the result without referring to the tournament director. That no one wanted, so the Rabbit had to give way, but he was determined, for all that, to see that justice prevailed. And if he couldn't do it on that board he would make sure of redressing the balance on the next one.

Hence his play, which looked to be foolproof, for could there be a more certain way of presenting the other side with a trick than by playing the jack from king-jack on an opponent's queen?

# Master Point Press on the Internet

www.masterpointpress.com

Our main site, with information about our books and software, reviews and more.

www.teachbridge.com

Our site for bridge teachers and students — free downloadable support material for our books, helpful articles, forums and more.

www.bridgeblogging.com

Read and comment on regular articles from MPP authors and other bridge notables.

www.ebooksbridge.com

Purchase downloadable electronic versions of MPP books and software.